The Healthy Kiwi Student

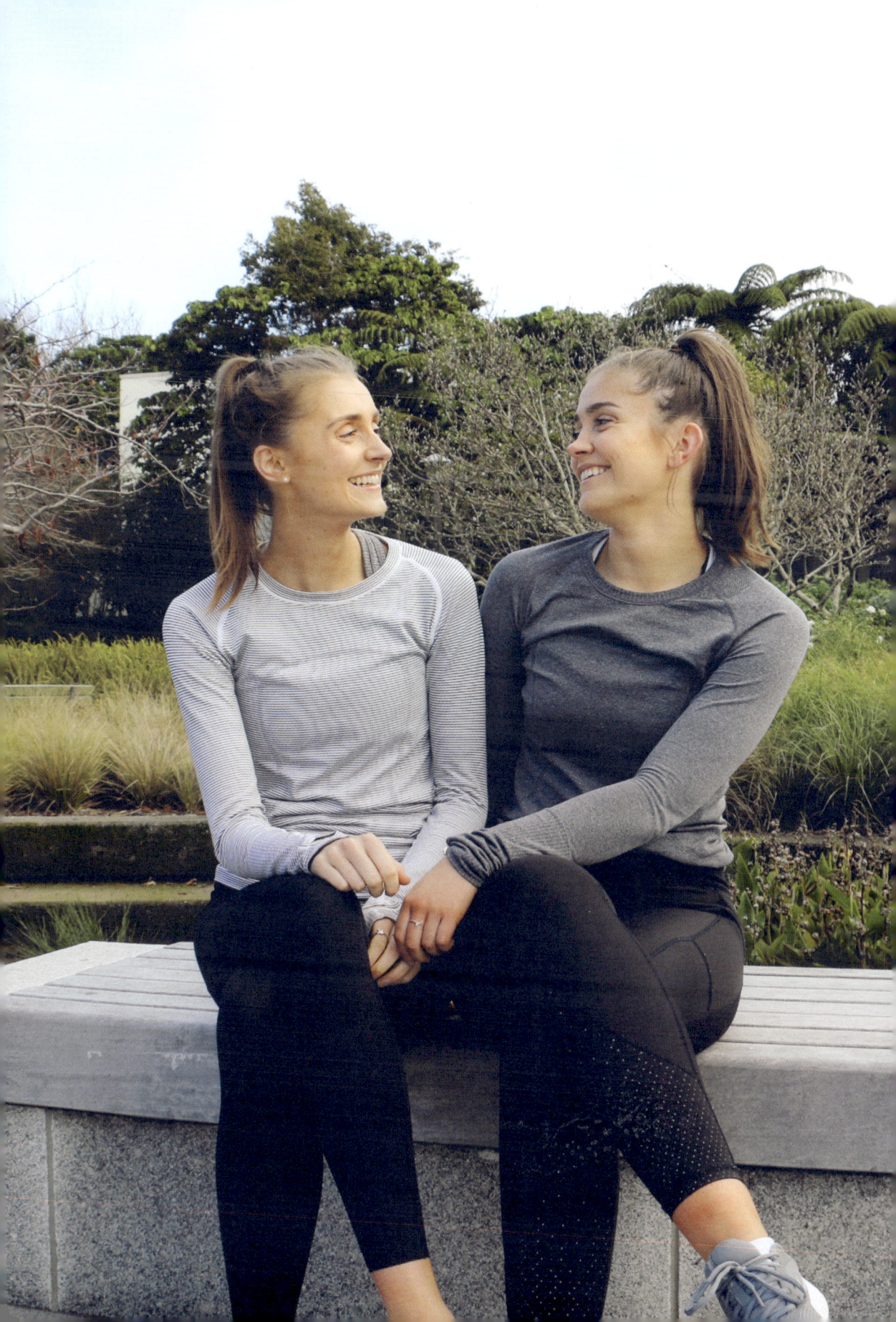

The Healthy Kiwi Student

Emily & Sophie Martin

A Food, Fitness & Lifestyle Guide from The Tasty Twins

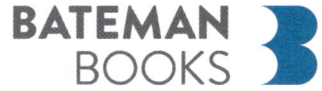

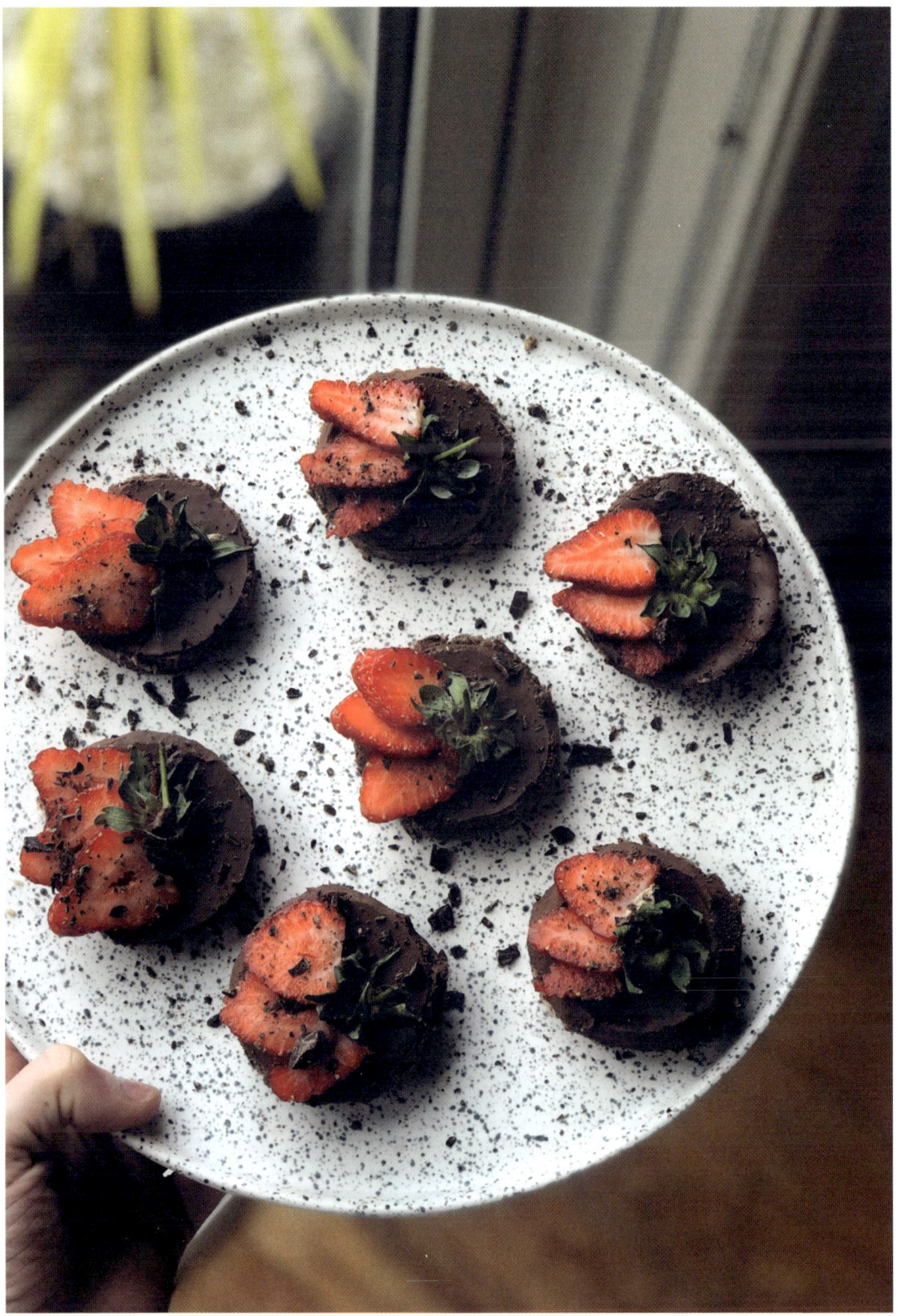

Contents

Introduction	6
Recipes	8
Tasty Twins' Food Tips and Tricks	9
Rise and Shine	12
Lunches on the Run	36
Feed the Flatties!	48
Simply Sweets	62
Absolute Bliss	94
Fitness	108
Tasty Twins' Exercise Tips and Tricks	110
Workouts	122
Mental Health	130
Soph's Story	131
Em's Story	132
Tasty Twins' Mental Health Tips and Tricks	133
Comparing Ourselves to Others	136
Failure	139
Eating	140
The Inside Scoop: Emma Ternouth	142
Stress	144
Self-care	148
Student Life	150
Study Tips	151
Budgeting	154
Flatting	155
Balance	156
Acknowledgements	159

Introduction

Hi everyone! Welcome to our book. We're *so* excited to be here. This is our actual, real-life book — how crazy is that? So, get yourself your favourite snack, find a comfy spot, and dive on in!

Before we get started, please allow us to introduce ourselves. We're Em and Soph, also known as the Tasty Twins from Instagram. We've been running an Instagram account for three years now; we started off posting our reviews of the Wellington cafe scene, and it just seemed to grow from there. Now we create all sorts of recipes, from raw treats to flat-friendly dishes, and we love to chat about all things mental and physical health. We also offer a bit of a glimpse into our lives as university students.

We've just finished our fourth year at the University of Otago, studying Consumer Food Science and Marketing (Soph) and Psychology (Em). After four years, we've seen it all; some . . . interesting . . . hall meals, crazy nights out and exhausting exam seasons. Uni has been a blast, but it's definitely full on, and there's lots to get your head around. It occurred to us that it would be super helpful for those leaving home and starting out their lives as tertiary students to have some tips, perhaps a book — a student survival guide, if you like. And we figured who better to write such a book than two sisters who are living that life already?! This guide is full of recipes for student-friendly meals and healthy treats, our top mental-health tips, workouts to get those endorphins going, and some tried-and-tested student life hacks.

But you don't have to be a uni student to use this book. Maybe you're simply keen to try some new recipes, discover some workout inspo, or you need a mental-health boost. Whatever you're looking for, we really hope this book provides the goods.

Lots of love,

Em and Soph. aka the Tasty Twins
instagram.com/tasty.twinsss

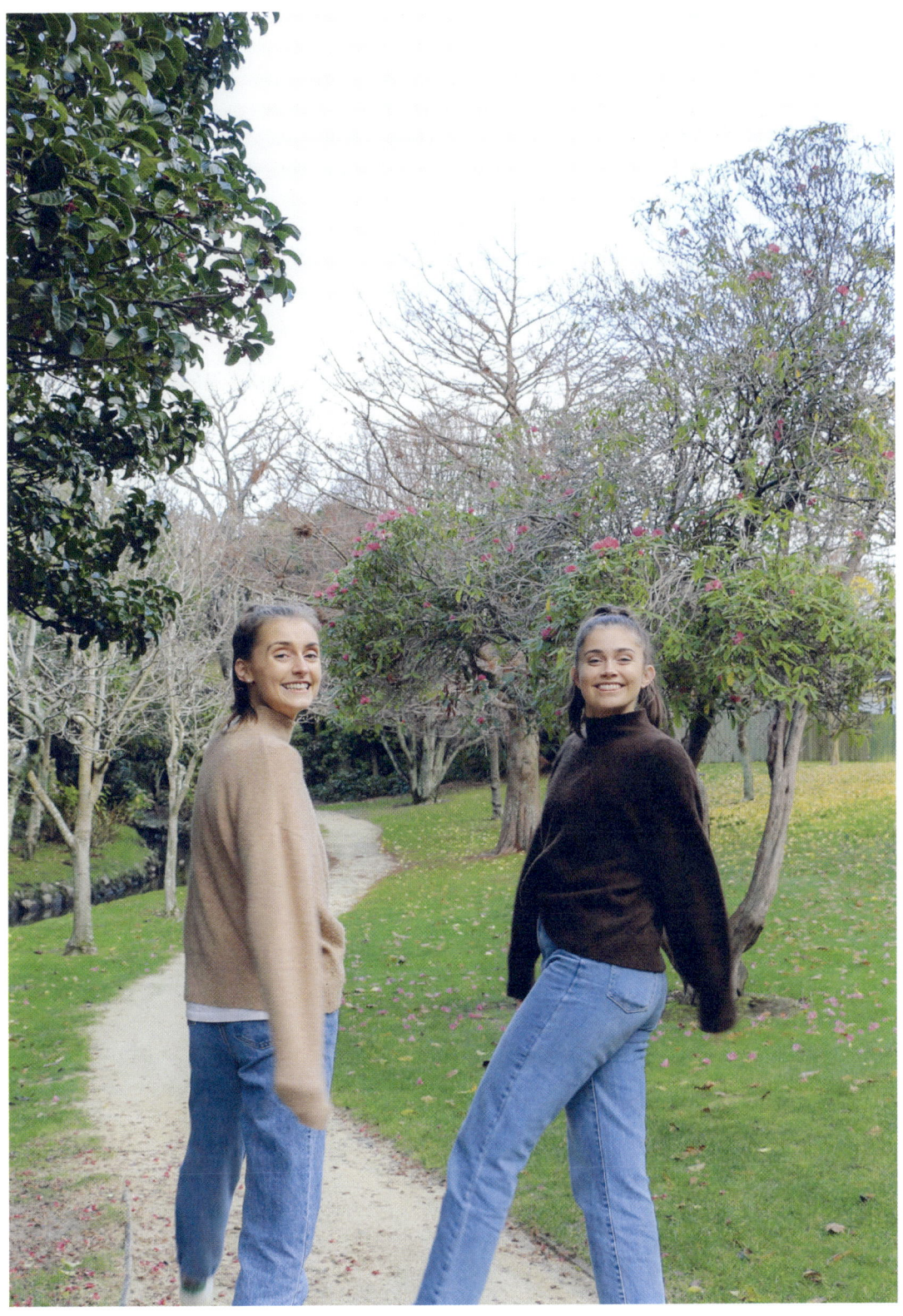

Recipes

You've moved out of home and suddenly you're completely in control of your own kitchen! But with study, socialising and every other aspect of student life to juggle, the last thing you want is to be slaving over a stove for hours a day. And while instant noodles are great as a last resort, it's ultra important to fuel your body and get the nutrients you need to thrive. So, we've compiled our go-to dishes for every meal of the day; they're quick, easy, affordable and, most of all, delicious! These meals are balanced and packed with nutritional goodness, and we even have some sweet treats and snacks to nourish your soul too.

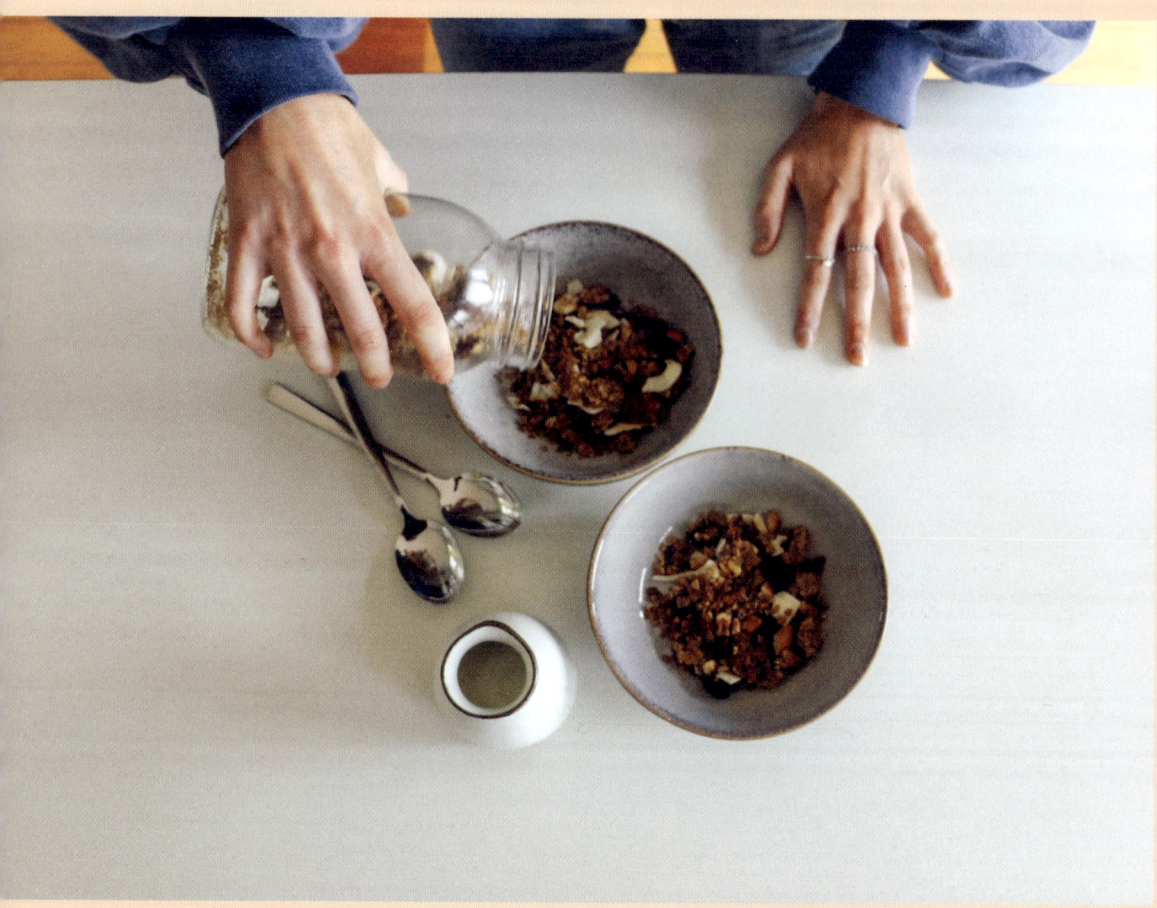

Tasty Twins' Food Tips & Tricks

NUTRITIONAL INFORMATION KEY
DF = dairy-free
RSF = refined-sugar-free
V = vegan
GF = gluten-free
PF = peanut-free

DIETARY ALTERNATIVES
Whatever your dietary requirements, our recipes are easy to tailor to your personal needs or preferences. This section offers you a variety of alternative options that you may like to try, which factor in food intolerances or preferences.

Liquid sweetener options:
Maple syrup (RSF, V, GF)
Rice malt syrup (RSF, V, GF)
Agave (RSF, V, GF)
Honey (RSF, GF)

Dry sweetener options:
White sugar
Coconut sugar (RSF, V, GF)
Brown sugar (V, GF)

Flour options:
Plain flour
Wholemeal flour
Ground almonds (GF)
Buckwheat flour (GF)
Oat flour (to make: grind rolled oats in a blender until finely milled)
LSA (which stands for: linseeds, sunflowers and almonds) (GF)

Milk options:
Cow's milk
Almond milk (V, DF)
Coconut milk (V, DF)
Soy milk (V, DF)
Oat milk (V, DF)

Oil options:
Olive oil
Melted coconut oil
Rice bran oil
Canola oil

Peanut butter options:
Almond butter (PF)
Tahini (PF — nut-free alternative that gives an earthy taste)

Rolled oat options:
Gluten-free oats (GF — available in organic shops and online)

Egg options:
Flaxseed or chia-seed eggs can be used in place of your regular eggs to make any creation vegan-friendly. These are very simple to make — just combine 1 tablespoon of ground flaxseed or chia seeds with 3 tablespoons of water, mix well, and leave for 15–30 minutes prior to use. Use this mixture in place of one egg in any recipe.

INGREDIENT SUBSTITUTIONS

Sometimes, you might have a craving for a particular recipe, but you may not have that one vital ingredient in the pantry. And, chances are, if you're living on a student budget, you'll always be on the lookout for a low-cost alternative. Below we've listed a few handy substitutes for some of our favourite ingredients.

Cacao nibs: Available in organic shops, these are raw cacao beans that give a crunch and a slight chocolate taste to your baking. Budget-friendly option = chocolate chips (perhaps not as 'healthy', but just as delicious!).

Cacao powder: This chocolatey powder is high in antioxidants and found in organic shops. Budget-friendly option = cocoa powder.

Coconut flakes: These crunchy chips are made from coconut flesh, and add awesome texture and flavour to your baking. Budget-friendly option = shredded or desiccated coconut.

Protein powder: While not an essential, protein powder is a great way to up the protein in your baking. This is useful for muscle recovery, and can be purchased in organic shops or online.
   Budget-friendly option = cocoa powder (for a chocolate flavour) or ground almonds. Some flavours we love to use are vanilla, chocolate and caramel.

RAW SLICES

Here are a couple of useful tips if you're keen to give a raw slice recipe a go:

- If you don't have protein powder handy, feel free to add a tablespoon of oat flour (oats ground into flour) or ground almonds instead.
- Make sure you allow plenty of time for each individual layer to set in the freezer before adding the next one.
- When you go to cut your slice, heat up a sharp knife under hot water and wipe it off before cutting.
- Slices are best stored in the freezer, and taken out to thaw in the fridge about an hour before eating.

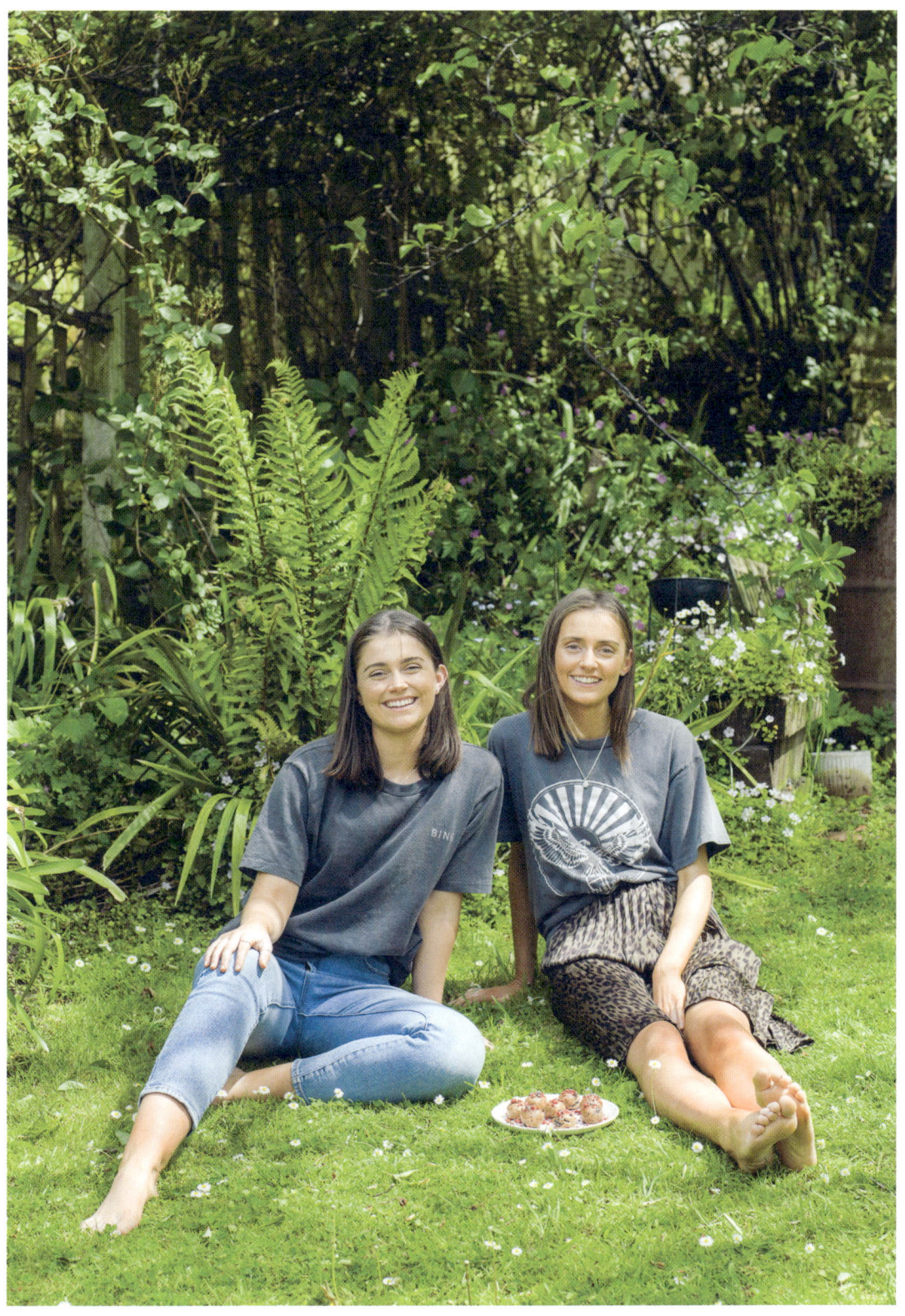

Rise and Shine

Breakfast is 100% our fave meal — there are just so many options. There's no better way to start the day than by fuelling your body with a bowl of oats, or digging into a stack of pancakes. We've created quite a few breakfast recipes in our time, and these are the best of them. From our go-to granola, to the best summer smoothie bowls, it's all here. So, get creating!

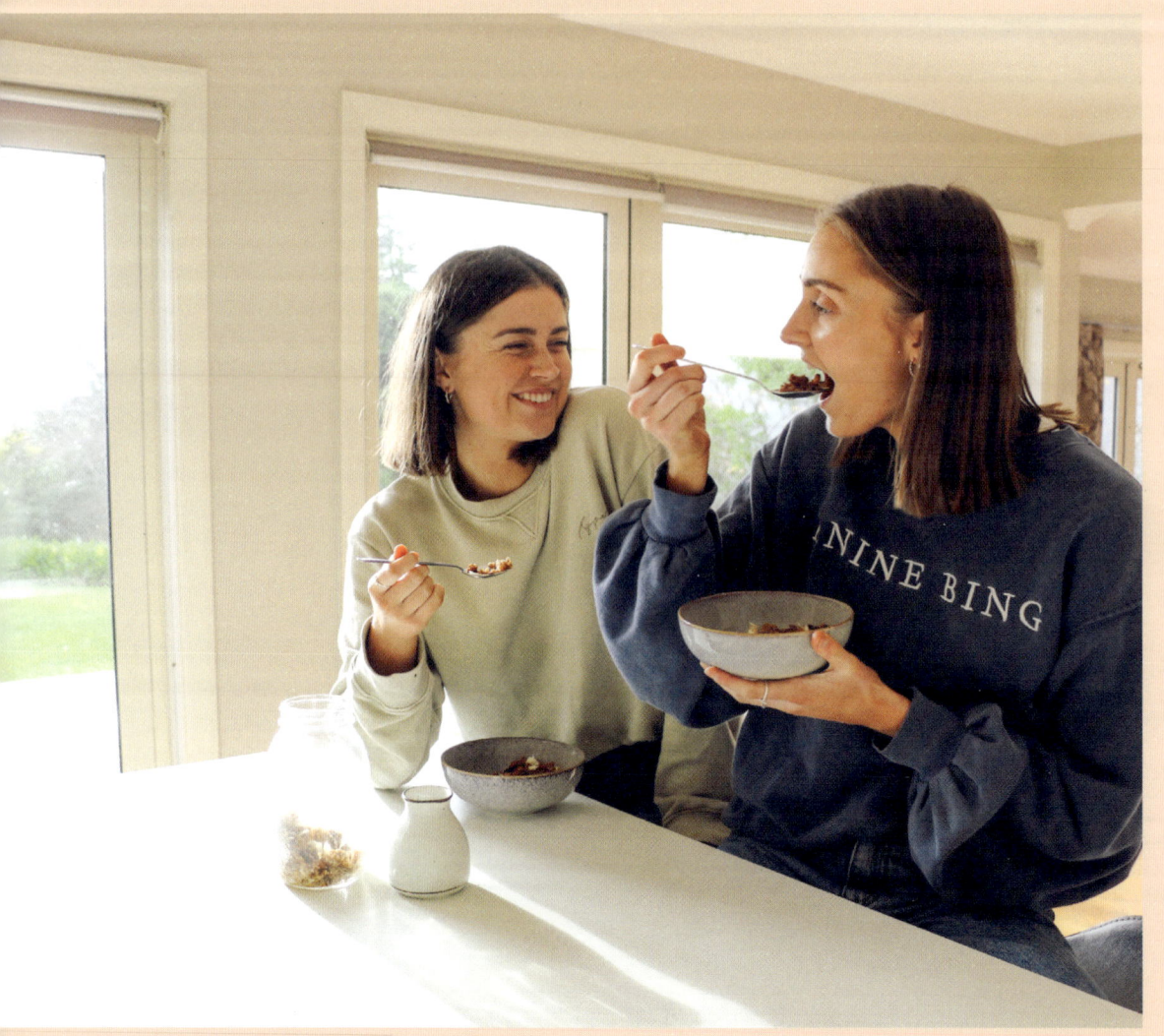

Peanut Butter & Banana Granola

½ cup peanut butter
1 Tbsp melted coconut oil or olive oil
1 large mashed banana
3 Tbsp maple syrup
2 cups rolled oats
1 cup roughly chopped nuts (we use almonds, walnuts, hazelnuts and cashews)
2 tsp cinnamon
1 tsp vanilla essence
¼ tsp salt

1. Preheat the oven to 160°C and line a baking tray with baking paper.
2. In a bowl combine the peanut butter, oil, mashed banana and maple syrup.
3. Add the remaining ingredients and mix well.
4. Spread the mixture onto prepared baking tray and place in the oven for 10–15 minutes or until golden brown.
5. Cool for 10 minutes.
6. Store or serve it up! We love pairing it with milk, seasonal fruit and a big dollop of peanut butter!

Makes/serves: 10 serves | Prep time: 5 minutes | Cook time: 10 minutes
Nutritional information: DF, RSF, V

Choc Crunch Granola

1½ cups rolled oats
1 cup roughly chopped nuts or seeds
2 Tbsp cacao powder
3 Tbsp maple syrup/honey
3 Tbsp peanut butter
3 Tbsp coconut oil, melted
1 Tbsp vanilla essence
100g chocolate, chopped
½ cup coconut thread

OPTIONAL TOPPINGS
sliced banana, peanut butter, freeze-dried raspberries

1. Preheat oven to 180°C. Combine oats, nuts or seeds, cacao powder, maple syrup or honey, peanut butter, oil and vanilla in a bowl.
2. Bake in the oven for 10–15 minutes.
3. Set aside to cool for 20–30 minutes.
4. Mix through the chocolate and coconut thread.
5. We love pairing this granola with sliced banana, milk or yoghurt, freeze-dried raspberries, and maybe a little extra peanut butter on the side.

Makes/serves: 10 serves | Prep time: 5 minutes | Cook time: 10 minutes
Nutritional information: DF, RSF, V

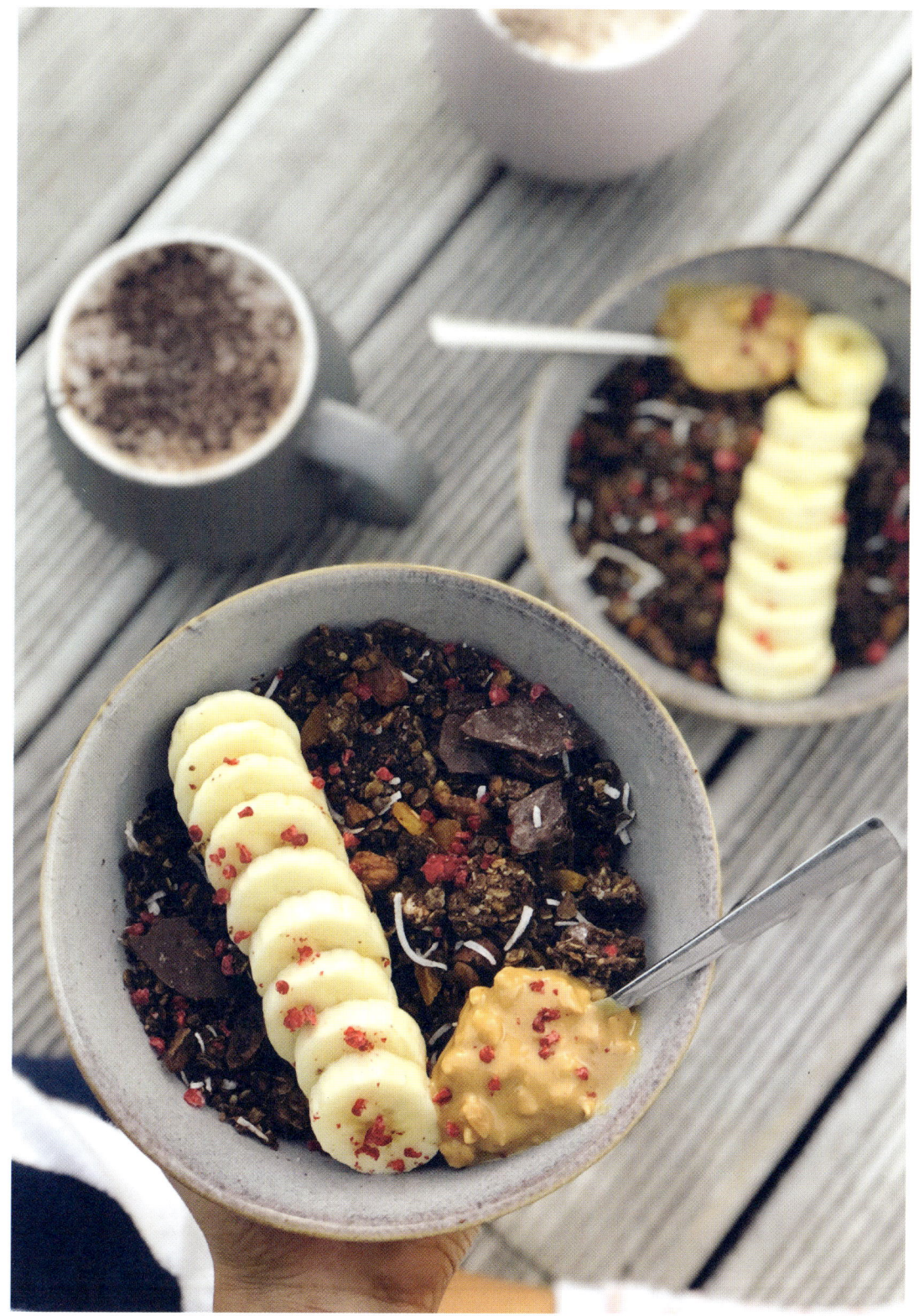

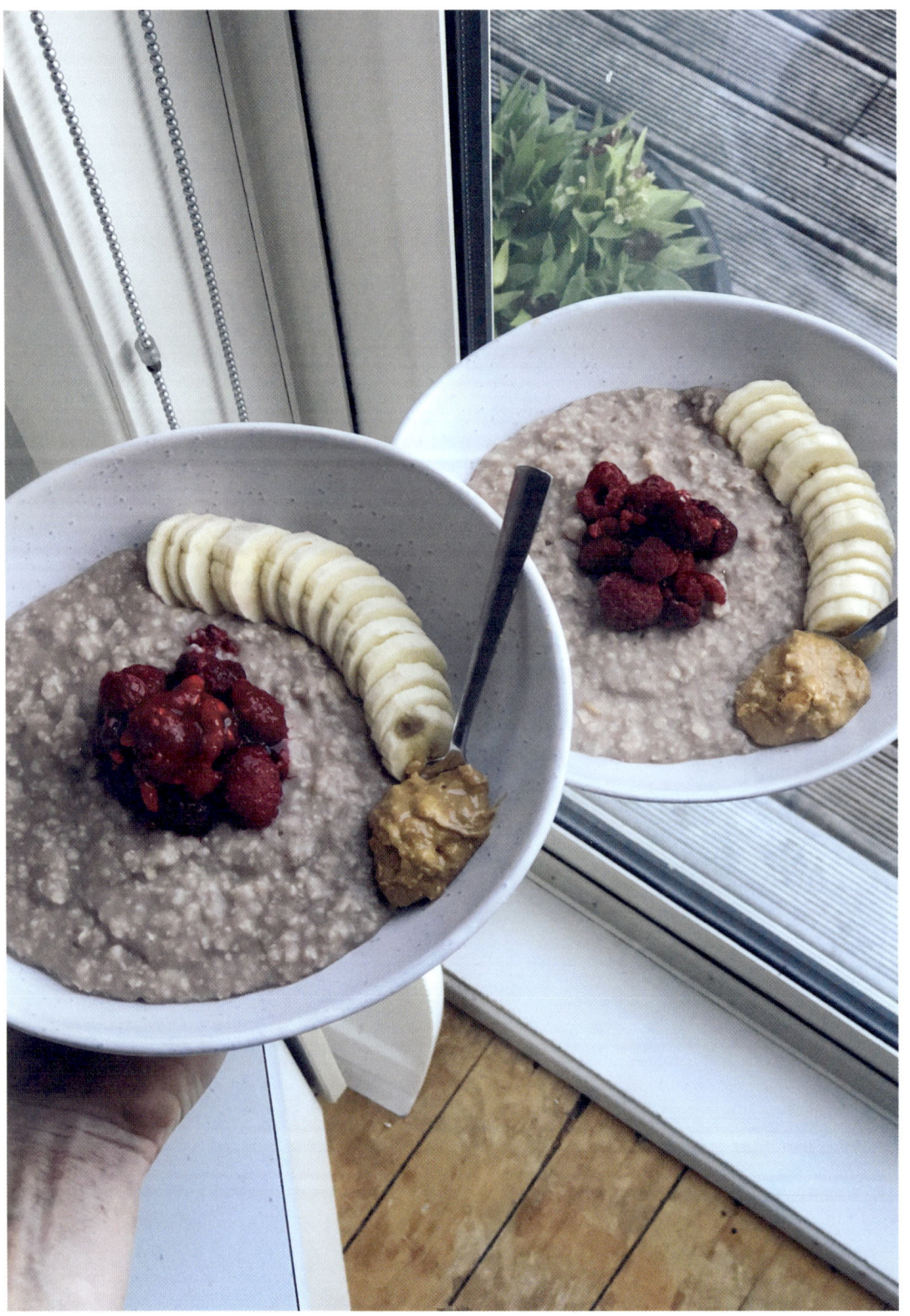

Classic Protein Oats

1 cup rolled oats
2⅓ cups water/milk of your choice (e.g. almond milk, oat milk or coconut milk)
2 Tbsp protein powder (we use Salted Caramel, Peanut Butter or Chocolate flavour)

OPTIONAL TOPPINGS
1 Tbsp peanut butter, mixed berries, banana, handful of chopped nuts

1. In a bowl, combine the oats, water/milk and protein powder. Mix well.
2. Place the bowl in the microwave for 1 minute. Remove and stir.
3. Place back in the microwave for another 1–2 minutes or until thick.
4. Top with whatever toppings you like and EAT!

Makes/serves: 2 | Prep time: 1 minute | Cook time: 1–2 minutes in microwave
Nutritional information: DF, RSF, V

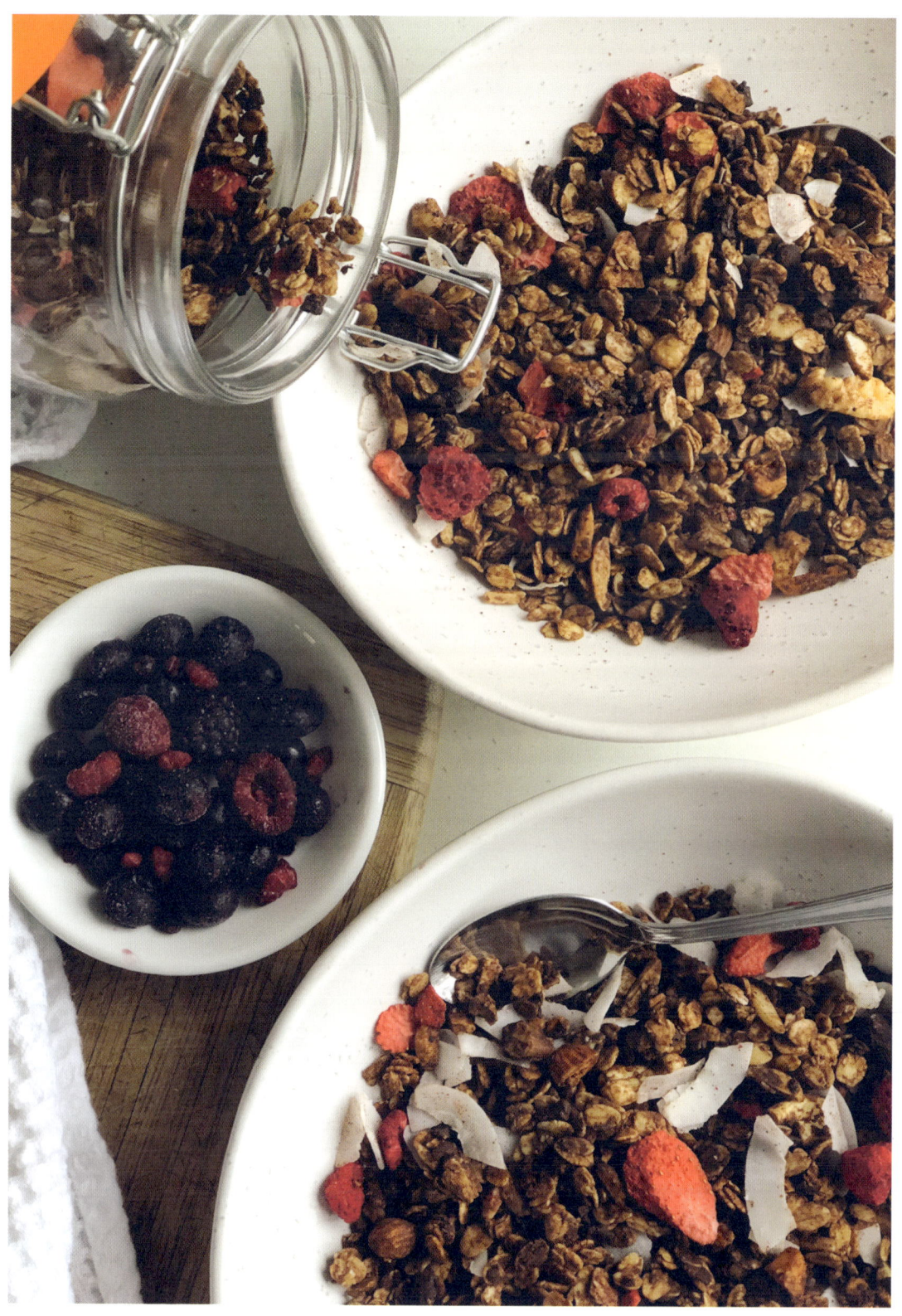

Coffee Peanut Butter Granola

1½ cups rolled oats
1 cup roughly chopped nuts
  (we use walnuts, almonds
  and cashews)
1 Tbsp ground coffee
1 Tbsp cacao powder
2 Tbsp peanut butter protein
  powder (optional)
¼ cup melted coconut oil
  or olive oil
¼ cup maple syrup, honey
  or rice malt syrup
½ cup coconut flakes
  or shredded coconut
½ cup cacao nibs
  or chocolate chips
handful of freeze-dried
  raspberries (optional)

1. Preheat oven to 160°C and line a baking tray with baking paper.
2. Combine the oats, nuts, coffee, cacao powder and protein powder in a bowl. Mix well.
3. Pour the coconut oil and maple syrup in and mix well.
4. Spread the mixture onto a baking tray and place in the oven for 10–15 minutes or until golden brown.
5. Cool for 10 minutes and then mix through the coconut, cacao nibs and raspberries (if using).
6. Enjoy with berries and yoghurt or milk.

Makes/serves: 10 serves | Prep time: 5 minutes | Cook time: 10 minutes
Nutritional information: DF, RSF, V

Vanilla Cinnamon Granola

2 cups rolled oats
1 cup roughly chopped nuts
   (we use peanuts, almonds
   and cashews)
⅓ cup honey or maple syrup
⅓ cup coconut
   or brown sugar
¼ cup melted coconut oil
1 Tbsp cinnamon
3 tsp vanilla essence
handful of coconut flakes
   (optional)

1. Preheat the oven to 160°C and line a baking tray with baking paper.
2. Combine all ingredients, except coconut flakes, in a bowl. Mix well.
3. Spread the mixture onto a baking tray and place in the oven for 10–15 minutes or until golden brown.
4. Cool for 10 minutes and then mix through the coconut flakes.
5. We love this for breakfast with banana and milk.

Makes/serves: 10 serves | Prep time: 5 minutes | Cook time: 10 minutes
Nutritional information: DF, RSF, V

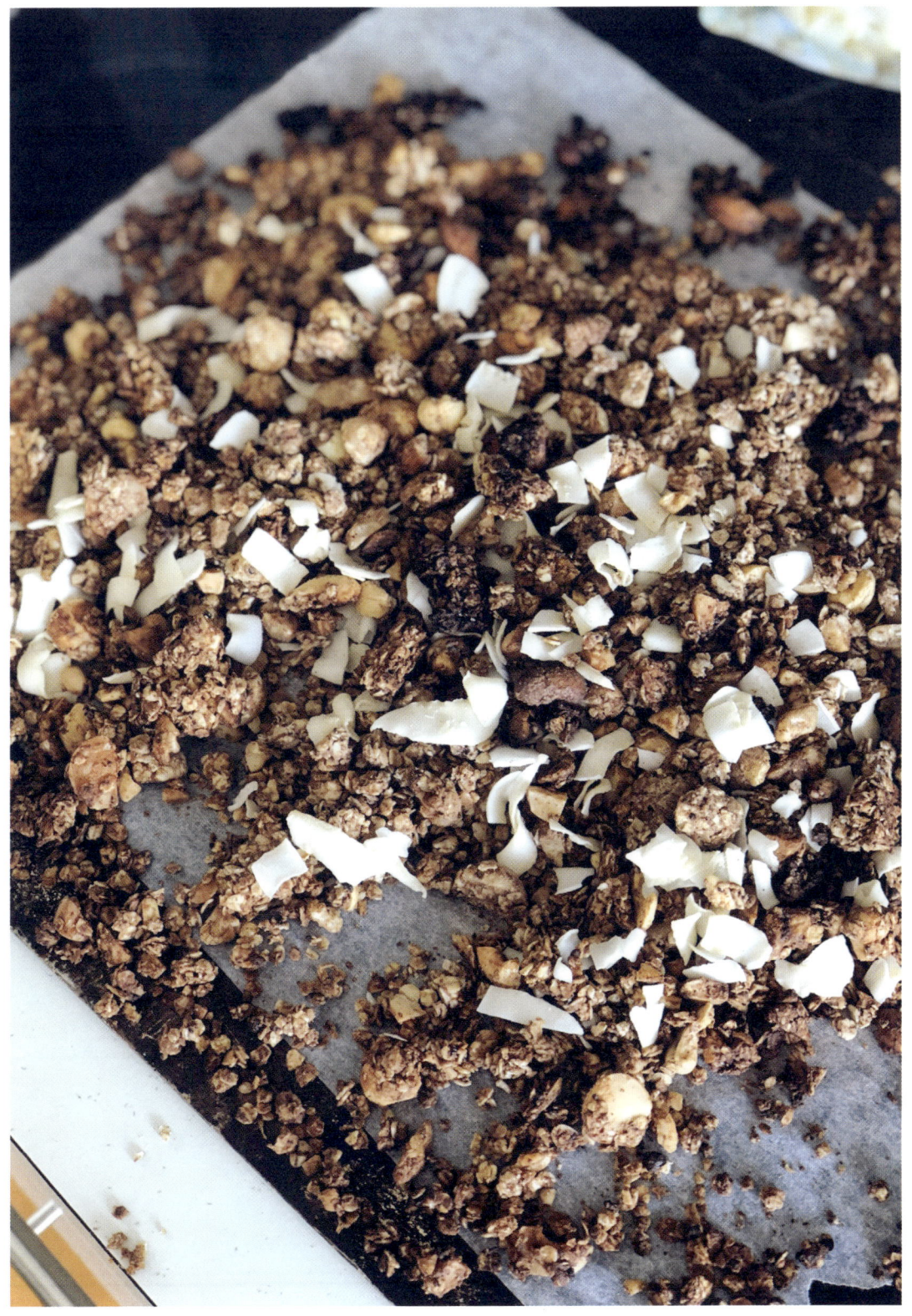

Green Smoothie Bowls

1 frozen zucchini
2 frozen bananas
handful of spinach
½ cup almond milk
1 scoop protein powder (optional)

OPTIONAL TOPPINGS
granola, peanut butter, chopped banana, berries

1. Blend the frozen zucchini, frozen bananas, spinach, almond milk and protein powder (if using) until smooth.
2. Pour into bowls and top with your favourite toppings.

Makes/serves: 2 serves | Prep time: 2 minutes
Nutritional information: DF, RSF, V

Fruit and Nut Muesli

1½ cups rolled oats
1 cup dried fruit (we use sultanas, cranberries, raisins)
½ cup chopped nuts (we use walnuts and sunflower seeds)
2 Tbsp honey
1 Tbsp cinnamon
1 tsp vanilla essence

1. Preheat the oven to 180°C. Line a baking tray with baking paper.
2. In a bowl combine all ingredients, pour onto the tray and bake in the oven for 10 minutes.
3. Enjoy topped with your favourite fruits and milk of your choice. You could even pack this one up for a breakfast on the go!

Makes/serves: 12 serves | Prep time: 2 minutes | Cook time: 10 minutes
Nutritional information: DF, RSF, V

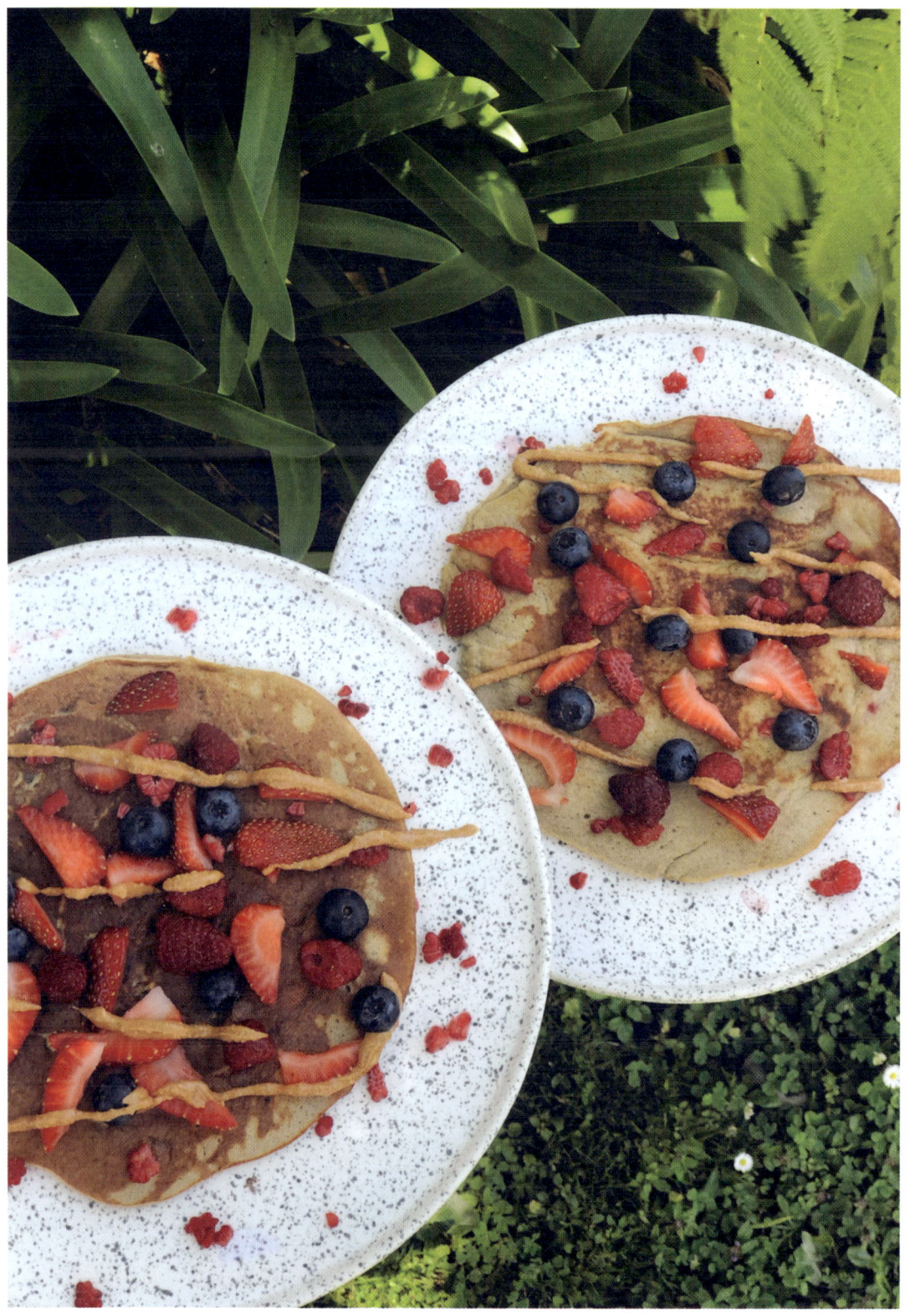

Protein Pancakes

1 banana
1 Tbsp protein powder
1 egg or 1 flaxseed/chia egg*
1 Tbsp coconut oil, melted

OPTIONAL TOPPINGS
peanut butter, berries, banana, a sprinkle of granola

1. Blend banana, protein powder and egg until smooth.
2. Heat the oil in a frying pan on a medium heat, and spoon half the mixture into the pan.
3. Fry each pancake for 2–3 minutes each side, or until they begin to bubble.
4. Repeat for all the remaining mixture.
5. Top with whatever you like!

*For instructions on making a flaxseed/chia egg, see p. 9

Makes/serves: 2 large pancakes or 8 small pancakes | Prep time: 2 minutes
Cook time: 10 minutes | Nutritional information: DF, RSF, GF

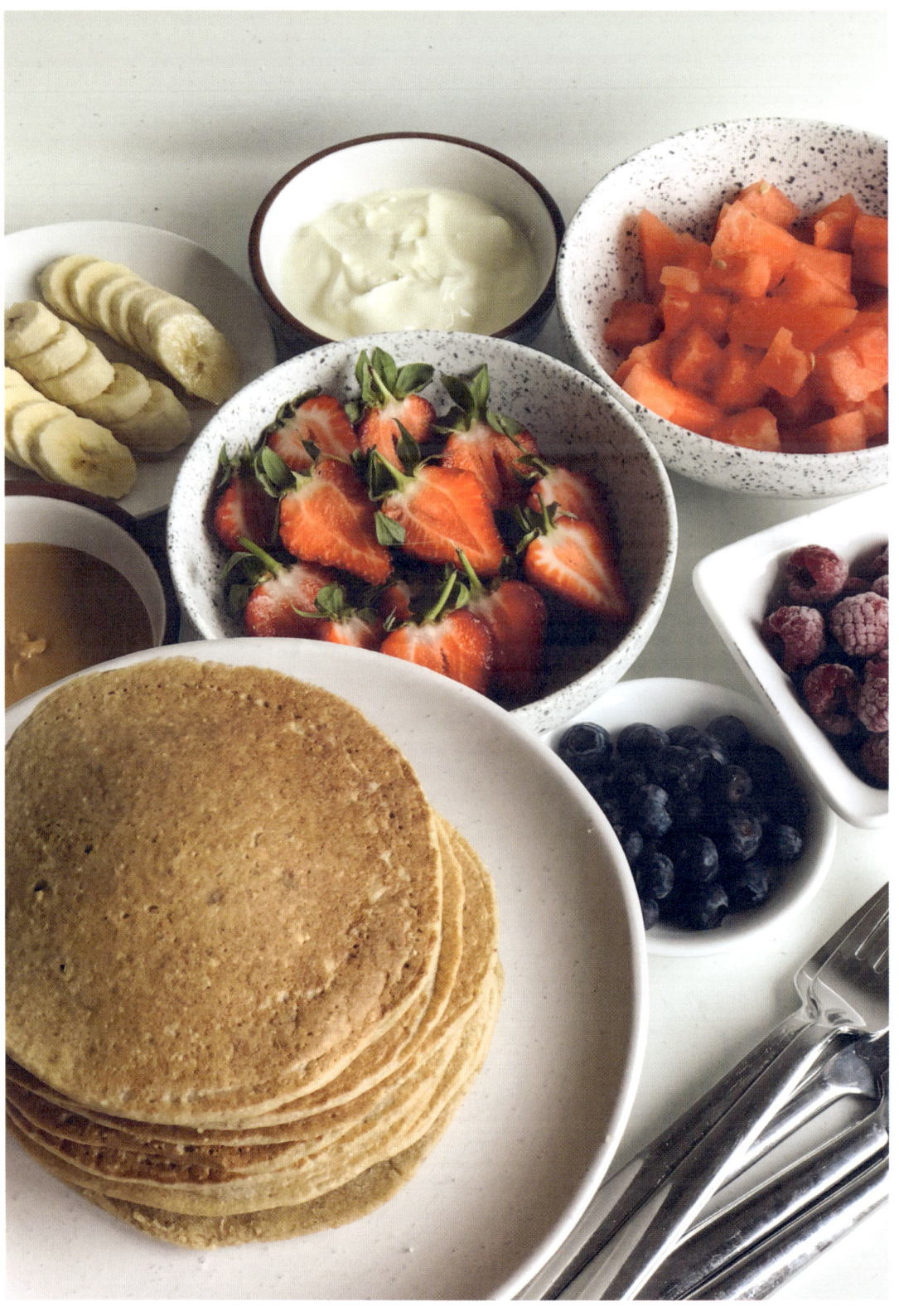

Oat Pancakes

1½ bananas
3½ cups rolled oats
1 Tbsp protein powder
1 tsp baking powder
1 tsp cinnamon
1 pinch of salt
1 egg, flaxseed or chia-seed egg (see p. 9)
1 tsp vanilla essence
1½ cups milk of choice (we used almond milk)
1 Tbsp coconut oil, melted

OPTIONAL TOPPINGS
watermelon, berries, banana, Greek yoghurt, peanut butter

1. Blend bananas, rolled oats, protein powder, baking powder, cinnamon, salt, egg, vanilla and almond milk until smooth.
2. Heat a pan with oil.
3. Pour enough batter into the pan to almost cover the base and cook over a medium heat for 3–4 minutes or until pancake starts to bubble on the top.
4. Then flip and cook the other side for another 3–4 minutes.
5. Repeat with remaining mixture until all batter is used up. Add more oil between pancakes if needed.
6. Serve with any toppings you like.

Makes/serves: 3 serves | Prep time: 2 minutes | Cook time: 10–15 minutes
Nutritional information: DF, RSF, V

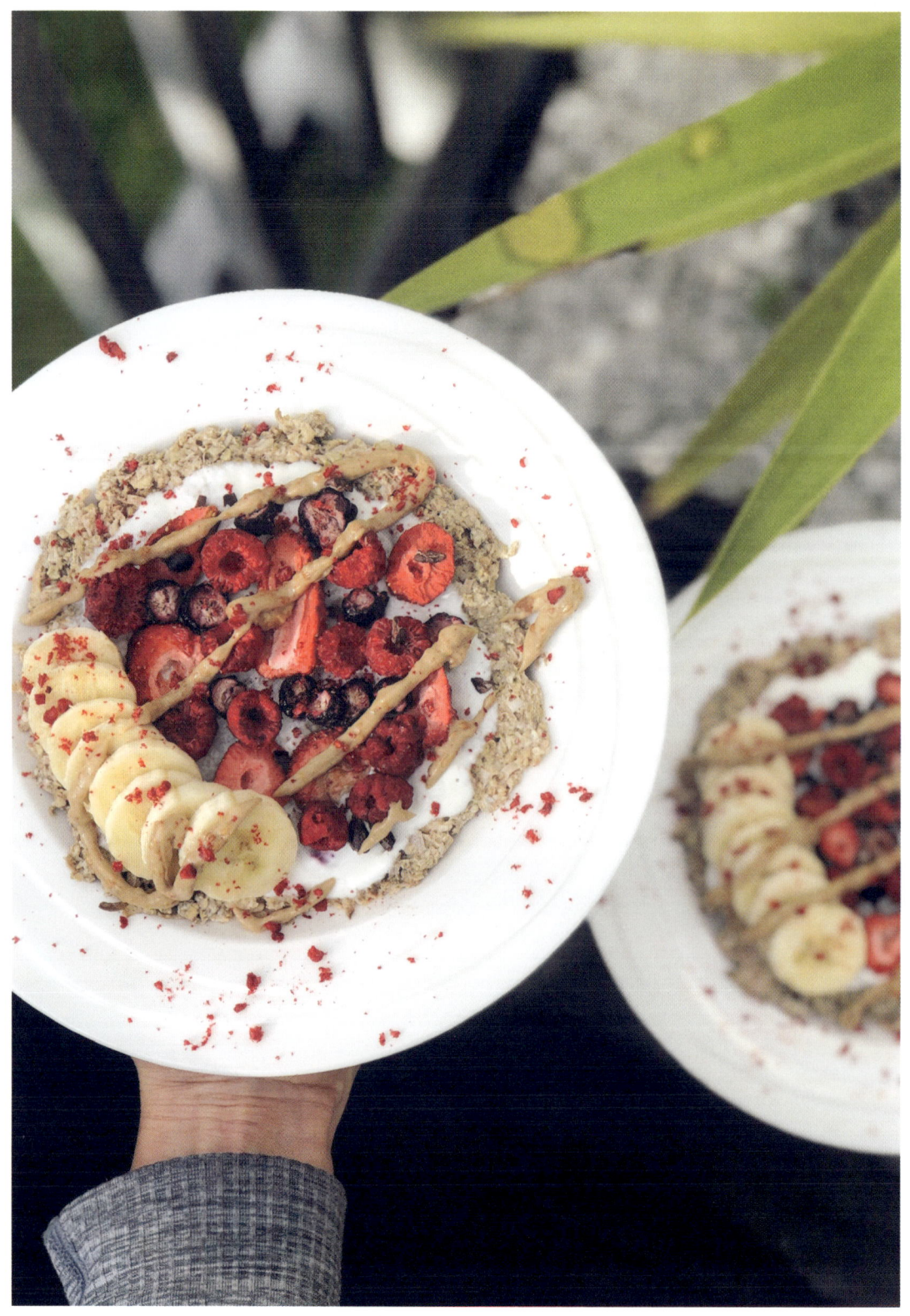

Coconut and Oat Breakfast 'Pizzas'

1 cup rolled oats
½ cup threaded coconut
½ cup almond milk
1 tsp vanilla essence
dash of cinnamon
1 tsp baking powder

OPTIONAL TOPPINGS
Greek yoghurt, sliced banana, peanut butter, berries

1. Preheat oven to 180°C. Line two baking trays with baking paper.
2. Mix all ingredients together until well combined.
3. Spread the mixture out to form two 'pizza bases' on prepared baking trays.
4. Place in the oven for 10 minutes until golden.
5. Top with your fave toppings.

Makes/serves: 2 serves | Prep time: 2 minutes | Cook time: 10 minutes
Nutritional information: DF, RSF, V

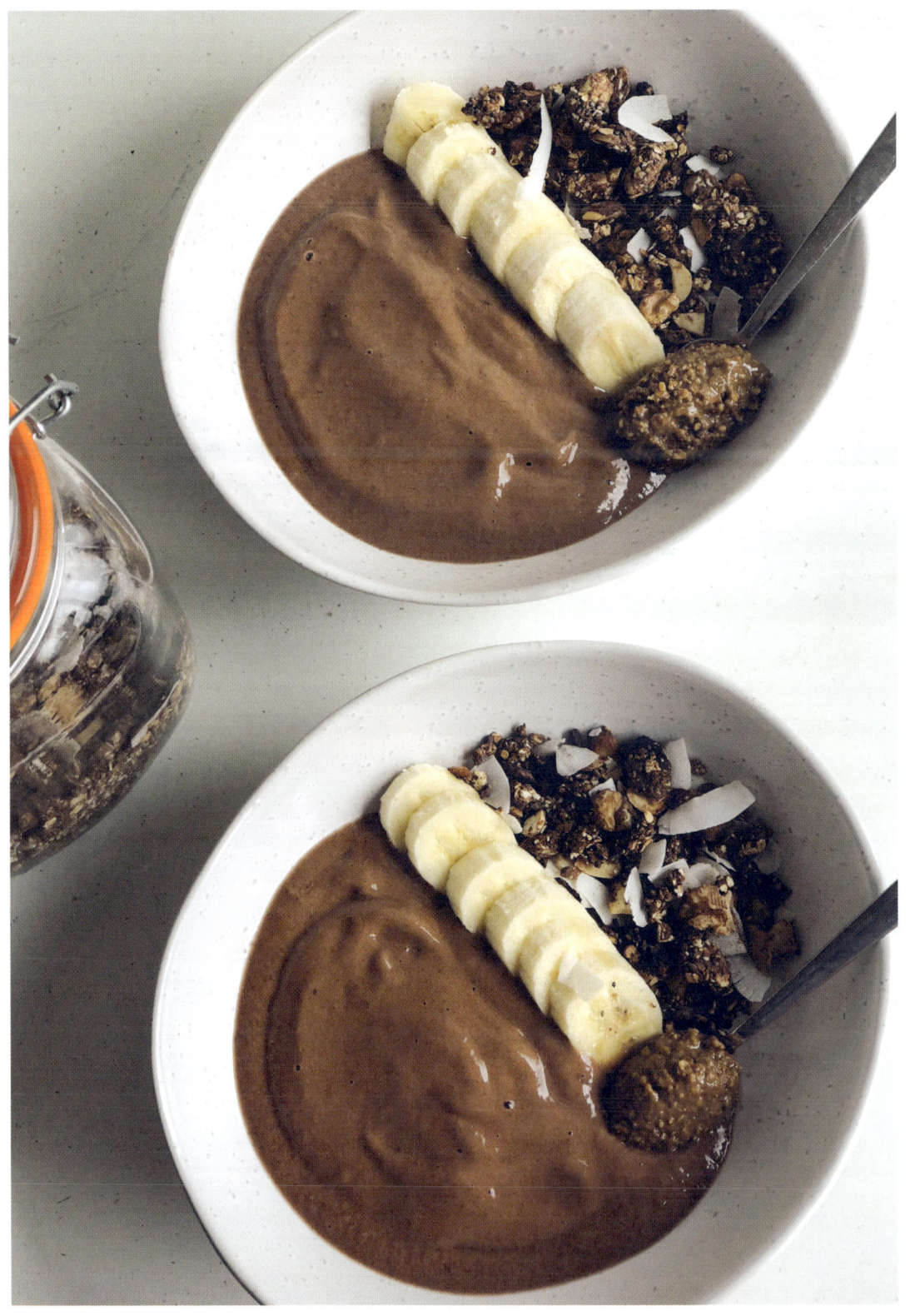

Choc Nana Smoothie Bowls

2 frozen bananas
1 Tbsp cacao powder
1 scoop chocolate protein powder
½ cup almond milk

OPTIONAL TOPPINGS
granola, peanut butter, banana

1. Blend the bananas, cacao powder, protein powder and almond milk until smooth.
2. Pour into bowls and top with your favourite topping.

Makes/serves: 2 serves | Prep time: 2 minutes
Nutritional information: DF, RSF, V

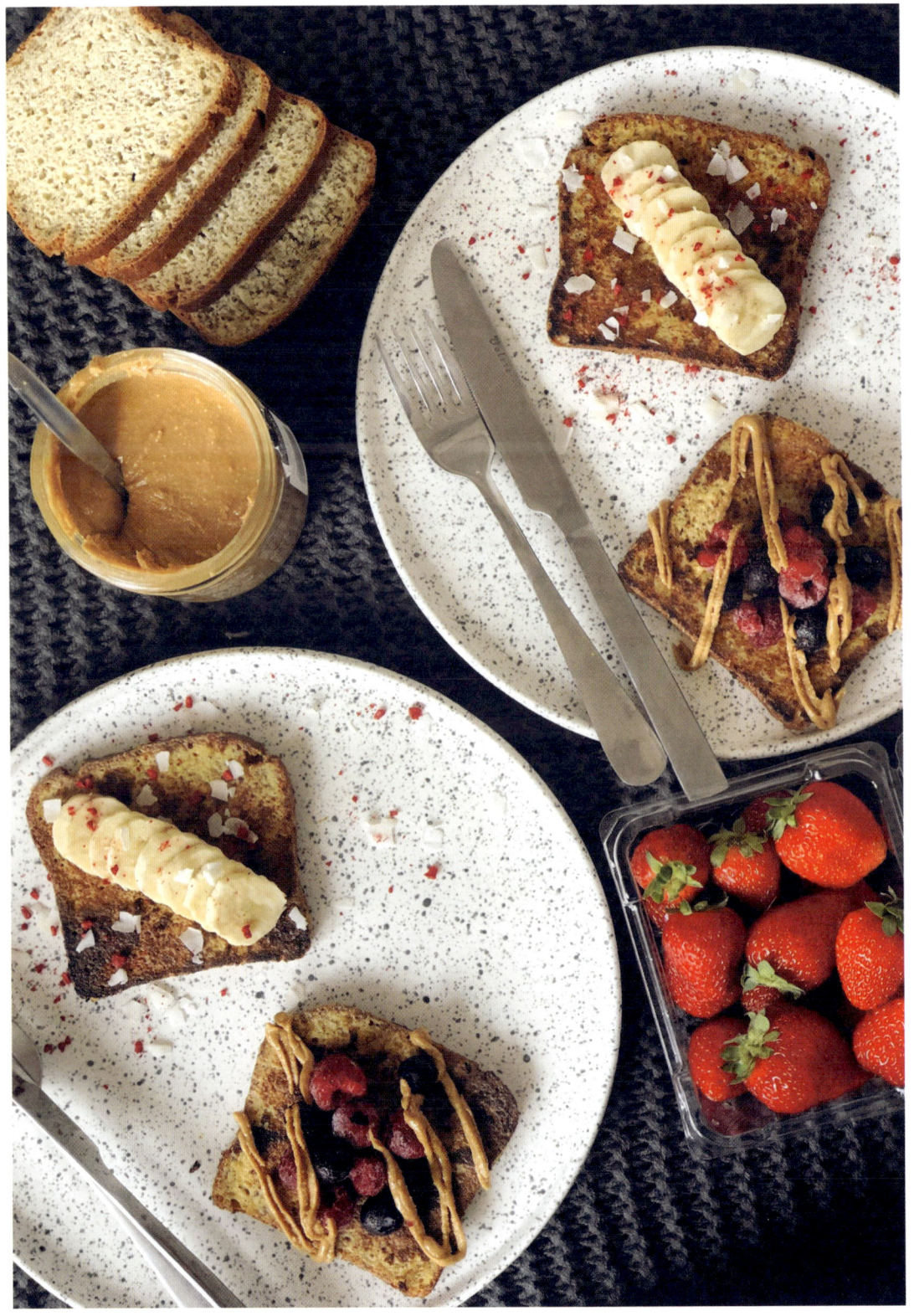

French Toast

2 eggs
¼ cup milk of choice
    (we use almond)
1 tsp cinnamon
4 pieces bread (use gluten-
    free bread if desired)

OPTIONAL TOPPINGS
peanut butter, banana,
    berries, coconut chips

1. Whisk eggs, milk and cinnamon in a bowl.
2. Coat bread in the egg mix.
3. Fry each side of the bread for 3–4 minutes or until browned.
4. Top with whatever you fancy!

Makes/serves: 2 serves | Prep time: 2 minutes | Cook time: 10 minutes
Nutritional information: RSF, can be made DF and GF

Savoury Buckwheat Pancakes

1 cup buckwheat flour
½ cup water
1 tsp paprika
1 tsp chilli powder
1 Tbsp coconut oil, melted

OPTIONAL TOPPINGS
avocado, hummus, tomatoes, chilli flakes

1. In a bowl combine buckwheat flour, water, paprika and chilli.
2. Heat a frying pan with oil on a medium heat, and pour half the mixture into the pan.
3. Cook for 2–3 minutes or until it starts to bubble, and then flip.
4. Repeat with the other half of the mixture.
5. Place on plates, add toppings and EAT!

Makes/serves: 2 large pancakes | Prep time: 2 minutes | Cook time: 6 minutes
Nutritional information: DF, RSF, V, GF

Smashed Peas on Toast

1 cup green peas
4 pieces of bread
juice of 1 lemon
salt and pepper to taste
handful of fresh coriander

OPTIONAL TOPPINGS
chopped cherry tomatoes, sliced radish

1. Bring the peas to the boil and rinse.
2. While the bread is in the toaster, use the back of a fork to mash the peas with a squeeze of lemon, salt, pepper and coriander.
3. Place the pea smash onto toast and top with cherry tomatoes and radish, if desired.

Makes/serves: 2 serves | Prep time: 2 minutes
Nutritional information: DF, RSF, V

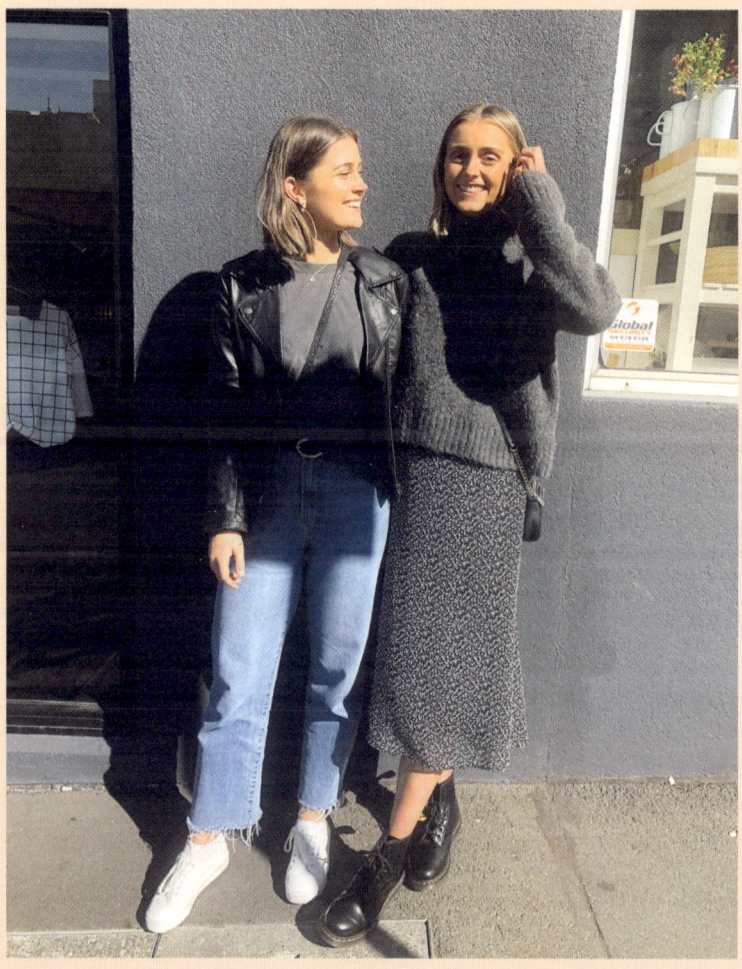

Lunches on the Run

We know what a rush it can be to get out the door to that morning lecture or gym class. But you can really save money if you make your lunch and take it with you, rather than buying it, and you have the added advantage of knowing what's in your lunchbox is healthy too! We recommend preparing these low-cost lunches the night before — that way, you can just grab a portion in the morning and away you go! All are super yum without needing to be reheated and guaranteed to fuel your brain and body with good energy.

One-tray Peanut, Lime, Chickpea and Pumpkin Salad

½ small pumpkin
½ broccoli
1 x 400g can chickpeas, drained and rinsed
olive oil
salt and pepper
½ bag spinach
½ chopped red cabbage
juice of 2 limes
½ cup chopped peanuts
lemon juice for squeezing over the top

1. Preheat oven to 180°C. Line a baking tray with baking paper.
2. Chop pumpkin and broccoli up into bite-sized pieces and place onto prepared baking tray. Add the chickpeas to the tray, drizzle with olive oil, sprinkle with salt and pepper and bake in the oven for 20 minutes.
3. In a large bowl combine the roast vegetables and chickpeas with spinach and red cabbage. Mix through the lime juice, peanuts and more salt and pepper.
4. Divide into three airtight containers and store in the fridge ready for lunches. Best eaten cold with a squeeze of lemon juice on top.

Makes/serves: 2–3 serves | Prep time: 10 minutes | Cook time: 20 minutes
Nutritional information: DF, RSF, V, GF

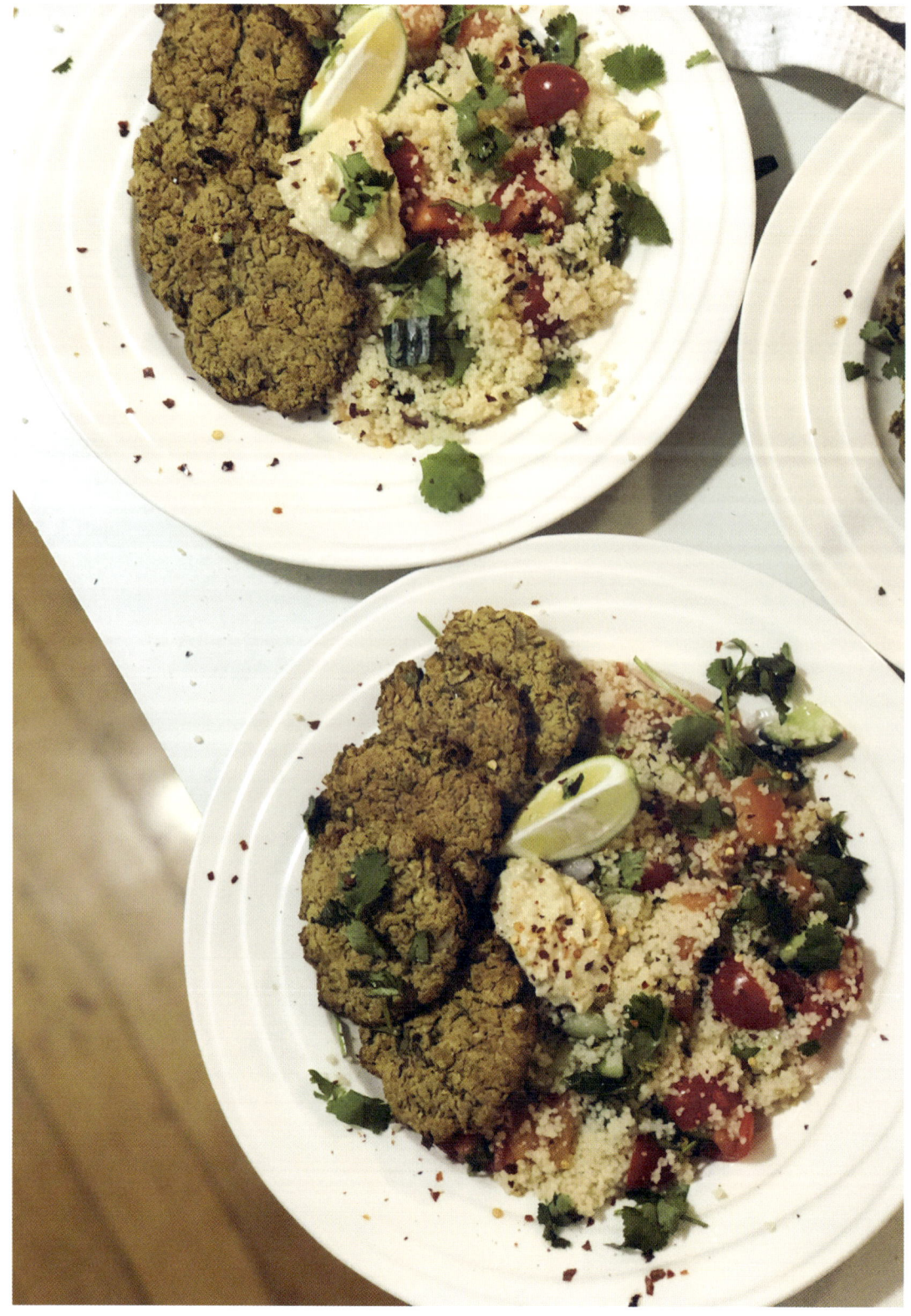

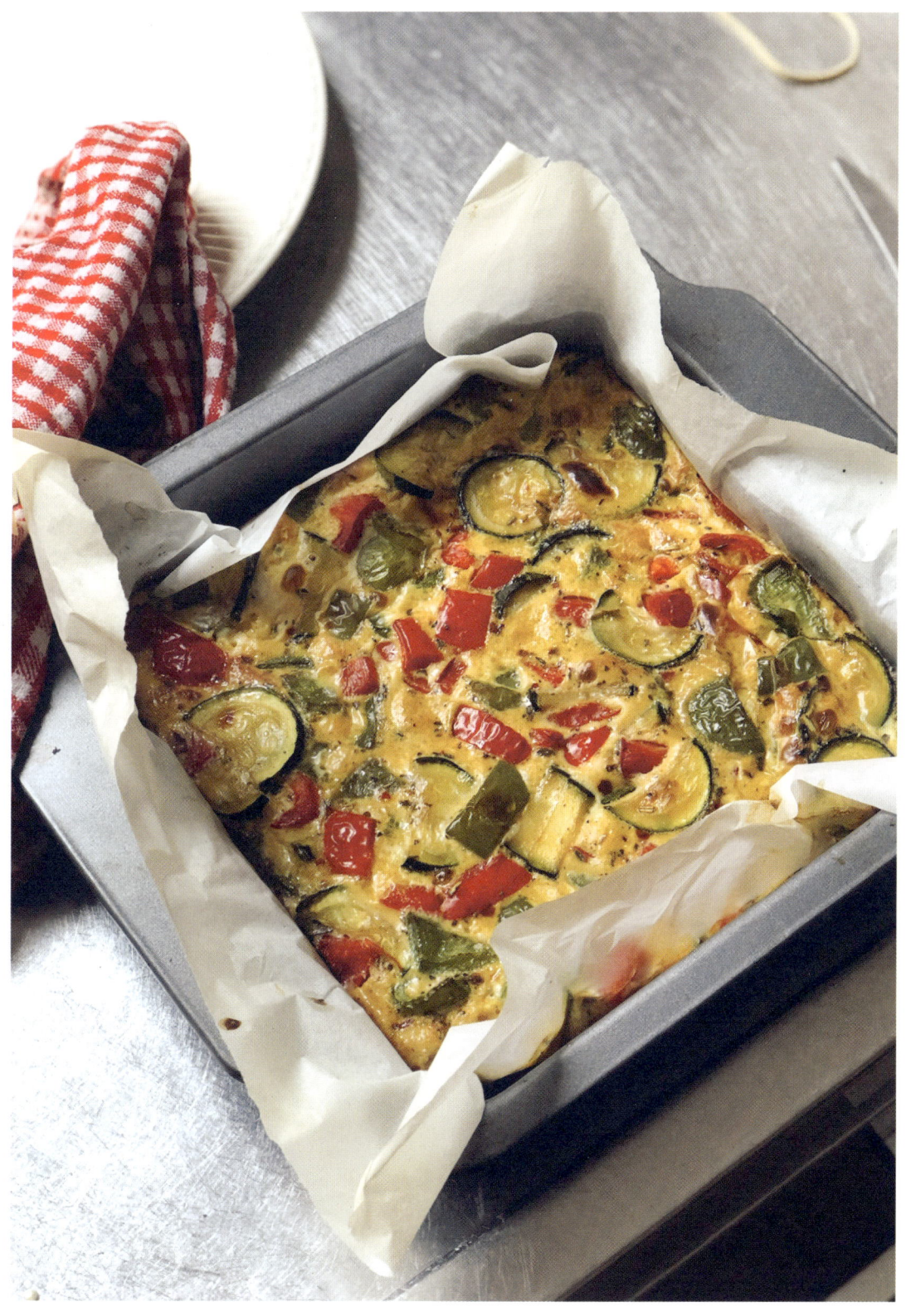

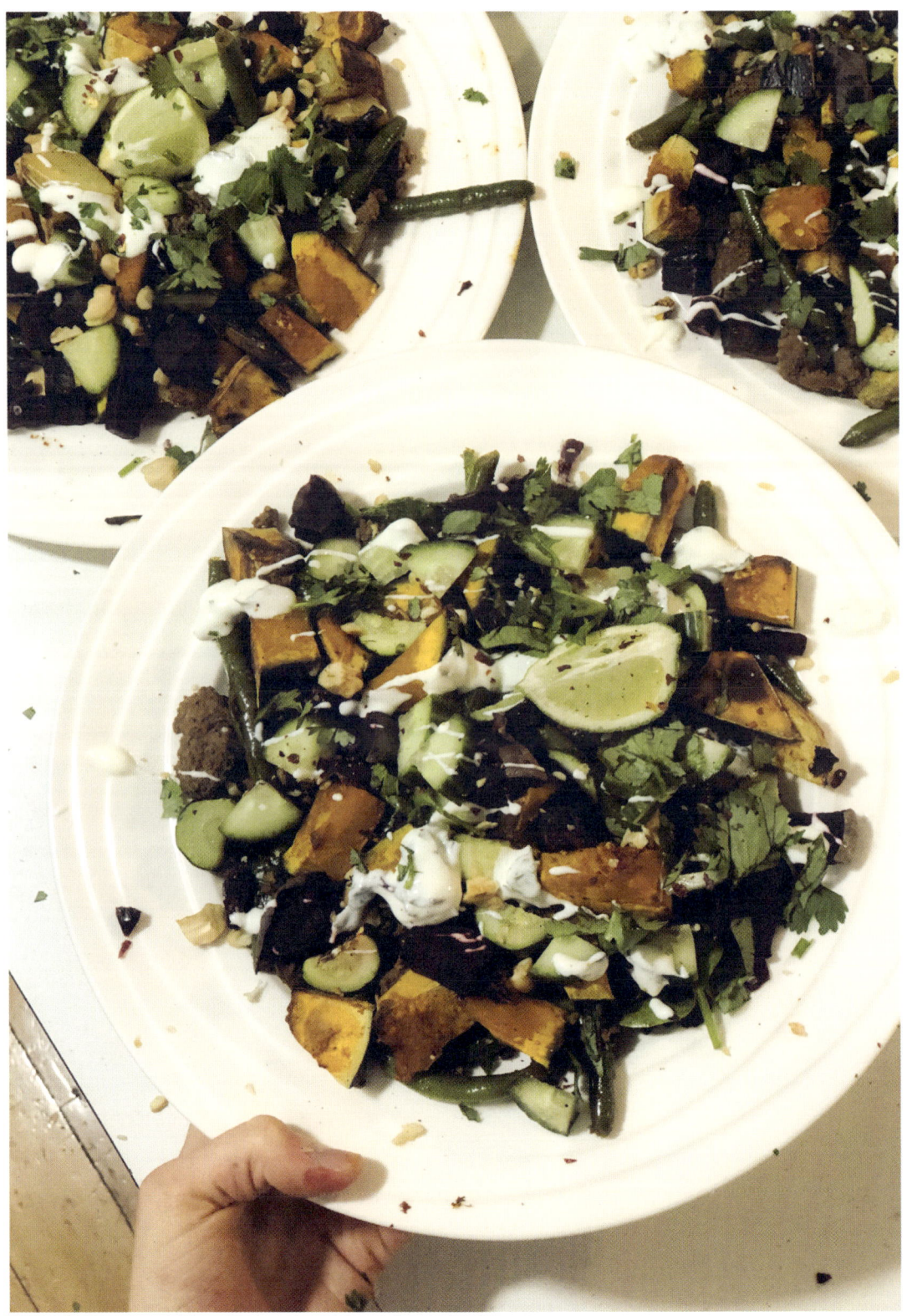

Roasted Chickpea, Beetroot and Pumpkin Salad

SALAD
1 beetroot
½ butternut pumpkin
1 x 400g can chickpeas, drained and rinsed
1 tsp chilli flakes
2 tsp paprika
2 tsp cumin
2 tsp ground coriander
2 Tbsp olive oil
1 cup green beans
½ cup chopped peanuts
½ cup cranberries
80g coriander

YOGHURT DRESSING
handful of mint
½ cup Greek yoghurt
juice of 1 lemon

1. Preheat oven to fan bake at 180°C. Line a baking tray with baking paper.
2. Chop the beetroot and pumpkin into 2cm cubes, and place onto prepared baking tray.
3. Add chickpeas, sprinkle over spices and olive oil and toss to coat. Place in the oven for 20–25 minutes. Remove from the oven and set aside to cool.
4. In a pan over a medium heat, gently soften the green beans with a splash of water and salt and pepper.
5. To make the dressing: finely chop the mint and combine with the yoghurt and lemon juice. Mix well.
6. Combine vegetables and chickpeas in a large bowl with the green beans, peanuts, cranberries and chopped coriander.
7. Just before serving, drizzle salad with dressing.
8. Transfer any remaining salad into an airtight container and store in the fridge.

Makes/serves: 4 serves | Prep time: 10 minutes | Cook time: 35 minutes
Nutritional information: DF, RSF

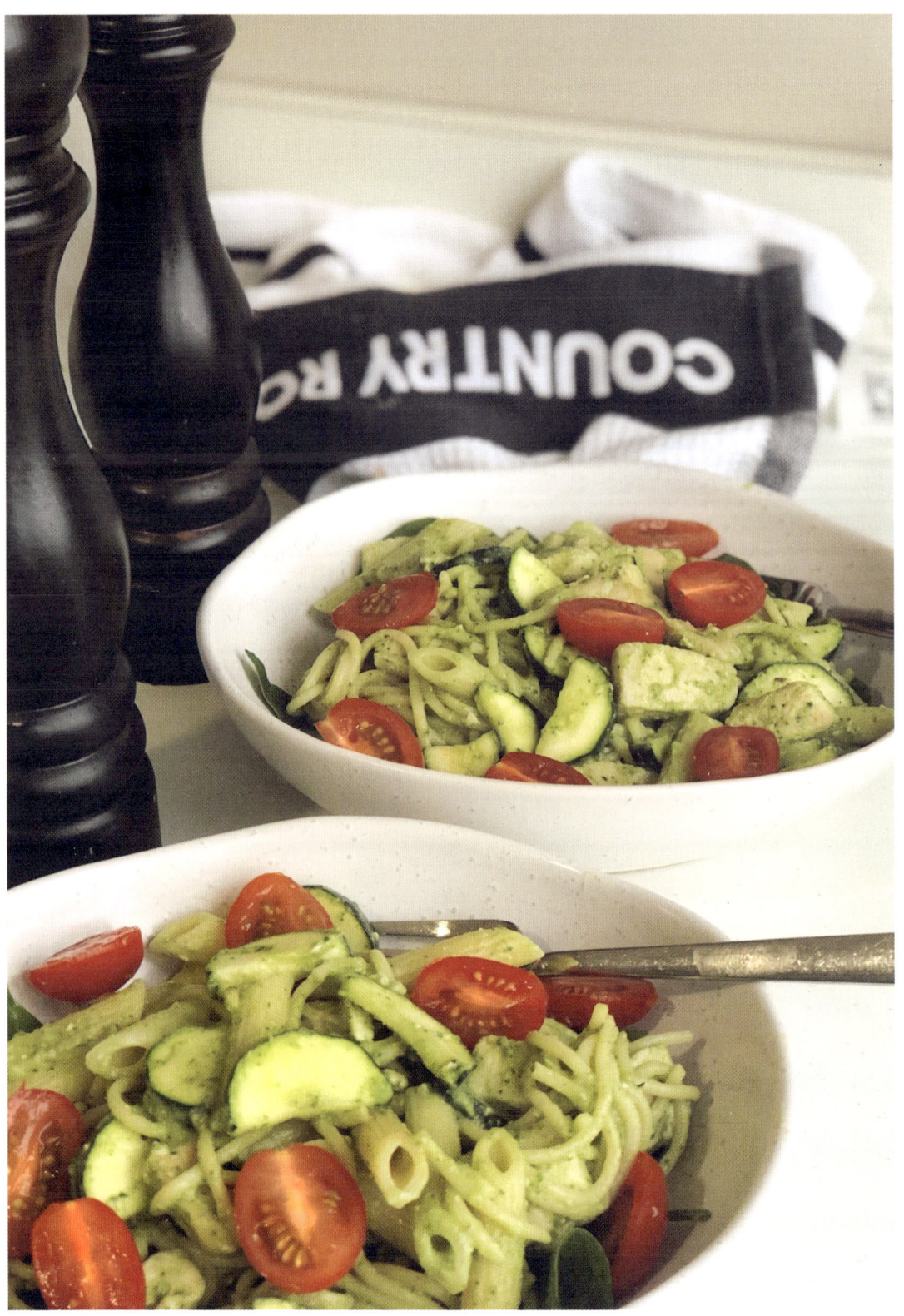

Creamy Avocado and Chicken Pasta

250g chicken breast
olive oil
250g pasta of choice
    (we use penne
    and spaghetti)
1 large avocado
1 lemon
salt and pepper to taste
100g spinach
100g zucchini
100g cherry tomatoes

1. Chop the chicken into bite-sized pieces and fry in a pan with a dash of olive oil for 10 minutes or until cooked through.
2. Boil water and cook pasta until al dente, then rinse.
3. Blend the avocado, lemon, salt and pepper until smooth. If it is too thick, add water to thin it out until the sauce is smooth and creamy.
4. Combine the chicken and pasta and mix through the avocado sauce, spinach, chopped zucchini and cherry tomatoes.
5. Divide evenly into 2–3 airtight containers and store in the fridge. Can be eaten cold or gently warmed in the microwave — the perfect lunch to take to uni or work.

Makes/serves: 2–3 serves | Prep time: 10 minutes | Cook time: 20 minutes
Nutritional information: DF, RSF

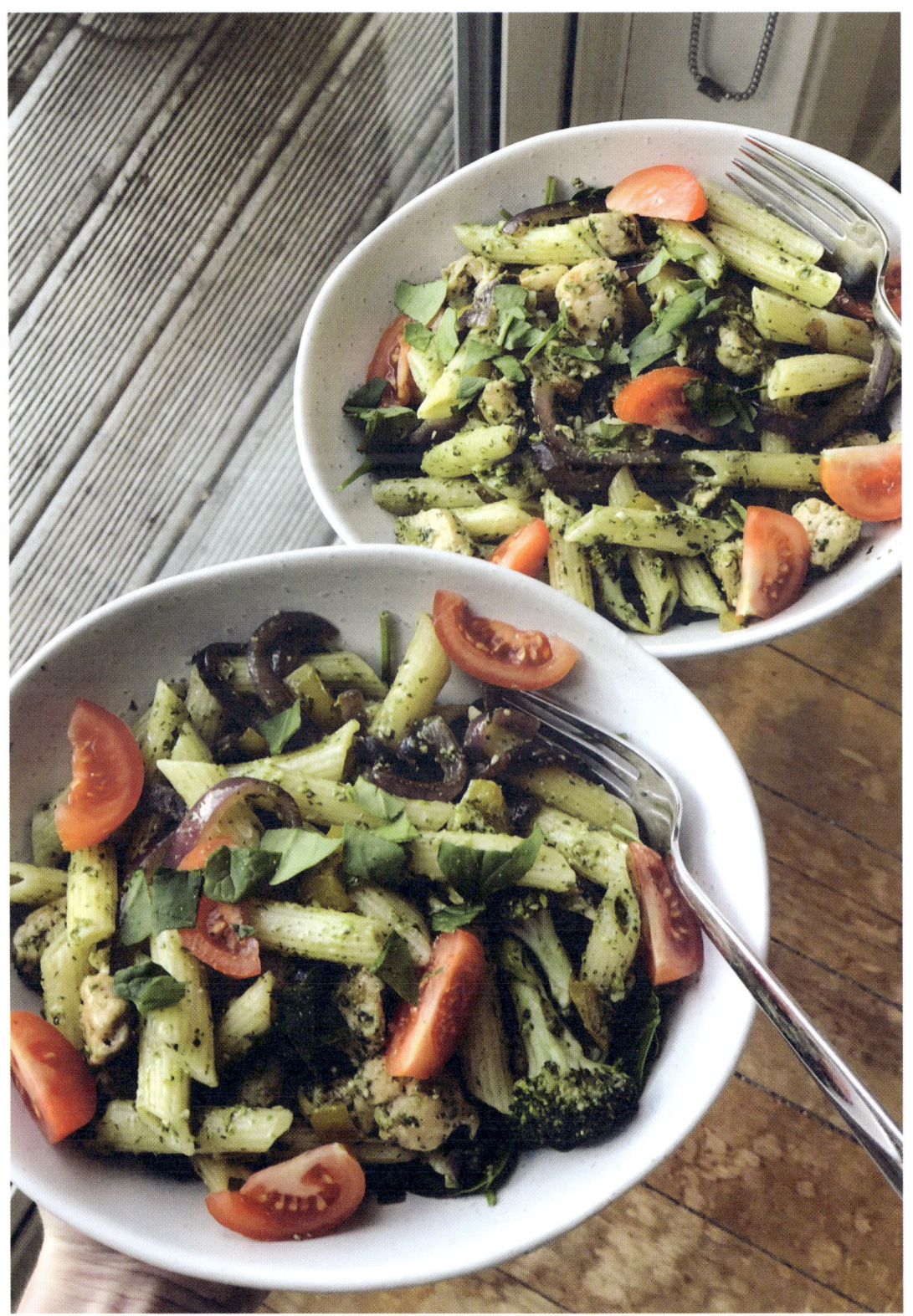

Pesto Pasta

500g chicken breast
1 cup broccoli
1 red onion
500g penne pasta
100g spinach
200g cherry tomatoes
100g pesto
handful of basil, torn

1. Preheat oven to 180°C. Chop the chicken into small pieces and fry in a pan with a dash of oil for around 10 minutes or until cooked through completely. Set aside.
2. Chop the broccoli and red onion into small chunks and place on a baking tray and bake in the oven for 20 minutes. Remove and set aside.
3. Add pasta to a pot of boiling salted water. Cook until just softened (around 8 minutes), drain and rinse.
4. In a bowl combine all ingredients. Scatter basil over the top.
5. Store in the fridge in an airtight container until ready to serve.

Makes/serves: 4–5 serves | Prep time: 10 minutes | Cook time: 30 minutes
Nutritional information: DF, RSF

Feed the Flatties!

With a couple of years of flatting behind us, we've had time to come up with some dinners that will make your flatmates smile, and which don't require you spending hours in the kitchen. We hope the following recipes help you keep your flat meals simple and inexpensive, yet still delicious.

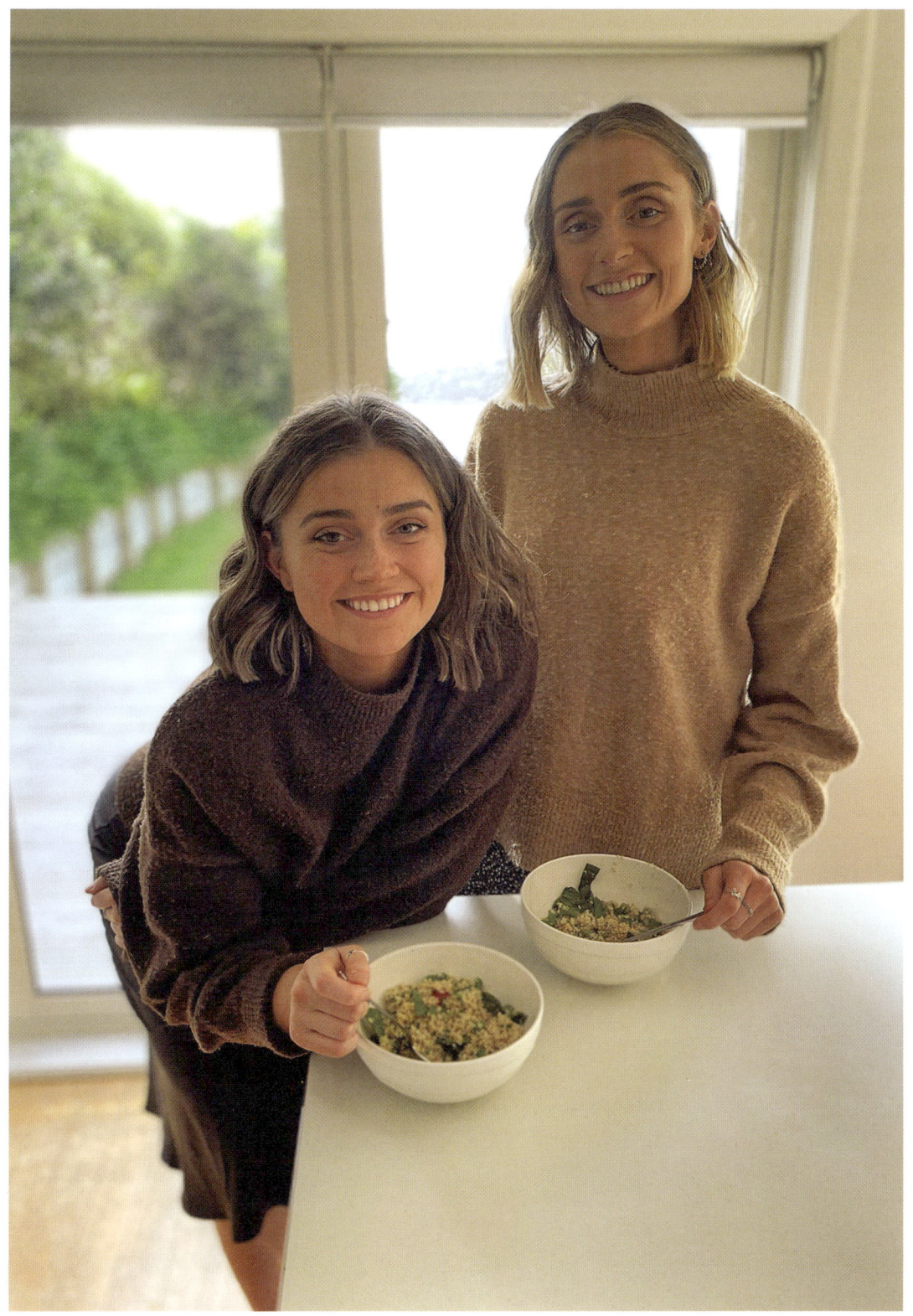

Loaded Wedges

6 medium-large potatoes
1 tbsp olive oil
2 tsp chilli powder
2 corn cobs
1 red onion
2 Tbsp water
1 tsp brown sugar
1 Tbsp balsamic vinegar
1 x 400g can red kidney beans
4 medium tomatoes

OPTIONAL EXTRAS
chopped tomato, mashed avocado, chopped coriander, lime wedges, chilli flakes

1. Preheat oven to 180°C. Line a baking tray with baking paper.
2. Chop potatoes into wedges, toss in olive oil and chilli powder and place on prepared baking tray. Bake in the oven for 25 minutes.
3. After 10 minutes, add the corn cobs to the baking tray and return to the oven for remaining 15 minutes.
4. While potatoes and corn are cooking, slice onion and fry in a frying pan with a dash of olive oil, water, brown sugar and balsamic vinegar. Cook until sticky.
5. Once the potatoes are cooked, rinse the red kidney beans and add them to the baking tray. Cook for a further 3 minutes then remove from the oven. When corn cobs are cool enough to handle, slice off kernels and return to potato mix.
6. Divide the potato wedges between 6 plates and spoon bean mixture on top.
7. Top with chopped tomato, mashed avocado, chopped coriander, lime wedges and chilli flakes if desired.

Makes/serves: 6 serves | Prep time: 10 minutes | Cook time: 25 minutes
Nutritional information: DF, RSF, V, G

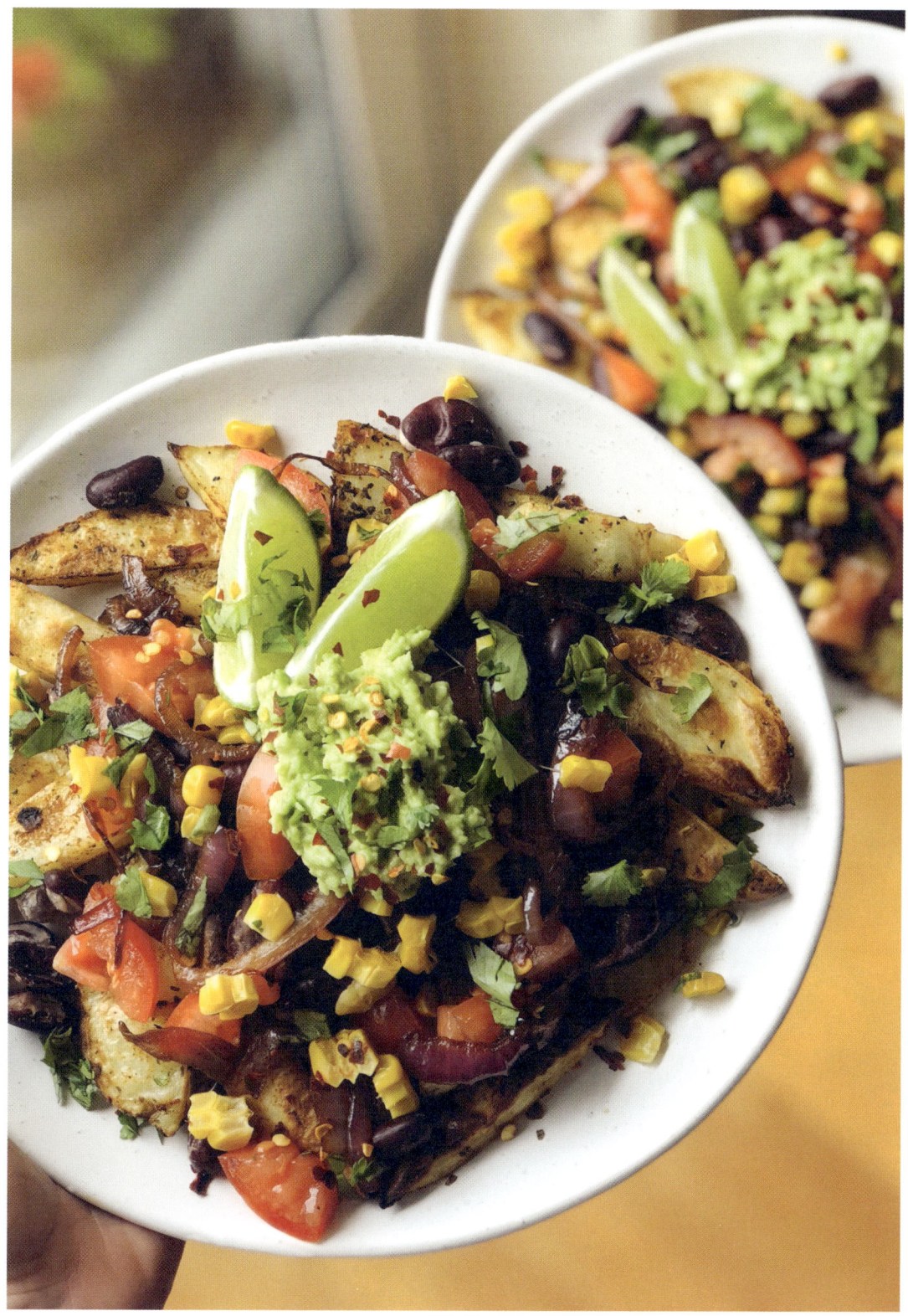

Em's Mexican Bowls

BEAN MIX
1 x 400g can chilli beans
1 x 400g can black beans
1 x 400g can corn kernels
2 x 400g cans diced tomatoes
1 tsp oregano
1 tsp coriander
1 tsp cumin
½ tsp ground chilli
2 cups rice
3½ cups water

SALAD
4–5 tomatoes
1 x onion
handful of fresh coriander
juice of 1 lime
2 Tbsp olive oil
1 x iceberg lettuce
2 x capsicums

1. Drain and rinse chilli beans, black beans and corn then add, along with canned tomatoes, to a frying pan. Add oregano and spices and leave to simmer for 20 minutes.
2. While the beans are simmering, add rice and water to a saucepan over a high heat. Stir constantly until boiling then cover with a lid and turn down to low. Simmer for 10 minutes, then remove from heat. Leave to sit (covered) for 5 minutes then uncover and fluff up with a fork.
3. To make the salad: Dice the tomatoes, onion and fresh coriander. Mix together and add the lime juice as well as the olive oil.
4. Chop up the lettuce, deseed and chop capsicums and toss through the salad.
5. Serve rice in bowls topped with beans and salad on the side and you're good to go!

Makes/serves: 6 serves | Prep time: 10 minutes | Cook time: 20 minutes
Nutritional information: DF, RSF, V

Veggie Nachos

NACHOS
olive oil
1 onion, finely chopped
1 zucchini, grated
1 red capsicum, deseeded and finely chopped
1 red chilli, finely chopped
2 carrots, grated
1 tsp cumin
1 tsp ground chilli
1 tsp paprika
1 x 400g can chilli beans
1 x 400g can diced tomatoes
1 x 300g packet corn chips
chopped coriander to serve
lemon wedges to serve

GUACAMOLE
1 large avocado
juice of 1 lemon
salt and pepper to taste

1. Heat a pan with a dash of olive oil and add onion. Cook until soft.
2. Add zucchini, capsicum, chilli, carrots and spices and cook for 3–4 minutes.
3. Add chilli beans and diced tomatoes and bring to the boil.
4. To make the guacamole, mash the avocado with the back of a fork and add lemon, salt and pepper.
5. Place a handful of corn chips in a bowl and add the bean mix on top.
6. Serve with a heaped tablespoon of guac, coriander and a lemon wedge!

Makes/serves: 4–5 serves | Prep time: 10 minutes | Cook time: 30 minutes
Nutritional information: DF, RSF, V

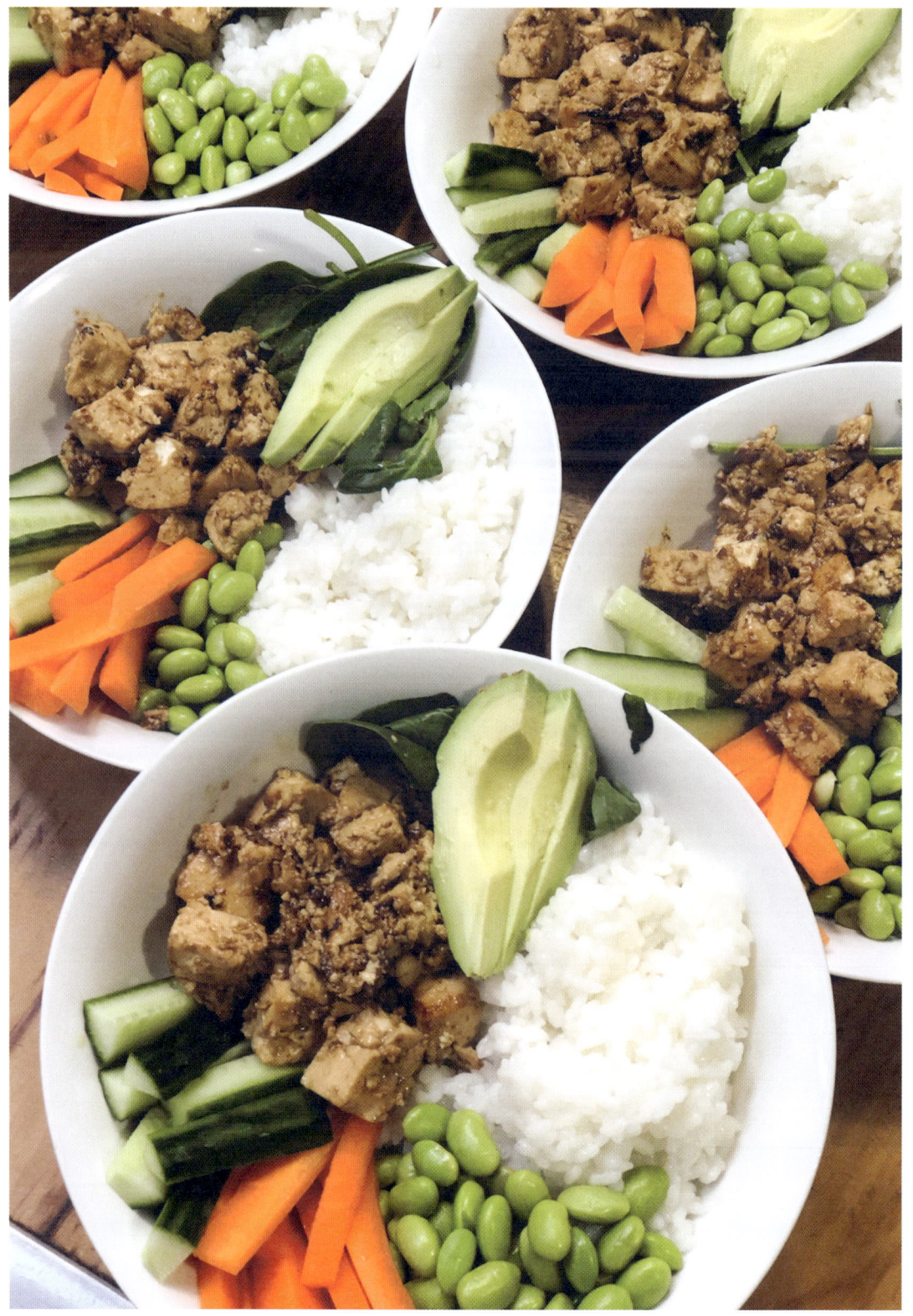

Teriyaki Tofu Donburi Bowls

olive oil for frying
1 x 450g block tofu
½ cup teriyaki sauce
2 x cups sushi rice
3 x cups water
sesame seeds (optional)

OPTIONAL VEGETABLES
carrot sticks, cucumber sticks, edamame beans, baby spinach, chopped cabbage, chopped broccoli, sliced avocado, dash of olive oil

1. Heat a dash of oil in a frying pan.
2. Slice tofu into cubes and cook for 2–3 minutes on each side until golden.
3. Add the teriyaki sauce to the pan and simmer for around 10 minutes.
4. While tofu is simmering, add sushi rice and water to a saucepan over a high heat. Boil, stirring regularly, for 10 minutes until soft. Drain well.
5. Prepare whatever veggies you like.
6. Add all components to a bowl and top with sesame seeds if desired.

Makes/serves: 5 serves | Prep time: 10 minutes | Cook time: 20 minutes
Nutritional information: DF, RSF, V

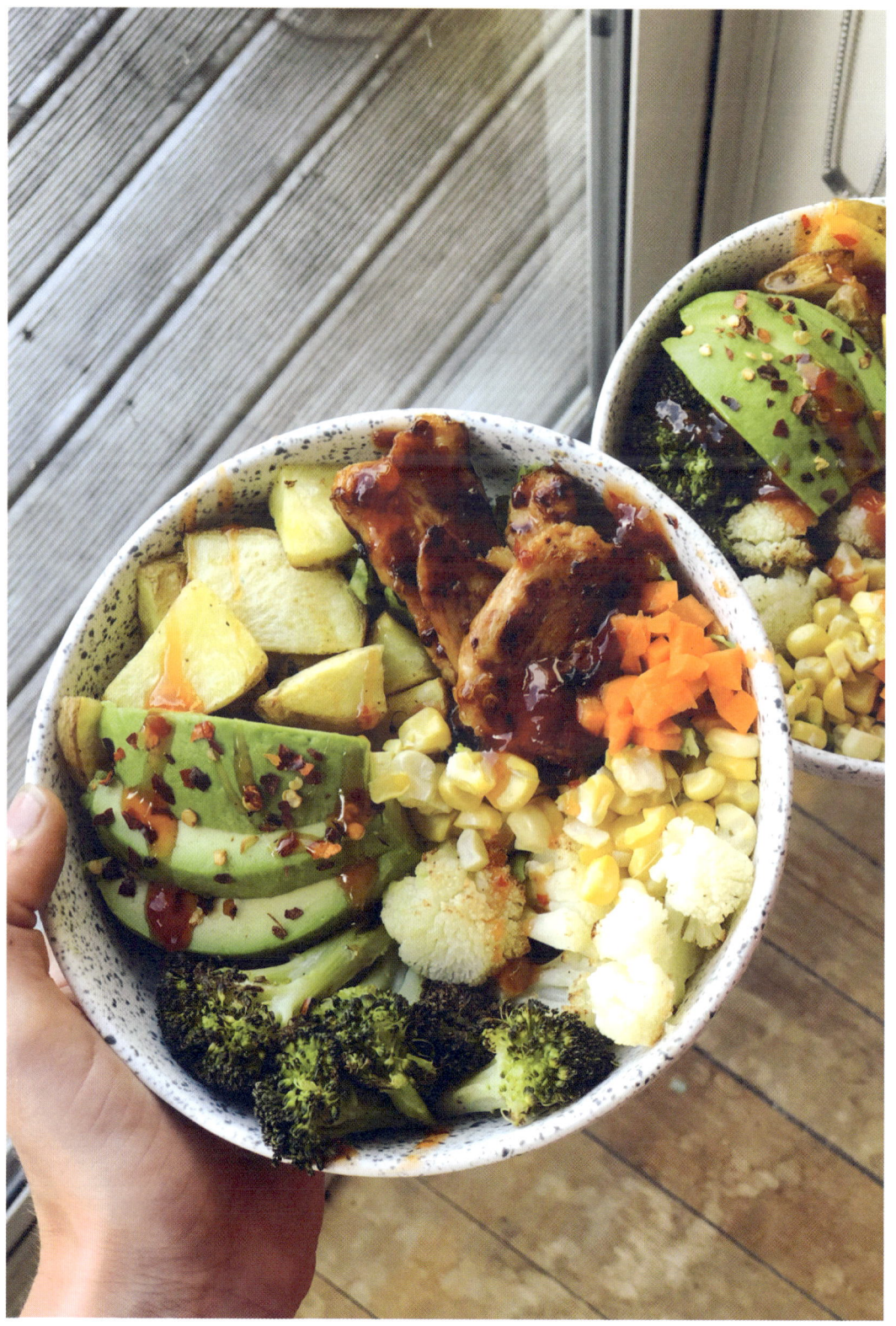

Sweet Chilli Chicken Nourish Bowls

3–4 medium–large potatoes
200g broccoli
200g cauliflower
1½ Tbsp olive oil
2 Tbsp sweet chilli sauce
1 tsp lime juice
400g chicken breast
2 carrots
1 avocado
1 x 400g can corn kernels

1. Preheat oven to 180°C. Chop potatoes, broccoli and cauliflower into bite-sized pieces. Place in a roasting dish with 1 tablespoon of the olive oil, salt and pepper. Bake in the oven for 20 minutes.
2. Mix sweet chilli sauce, lime juice and remaining olive oil.
3. Chop chicken into small pieces and coat with sweet chilli mixture. Cook in a frying pan over a medium heat until lightly brown and cooked through.
4. Dice carrots, slice avocado and rinse corn.
5. Mix all components in a bowl. You can add more sweet chilli if you like!

Makes/serves: 5 serves | Prep time: 10 minutes | Cook time: 20 minutes
Nutritional information: DF, RSF, GF

Corn Fritters with Black Rice Salad

FRITTERS
2 cups corn
2 eggs
3 Tbsp oil
1 Tbsp flour
1 tsp smoked paprika
1 tsp chilli powder
1 tsp ground coriander
zest of 1 lemon

BLACK RICE SALAD
1½ cups black rice
1 chopped cucumber
3 chopped tomatoes
juice of 1 lemon
sliced avocado
lemon wedges to serve
handful of coriander
    to garnish

1. To make the fritters: preheat oven to 180°C. Line a baking tray with baking paper.
2. Combine all fritter ingredients in a bowl.
3. Add heaped tablespoonfuls of mixture onto the prepared tray.
4. Cook in the oven for 5–8 minutes or until lightly brown on top, then flip and cook for another 5–8 minutes.
5. While the fritters are in the oven, boil the rice (see p. 52).
6. Once the rice has cooked, mix through the cucumber, tomatoes and lemon juice. Set aside.
7. Dish up! Serve fritters with black rice salad, sliced avocado and a lemon wedge on the side. Garnish with coriander.

Makes/serves: 10–12 fritters | Prep time: 10 minutes | Cook time: 15 minutes
Nutritional information: DF, RSF

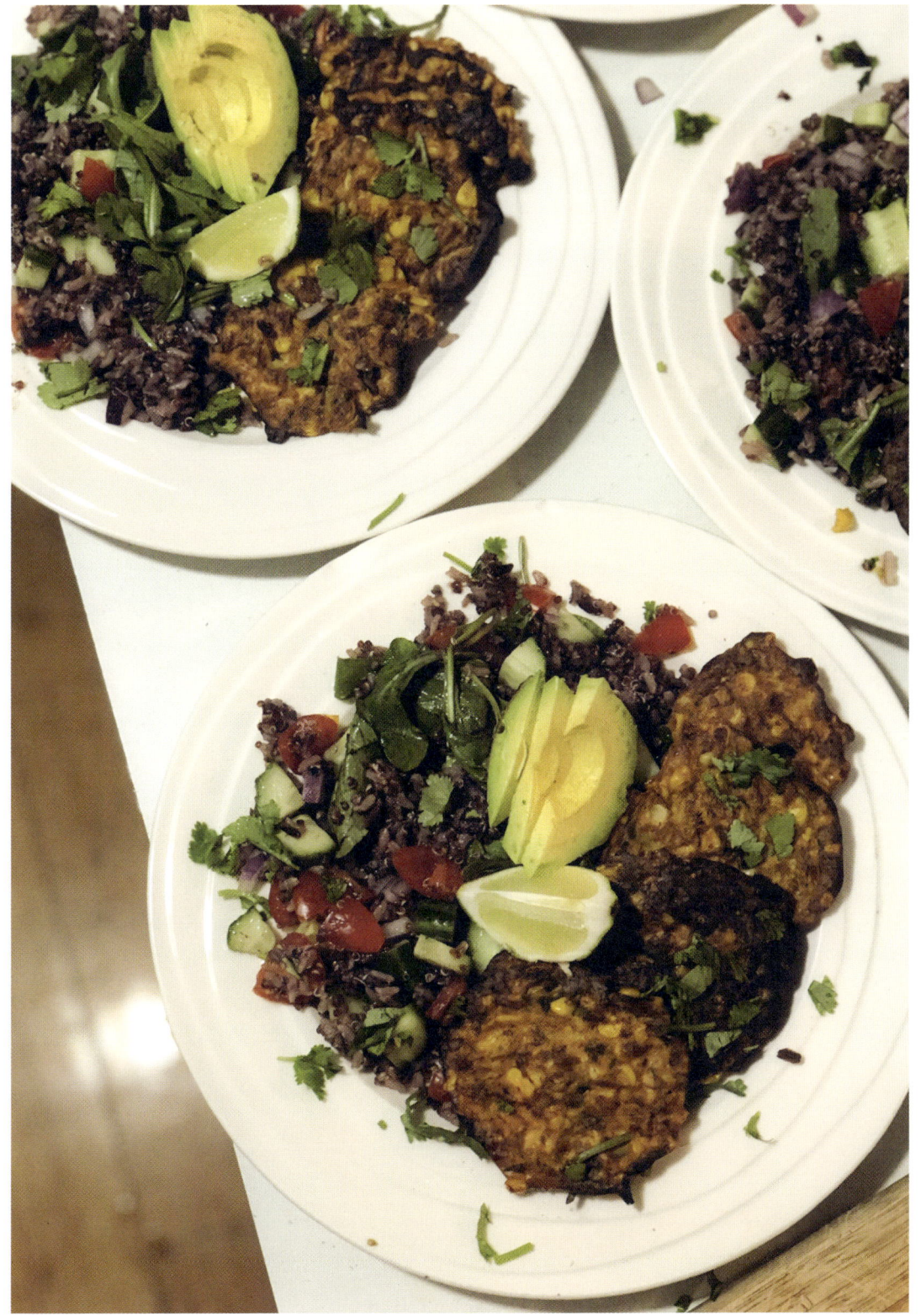

Lentil Bolognese

1 onion, finely chopped
1 capsicum, deseeded and finely chopped
1 zucchini, finely chopped
2 carrots, grated
2 tsp chilli powder
2 tsp paprika
1 tsp ground coriander
1 Tbsp mixed herbs
2 tsp ground basil
300g spaghetti
2 x 400g cans diced tomatoes
2 x 400g cans brown lentils, drained
fresh basil and coriander, chopped (optional)

1. In a large frying pan, with a splash of oil, fry onion, capsicum, zucchini, carrots, chilli powder, paprika, ground coriander, mixed herbs and ground basil for 5 minutes, or until brown.
2. While this browns, bring a saucepan of water to the boil and cook spaghetti as per packet instructions.
3. Add tinned tomatoes and lentils to the veggie mix and bring to the boil (add ½ cup water if needed).
4. Dish up and serve topped with fresh basil and coriander if desired

Makes/serves: 4 serves | Prep time: 20 minutes | Cook time: 20 minutes
Nutritional information: DF, RSF, V

Creamy Red Chickpea Curry

2 x 400g cans chickpeas
2½ cups basmati rice, rinsed
4 cups cold water
1½ cups cauliflower
½ cup mixed vegetables
2–3 Tbsp red curry paste
1 x 400g can coconut milk
120g spinach

1. Preheat oven to 180°C. Line a baking tray with baking paper.
2. Rinse chickpeas and place onto prepared baking tray. Roast in the oven for 15 minutes.
3. Place the rice in a saucepan with the water and stir constantly over a high heat until it boils. Once it boils, cover with a lid and turn the heat to low. Simmer, covered, for 12 minutes without lifting the lid then remove from heat. After 5 minutes, remove lid and fluff rice up with a fork.
4. Chop the cauliflower into small florets and combine in a large frying pan with mixed vegetables, red curry paste and coconut milk. Bring to the boil.
5. Once the chickpeas are crispy, add to the frying pan and combine.
6. Serve curry with rice on the side, and top with a handful of spinach.

Makes/serves: 5 serves | Prep time: 10 minutes | Cook time: 20 minutes
Nutritional information: DF, RSF, V

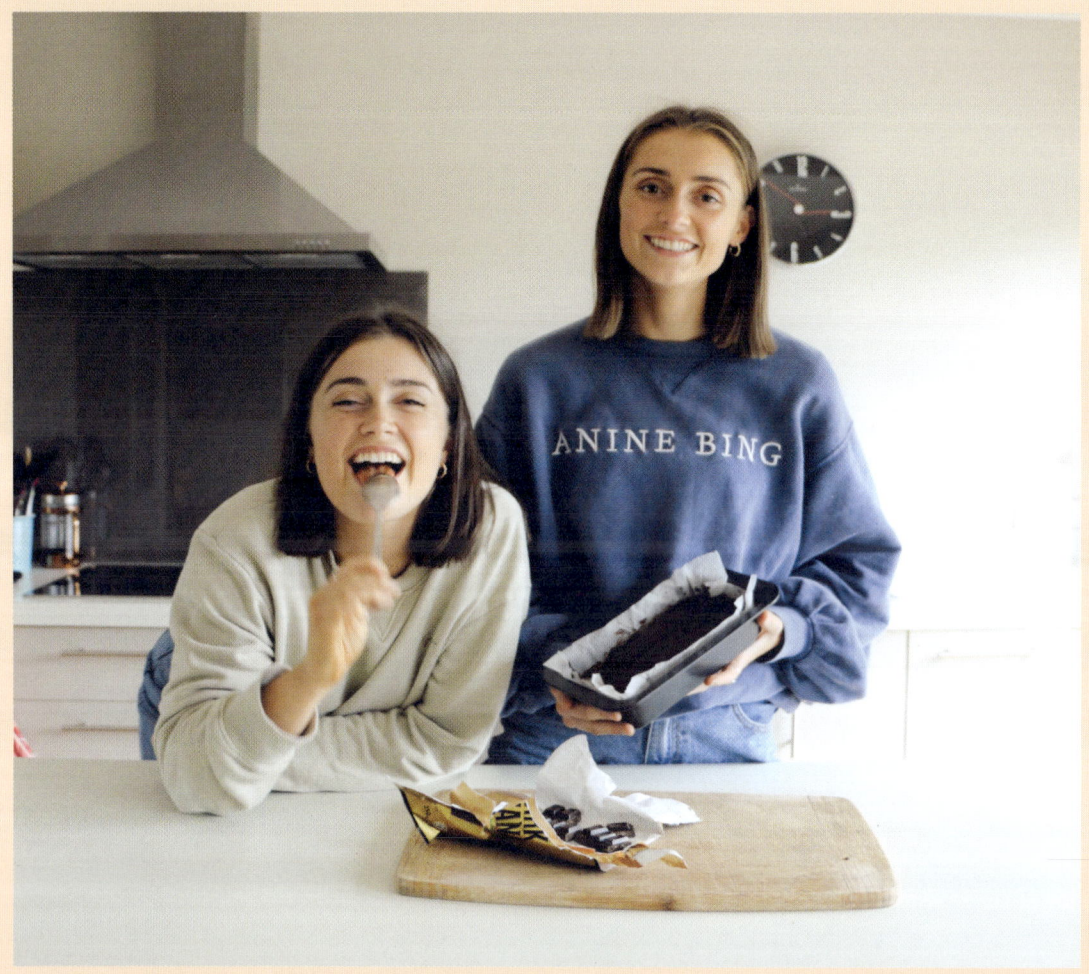

Simply Sweets

Okay, we know we said breakfast is our fave meal of the day, but dessert easily takes the cake (excuse the pun) for our favourite recipes to create. For those with a serious sweet tooth like us — look no further! Whether a Raw Peanut Butter and Jelly Slice sounds like your thing, or you're more of a Salted Caramel Brownie fan, this section has a (healthy-ish) treat for everyone.

Afghans

2 cups flour of choice (e.g. buckwheat flour or plain flour, or even ground almonds)
½ cup cacao powder
1½ cups cornflakes
1½ cups chopped dark chocolate
¾ cup melted coconut oil/dairy-free butter
¾ cup coconut sugar/brown sugar
1 tsp vanilla essence
⅓ cup almond butter
¼ cup almond milk or cow's milk (optional)
¾ cup coconut cream
handful of walnuts, halved

1. Preheat oven to 180°C. Line a baking tray with baking paper.
2. Combine flour, cacao powder, cornflakes and half a cup of chopped dark chocolate in a bowl.
3. In a separate bowl combine melted oil or butter with coconut sugar or brown sugar and vanilla essence.
4. Combine the dry and wet ingredients together, and add the almond butter. If the mixture is dry and crumbly, add milk until it is moist.
5. Roll mixture into balls, place on prepared tray and cook in oven for 10–15 minutes.
6. Remove from the oven and set aside to cool.
7. Melt the remainder of the dark chocolate and combine with coconut cream to create the icing. Ice biscuits and top with walnuts.

Makes/serves: 20 cookies | Prep time: 10 minutes | Cook time: 15 minutes
Nutritional information: DF, RSF, V

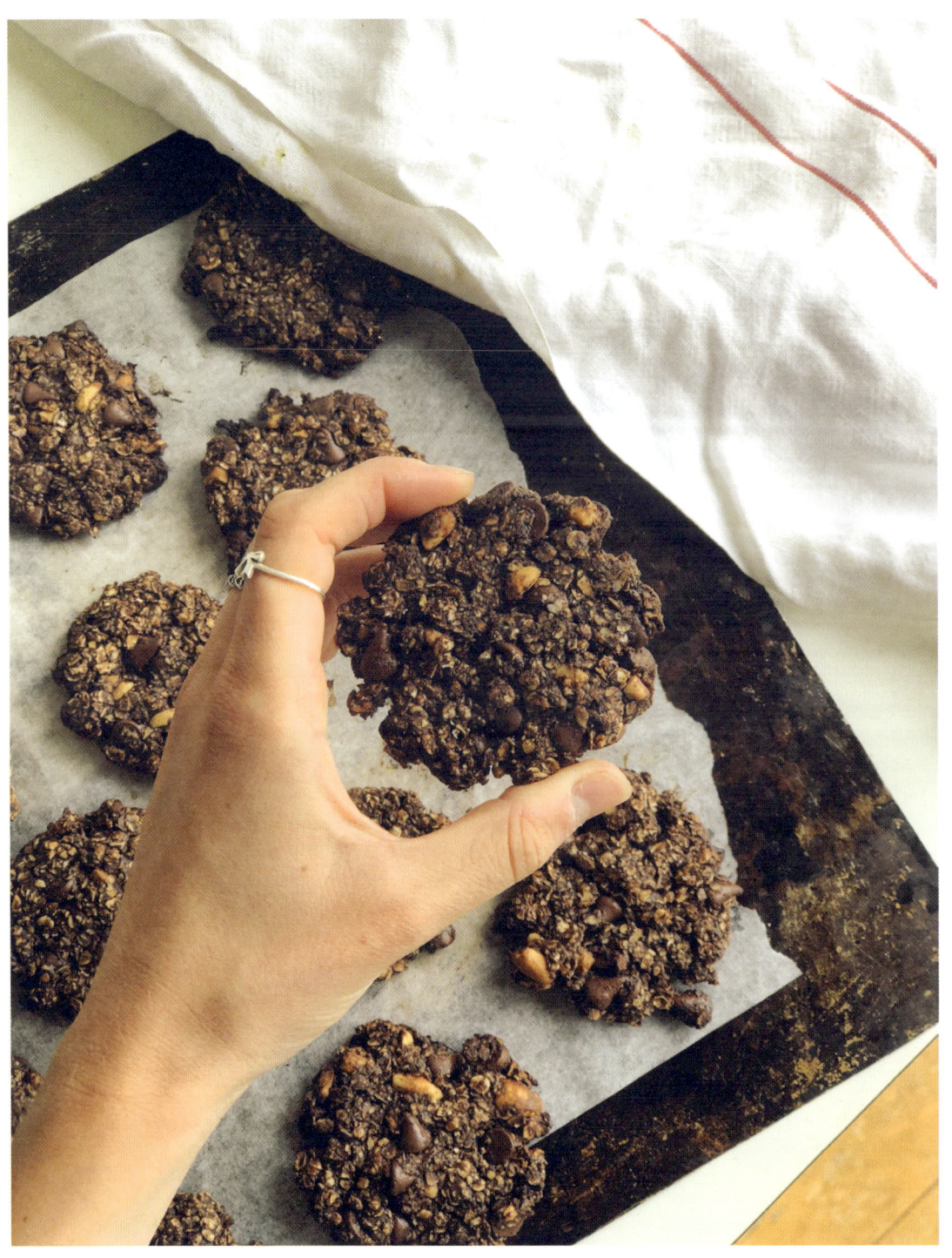

Six-ingredient Choc and Peanut Butter Cookies

2 cups rolled oats
¾ cup chopped dark chocolate
3 Tbsp peanut butter
3 Tbsp liquid sweetener, e.g. maple syrup/honey/agave
2 Tbsp coconut oil
1 egg
pinch of salt

1. Preheat oven to 180°C. Line a baking tray with baking paper.
2. Combine all ingredients in a bowl and mix well.
3. Roll mixture into balls, place on a lined baking tray and bake in the oven for 10 minutes until golden.
4. EAT!

Makes/serves: 15 cookies | Prep time: 10 minutes | Cook time: 10 minutes
Nutritional information: DF, RSF, GF

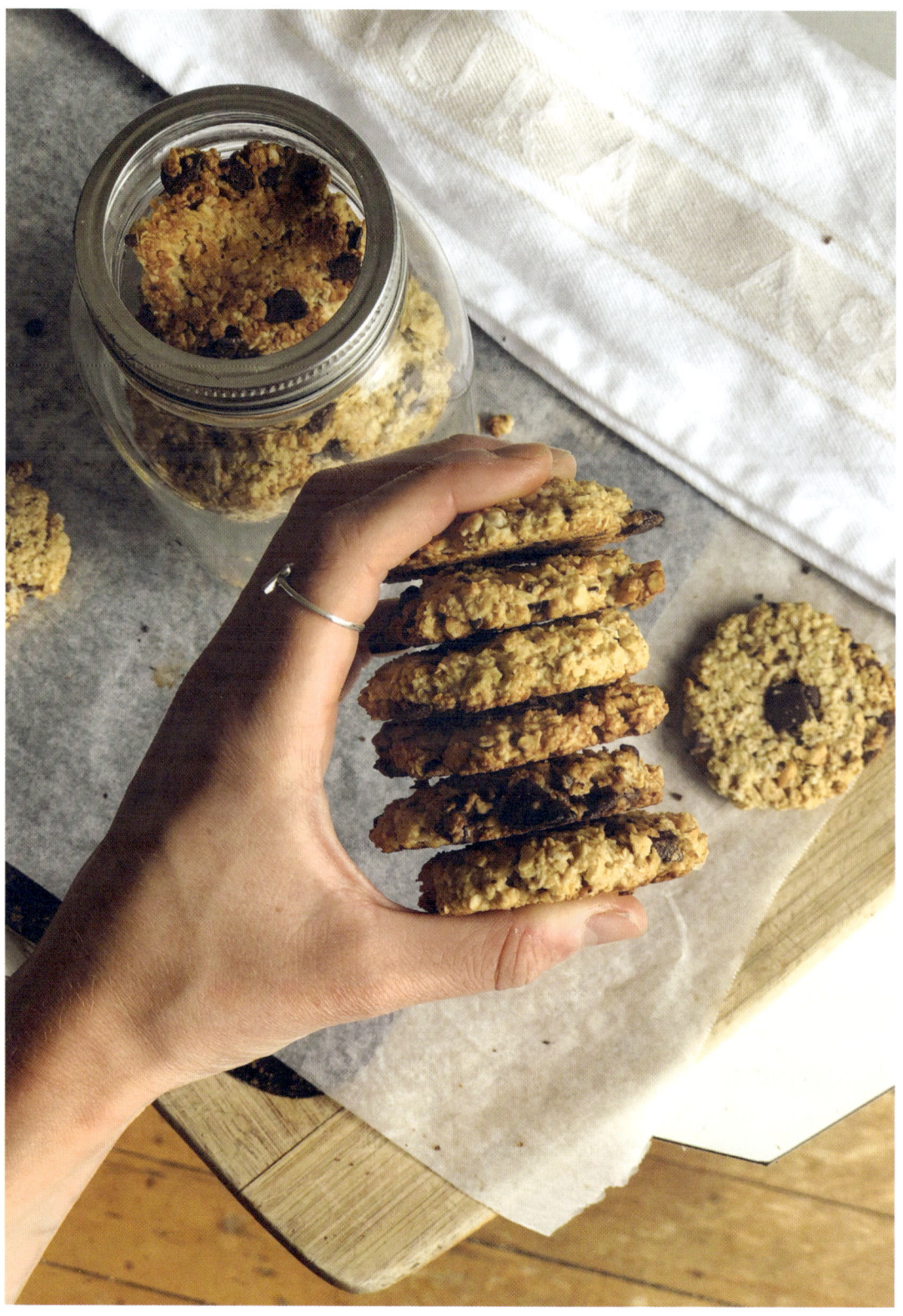

Chocolate Chunk Cookies

¾ cup almond butter
2 eggs
½ cup melted coconut oil
2 Tbsp liquid sweetener, e.g. rice malt syrup/maple syrup/honey
1 Tbsp chocolate protein powder
1 cup flour of choice or ground almonds
2 Tbsp cacao powder
1 tsp baking powder
½ cup chopped dark chocolate

1. Preheat the oven to 180°C and line a baking tray with baking paper.
2. Combine almond butter, eggs, oil and liquid sweetener in a bowl and mix well.
3. Add protein powder, flour, cacao powder, baking powder and dark chocolate to the mixture.
4. Roll the mixture into ping pong-ball-sized balls and place onto the baking tray.
5. Press each cookie down with the back of a fork and bake in the oven for 10–12 minutes.

Makes/serves: 10–12 cookies | Prep time: 5 minutes | Cook time: 10–15 minutes
Nutritional information: GF, DF, RSF

Buckwheat Chocolate Chip Cookies

¾ cup coconut sugar
⅓ cup melted coconut oil
1 egg
1 tsp vanilla essence
1 cup buckwheat flour
½ tsp baking soda
½ tsp salt
1 cup chopped dark chocolate

1. Preheat the oven to 180°C and line a baking tray with baking paper.
2. Combine coconut sugar, coconut oil, egg and vanilla and mix until the mixture becomes a caramel colour.
3. To the above mixture, add buckwheat flour, baking soda, salt and dark chocolate.
4. Roll into balls, place on a baking tray, and flatten with the back of a fork. Place in the oven and bake for 8–10 minutes.

Makes/serves: 18 cookies | Prep time: 5 minutes | Cook time: 10 minutes
Nutritional information: GF, DF, RSF

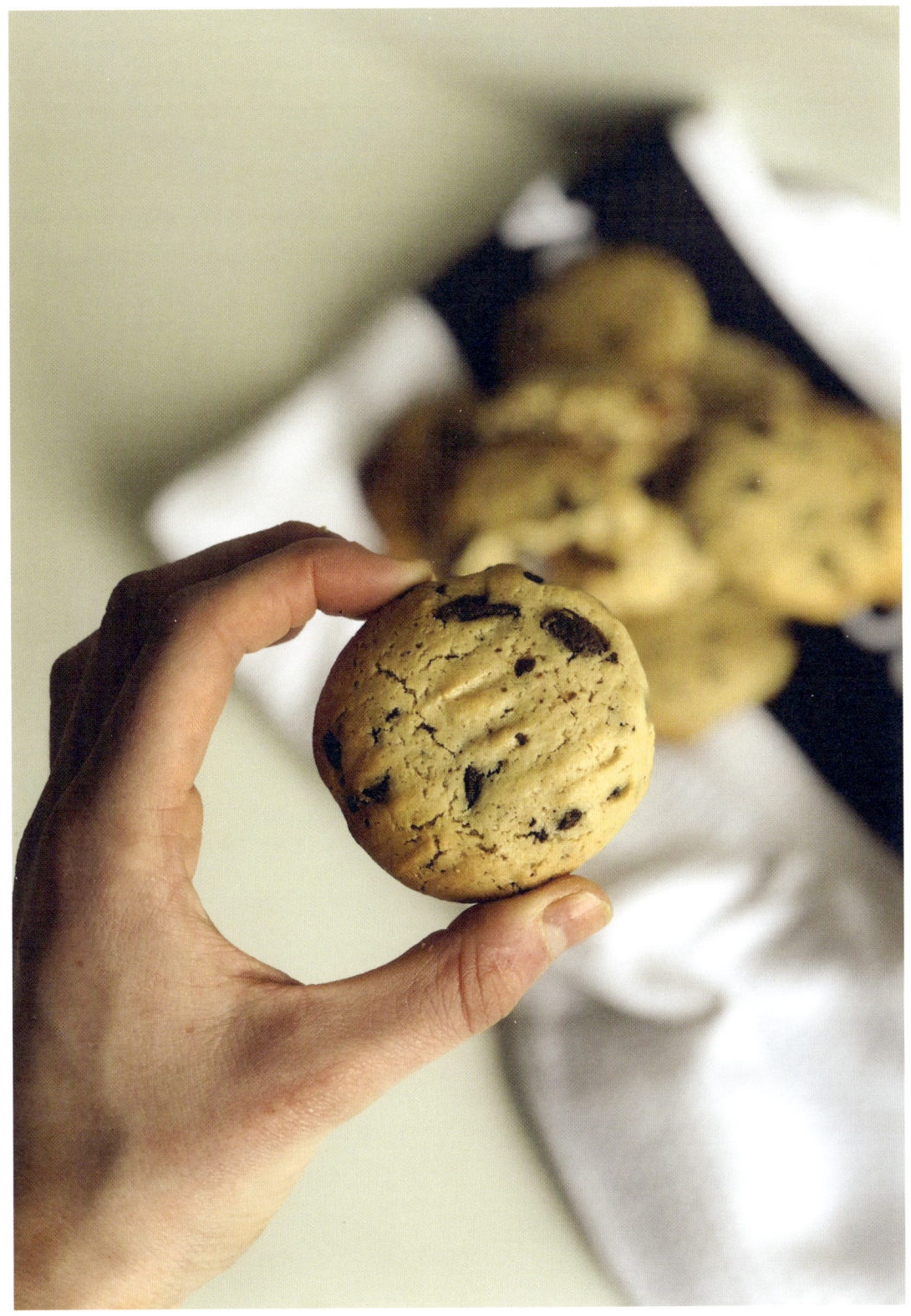

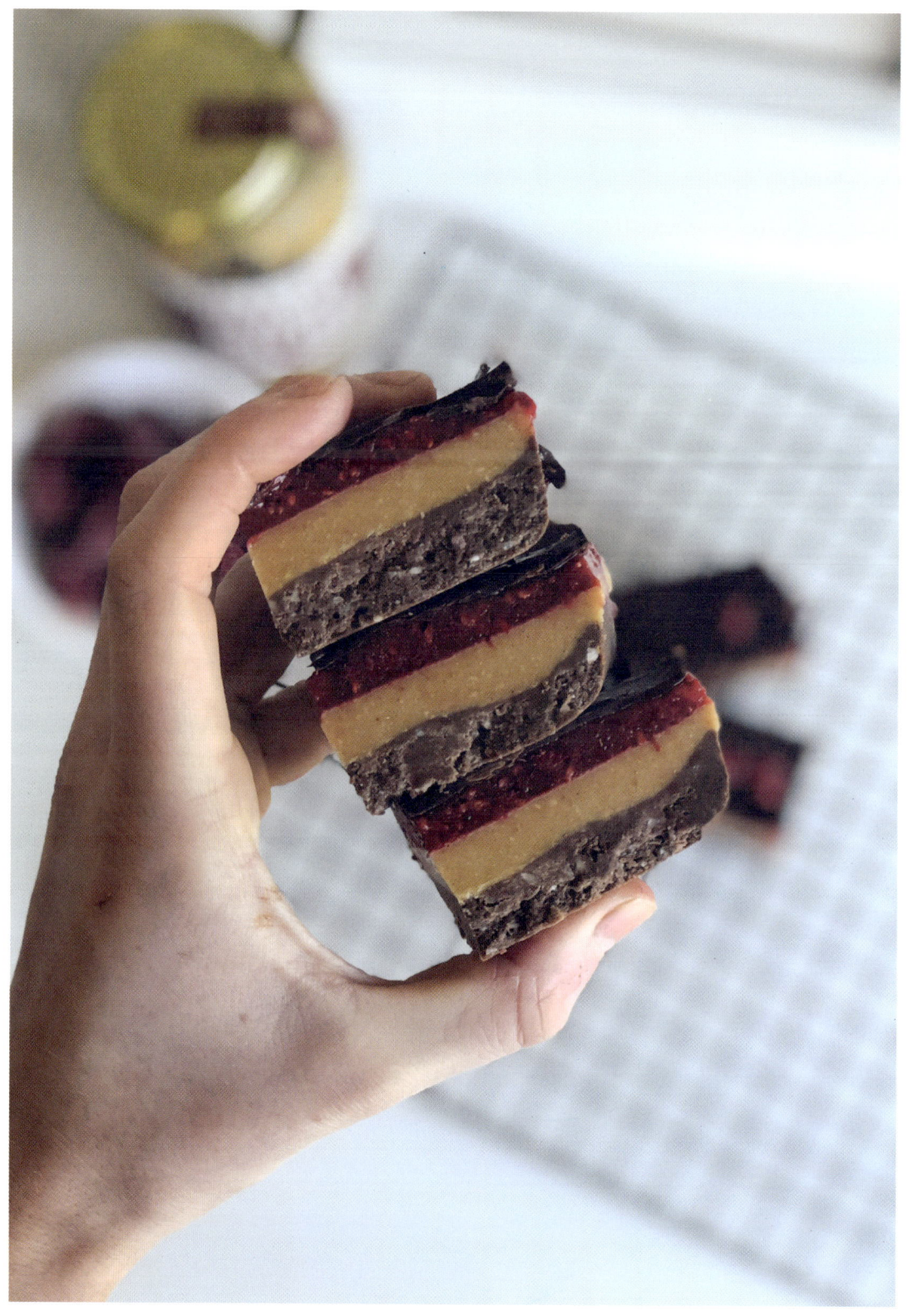

Raw Peanut Butter and Jelly Slice

BASE
1 cup ground almonds
2 scoops chocolate protein powder
3 Tbsp maple syrup
2 Tbsp melted coconut oil
2 Tbsp cacao powder
⅓ cup almond milk

PEANUT BUTTER LAYER
6 Tbsp smooth peanut butter
2 Tbsp maple syrup
1 Tbsp coconut oil

JELLY LAYER
1 cup raspberries
2 Tbsp maple syrup
1 tsp lemon juice

CHOC TOP
100g dark chocolate, melted

1. Line a slice tin with baking paper.
2. Combine all the base ingredients in a bowl and pat into the bottom of prepared tin.
3. Combine all the peanut butter layer ingredients in another bowl and pour on top of the base layer. Set in the freezer for 2 hours.
4. Combine all the jelly layer ingredients and blend in a food processor or by using a stick blender then pour on top of the peanut butter layer. Set in the fridge for a further 2 hours.
5. Pour melted chocolate on top of the jelly layer. Set in the fridge for 30–60 minutes.
6. Slice with a warm knife and EAT!

Makes/serves: 16 pieces | Prep time: 5 minutes | Set time: 5 hours in total
Nutritional information: GF, DF, RSF, V

Chocolate Avocado Mousse Tart

BASE
1 cup mixed nuts (we use almonds and cashews)
1 cup dates
1 Tbsp cacao powder
1 Tbsp coconut oil, melted

CHOCOLATE MOUSSE
1 large avocado
¾ cup coconut cream
100g dark chocolate, melted
2 Tbsp maple syrup
1 Tbsp cacao powder

OPTIONAL TOPPINGS
cacao nibs, chopped nuts, freeze-dried raspberries

1. Line a slice tin with baking paper.
2. Using a food processor or stick blender, blend all the base ingredients to fine crumbs. Pat into the bottom of prepared tin.
3. Blend the chocolate mousse ingredients until silky smooth. Pour on top of the base layer and set in the freezer for 1–2 hours.
4. Top with whatever you like!

Makes/serves: 12 pieces | Prep time: 5 minutes | Set time: 1–2 hours
Nutritional information: GF, DF, RSF, V

Peanut Butter and Choc Rice Crackle Slice

1½ cups brown rice puffs or rice bubbles
¾ cup peanut butter
¼ cup chia seeds
1 Tbsp maple syrup
100g dark chocolate, melted
1 Tbsp coconut oil, melted

1. Line a slice tin with baking paper.
2. In a bowl combine rice puffs, peanut butter, chia seeds and maple syrup.
3. Pat into tin and drizzle dark chocolate and coconut oil on top.
4. Set in the fridge for 30–60 minutes.
5. Take out and slice into rectangular pieces using a hot knife.

Makes/serves: 12 pieces | Prep time: 10 minutes | Setting time: 30 minutes
Nutritional information: DF, RSF, V, GF

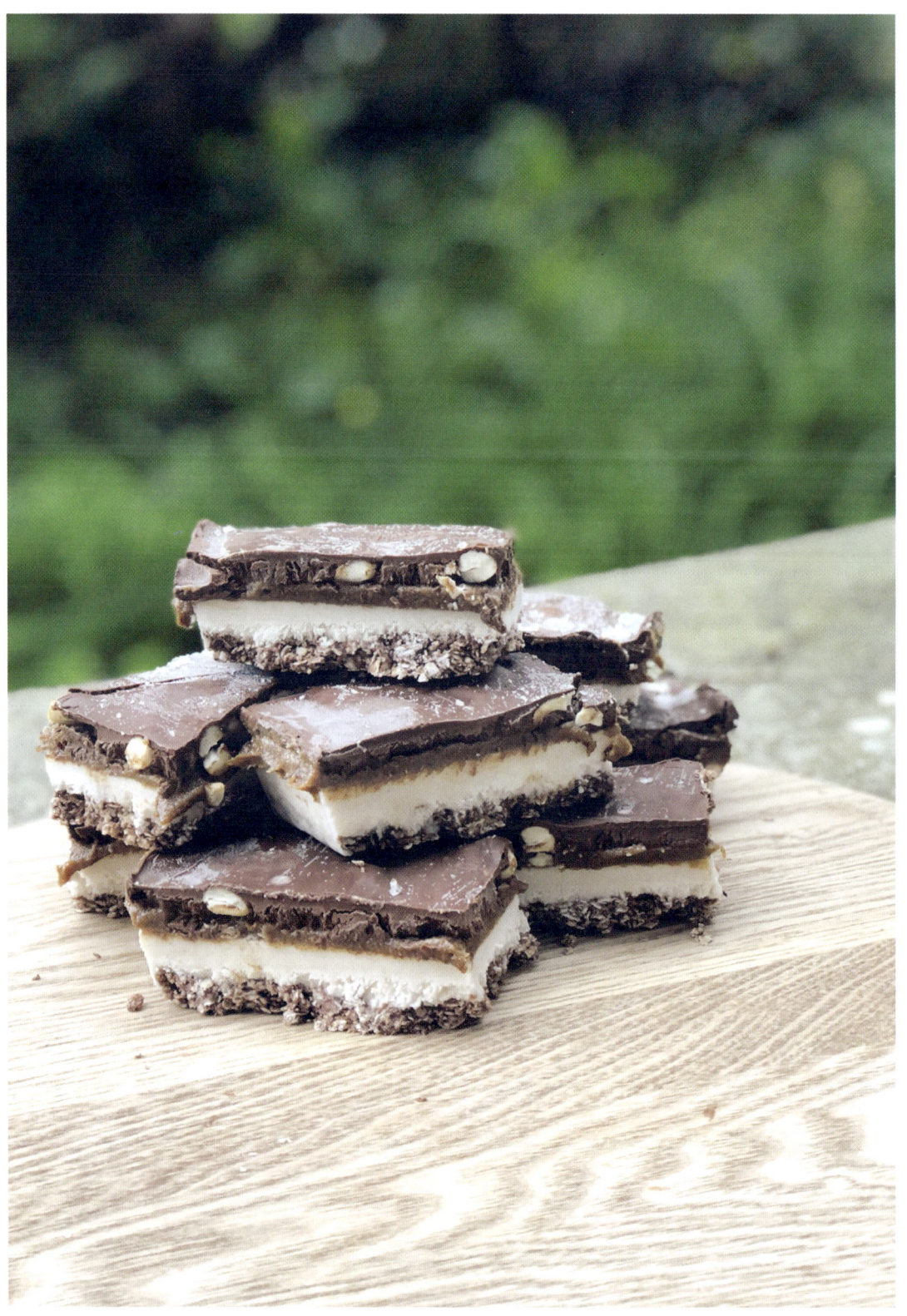

Raw Nutty Caramel Slice

BASE
1½ cups rolled oats
½ cup melted coconut oil
2 Tbsp cacao powder
1½ Tbsp maple syrup

VANILLA LAYER
1½ cups soaked cashews
⅓ cup melted coconut oil
2 Tbsp maple syrup
1 tsp vanilla essence

CARAMEL
1½ cups soaked dates
½ cup almond milk
2 Tbsp maple syrup
1 Tbsp tahini
pinch of salt

CHOCOLATE
100g dark chocolate, melted
¾ cup coconut cream
½ cup chopped peanuts

1. Place dates in a medium bowl, cover with boiling water and leave to soak for 30 minutes.
2. Line a slice tin with baking paper.
3. Using a food processor or stick blender, blend all base ingredients together until smooth then pat into the bottom of prepared tin.
4. Blend all vanilla layer ingredients together until smooth and pour on top of the base layer.
5. Set in the fridge for 1–2 hours.
6. Blend all caramel layer ingredients until smooth and pour on top of the vanilla layer.
7. Set in the fridge for another 1–2 hours.
8. Combine melted chocolate with coconut cream and chopped peanuts.
9. Mix through peanuts and pour on top of caramel layer.
10. Slice with a warm knife and EAT!

Makes/serves: 12–14 pieces | Prep time: 15 minutes | Set time: 2–4 hours
Nutritional information: DF, RSF, V

Choc Pineapple Slice

BASE
1 cup ground almonds, LSA or ground rolled oats
½ cup desiccated coconut
3 Tbsp maple syrup
3 Tbsp coconut oil, melted
2 Tbsp cacao powder
1 tsp vanilla essence
1 Tbsp water (if too dry)

PINEAPPLE LAYER
500g chopped pineapple
½ cup cashews soaked in water for 15–30 minutes
½ cup coconut cream
2 Tbsp maple syrup
1 Tbsp coconut oil, melted
1 tsp vanilla essence

CHOC TOP
¾ cup coconut cream
100g dark chocolate, melted

1. Preheat oven to 180°C. Line a slice tin with baking paper.
2. Combine all base ingredients and mix well.
3. Pat down the mixture into the bottom of tin and place in the oven for 10 minutes or until golden brown.
4. Remove from the oven and set aside to cool for 10 minutes.
5. Blend all pineapple layer ingredients until smooth and pour on top of the base layer.
6. Set in the freezer for 1–2 hours.
7. For the choc top, combine melted chocolate with the coconut cream. Add this on top of the pineapple layer and allow to set for another 1–2 hours.
8. Slice and EAT!

Makes/serves: 10–12 serves | Prep time: 20 minutes | Set time: 2 hours
Nutritional information: DF, RSF, V

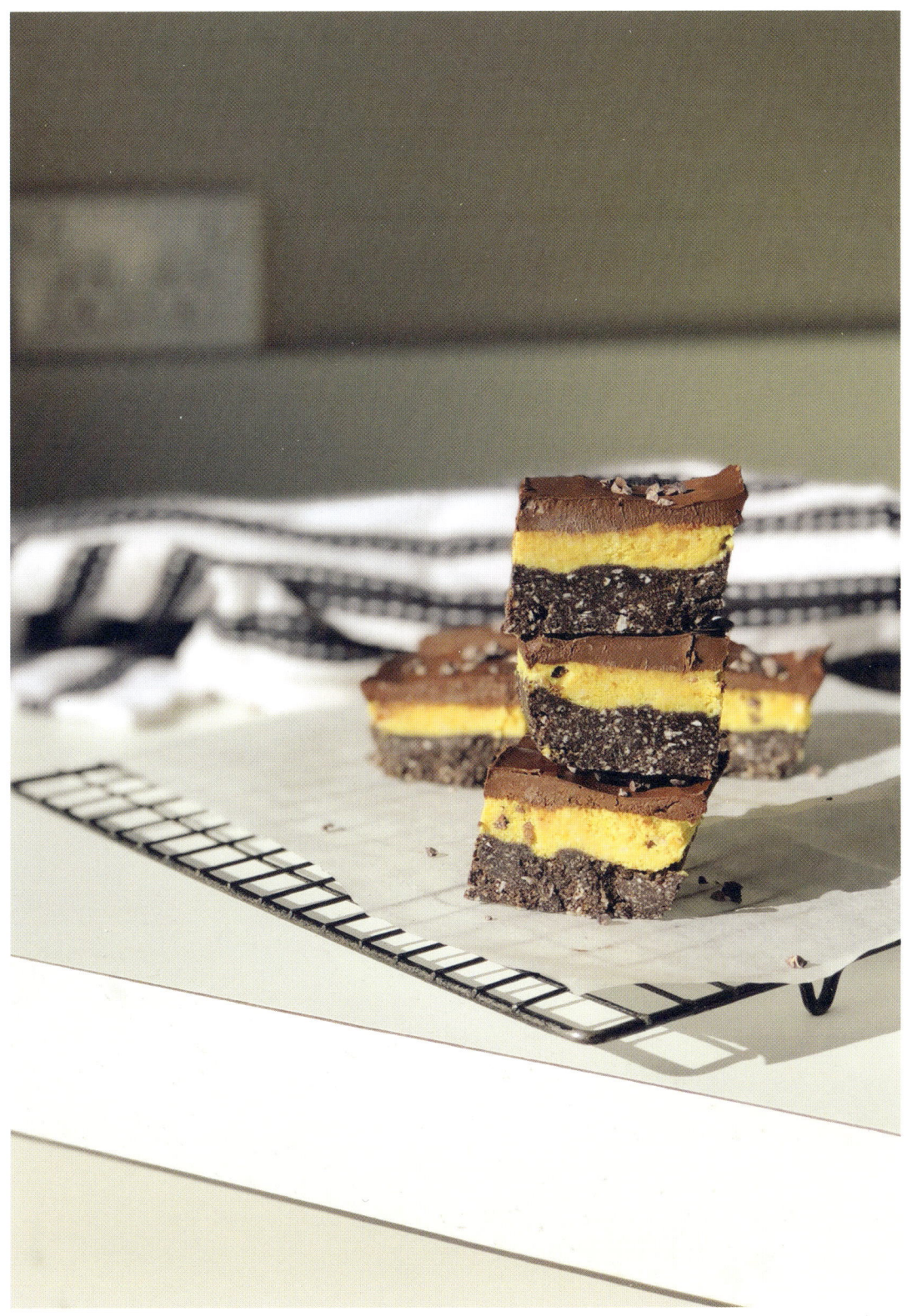

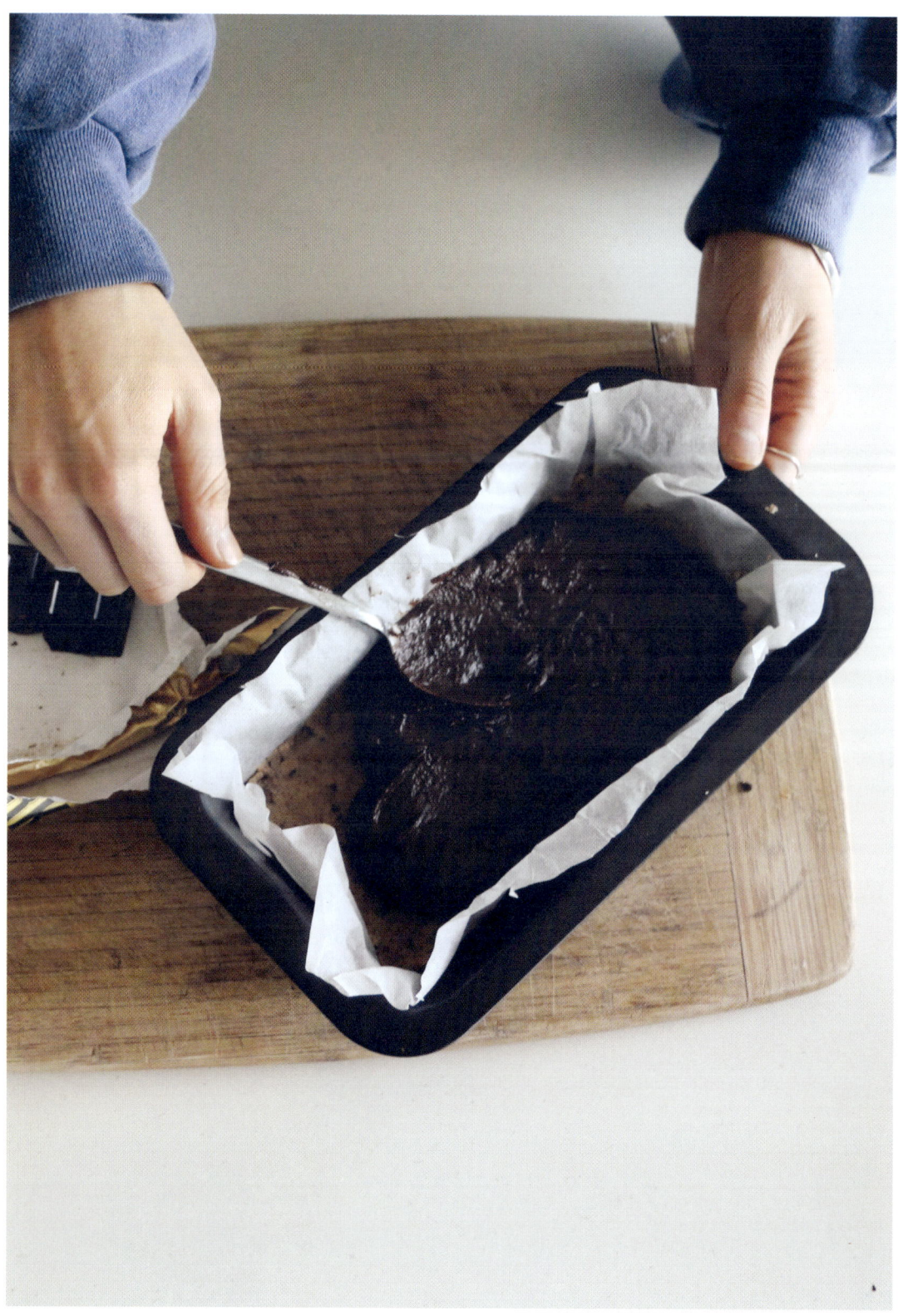

Raw Cookie Dough Slice

BASE
1 cup ground almonds
½ cup peanut butter
1 Tbsp maple syrup
2 scoops protein powder
handful of chopped dark chocolate
dash of almond milk (if too dry)

CHOCOLATE TOPPING
100g dark chocolate, melted
¾ cup coconut cream

1. Combine all base ingredients in a bowl. Line a loaf tin with baking paper.
2. Pat into the bottom of prepared tray and set in the fridge.
3. Combine the melted dark chocolate with the coconut cream, pour on top and set in the fridge for a further 30 minutes.
4. Remove from the fridge, slice and EAT!

Makes/serves: 12–14 slices | Prep time: 20 minutes | Set time: 1 hour
Nutritional information: DF, RSF, GF, V option

Lemon and Berry Loaves

2 eggs
⅓ cup melted coconut oil/ olive oil
½ cup milk of choice
½ cup liquid honey/maple syrup
1 tsp vanilla essence
1 lemon (juice and zest)
1½ cups ground rolled oats/ ground almonds/or flour of your choice
1 tsp baking powder
¾ cup frozen berries (blueberries work well)

1. Preheat oven to 180°C.
2. Beat the eggs and combine in a bowl with oil, milk, honey or maple syrup, vanilla and lemon.
3. Add the oats and baking powder to the mixture.
4. Gently stir through the berries.
5. Pour into a friand or mini loaf tin and bake for 10–15 minutes or until golden on top.

Makes/serves: 6 mini loaves/1 medium-sized loaf | Prep time: 15 minutes
Cook time: 10–15 minutes | Nutritional information: DF, RSF

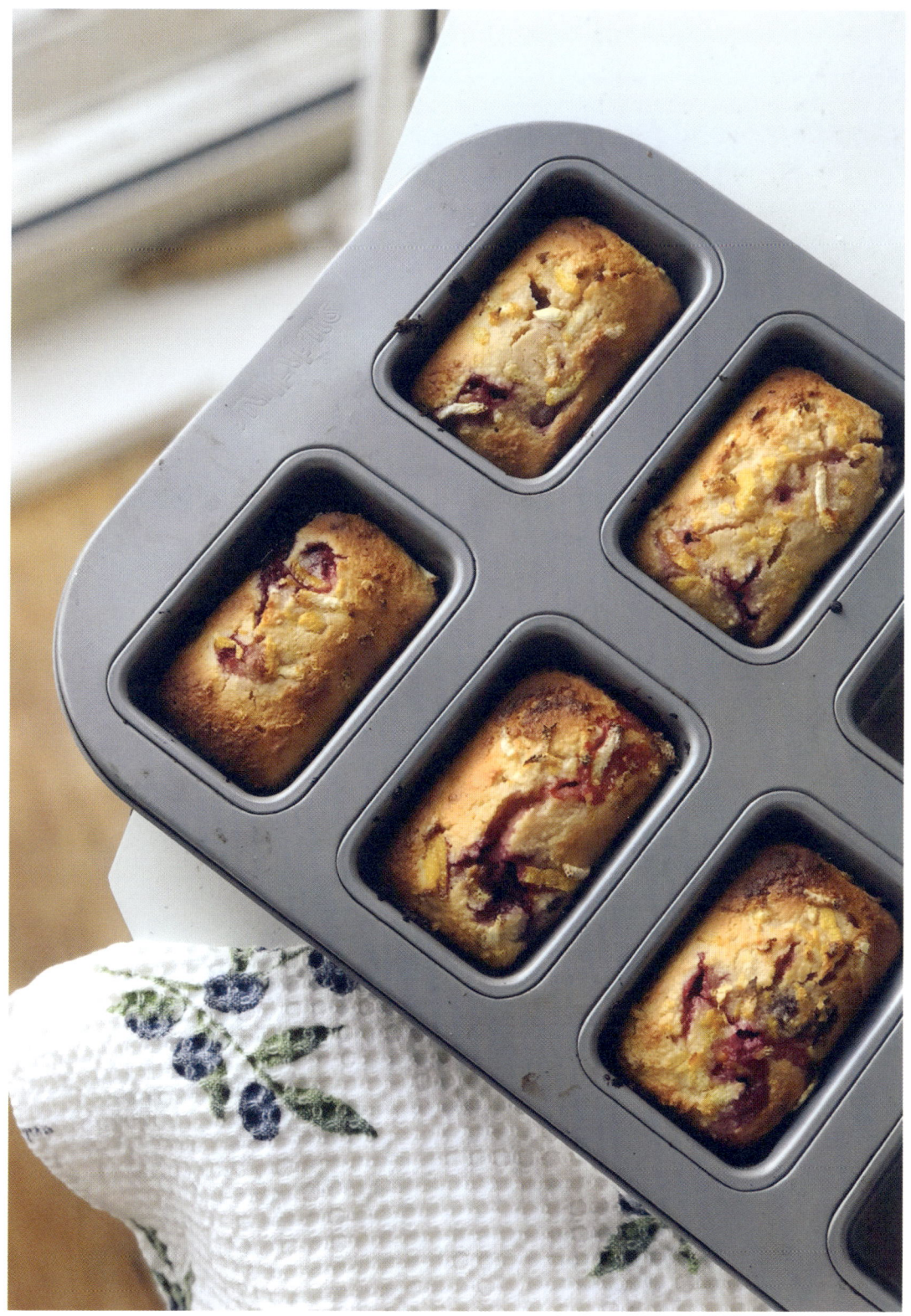

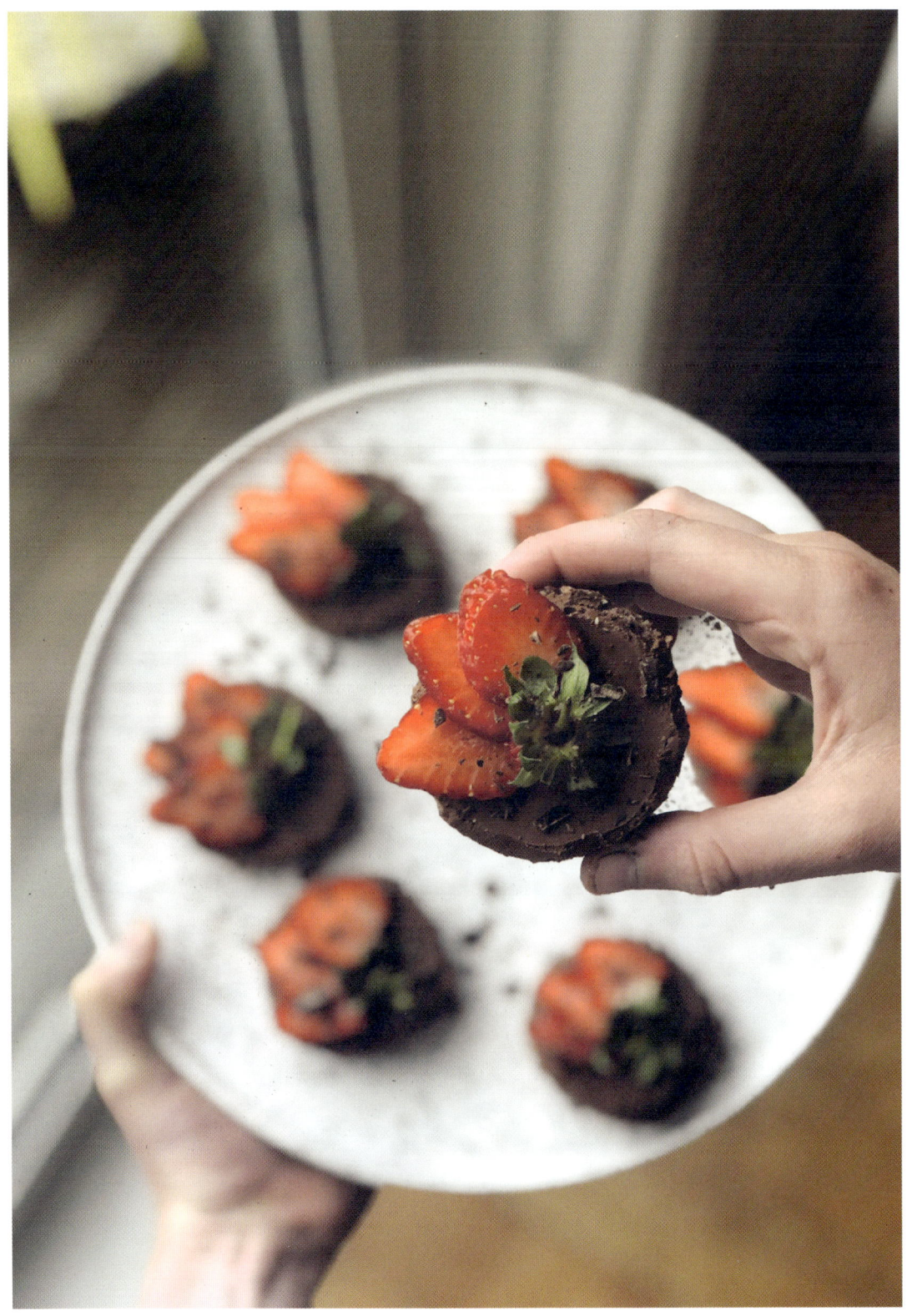

Mini Chocolate Tarts

BASE
1½ cups ground almonds/ oat flour
4 Tbsp maple syrup
4 Tbsp almond milk
½ cup peanut butter
¼ cup cacao powder

CHOCOLATE LAYER
100g dark chocolate, melted
¾ cup coconut cream
sliced strawberries to serve

1. In a bowl, combine all the base ingredients. Pat this mixture into muffin cases in a muffin tin. Set aside.
2. For the chocolate layer, melt the dark chocolate and combine with coconut cream. Pour this on top of the base and set in the fridge/freezer for another hour until set.
3. Remove from the freezer and top with sliced strawberries.
4. Remove muffin cases and enjoy!

Makes/serves: 8 tarts | Prep time: 20 minutes | Setting time: 2 hours
Nutritional information: DF, RSF, V, GF

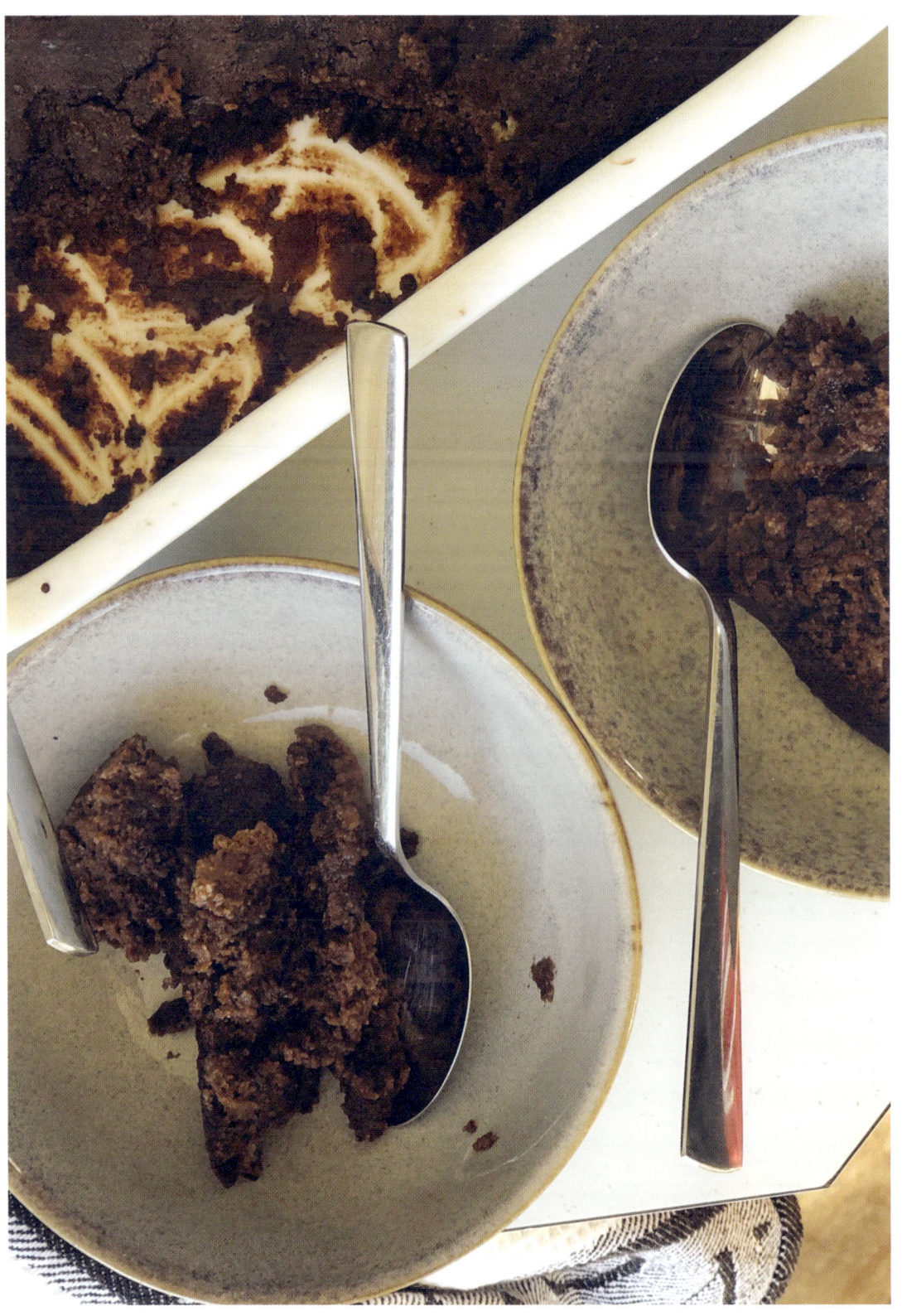

Chocolate Pudding

PUDDING
1¾ cup ground almonds or flour of your choice
⅓ cup melted coconut oil
3 Tbsp cacao powder
3½ Tbsp coconut sugar/brown sugar
2 tsp baking powder
⅓ cup chocolate chips (optional)

TOPPING
¾ cup boiling water
¼ cup maple syrup/rice malt syrup/honey
2 Tbsp cacao powder

1. Preheat oven to 180°C.
2. Stir all pudding ingredients together until combined.
3. Pour mixture into a large dish. If you like, sprinkle with chocolate chips as well.
4. Combine topping ingredients and pour on top of pudding mixture.
5. Bake in the oven for 25–30 minutes.
6. Dig in!

Makes/serves: 6 servings | Prep time: 10 minutes | Cook time: 25–30 minutes
Nutritional information: DF, RSF, GF

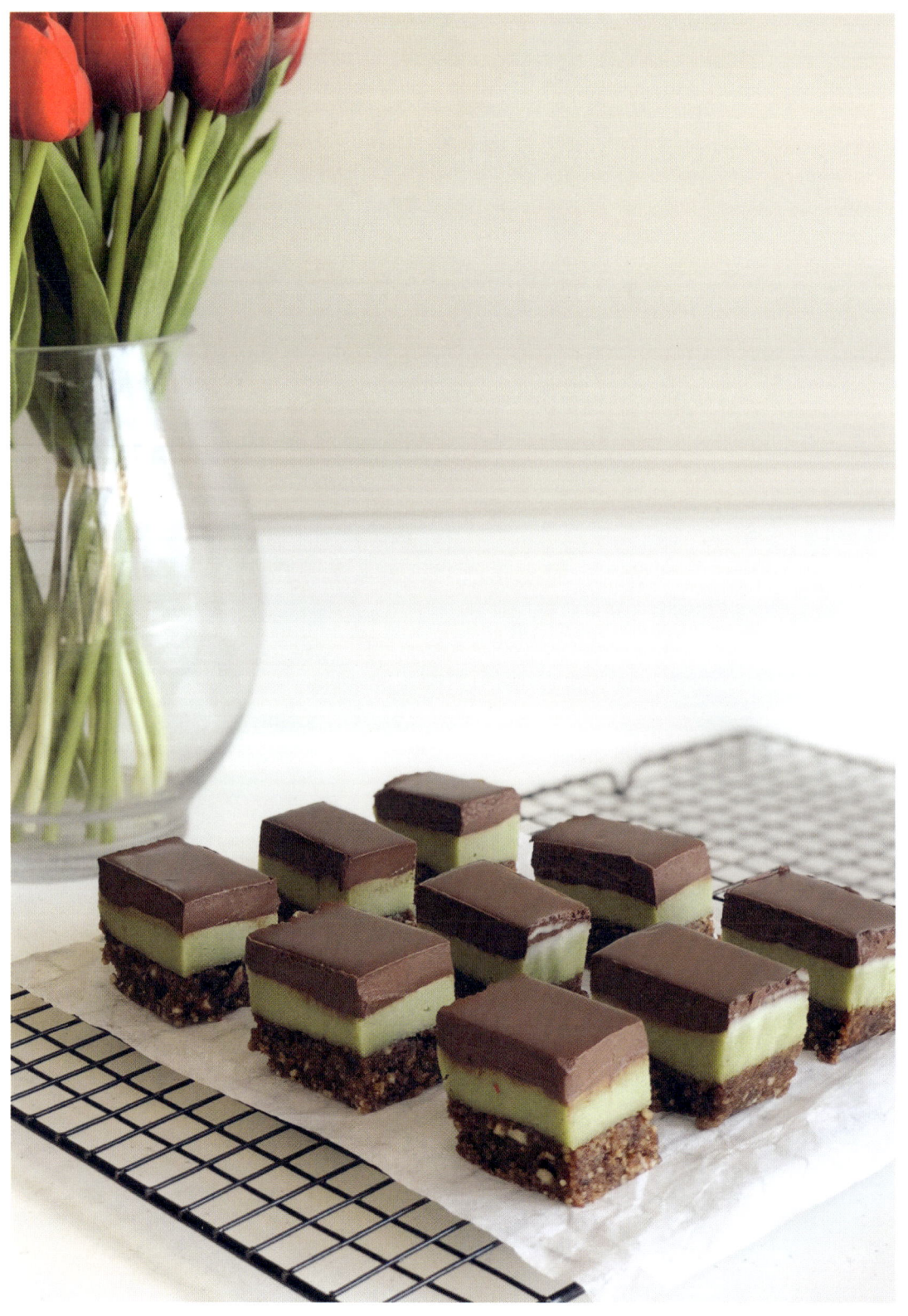

Raw Peppermint Slice

BASE
1 cup mixed nuts
1 cup dates
1 Tbsp cacao powder
2 Tbsp warm water

PEPPERMINT LAYER
1½ cups soaked cashews
 (soak for ½ hour in boiling
 water prior to use)
½ cup melted coconut oil
2 Tbsp cacao butter
½ tsp sea salt
1 tsp vanilla essence
2 drops peppermint essence
1 tsp matcha (optional,
 to give green colour)

CHOCOLATE GANACHE
100g dark chocolate, melted
¾ cup coconut cream

1. Line a slice tin with baking paper.
2. Blend base ingredients in a food processor or with a stick blender until firm. Pat into the base of prepared tin.
3. Blend the peppermint layer ingredients until smooth and pour on top of the base layer. Set in the fridge for 1 hour.
4. Melt dark chocolate and combine with coconut cream for the ganache. Pour on top of the peppermint layer and set in the fridge/freezer for another hour until set.
5. Remove from the fridge, slice with a warm knife and EAT!

Makes/serves: 12 large slices | Prep time: 20 minutes | Set time: 1–2 hours
Nutritional information: DF, GF, V, RSF

Lemon Raspberry Tart

BASE
2 cups ground almonds/
 ground oats/LSA
2 Tbsp coconut oil, melted
2 Tbsp maple syrup
1 Tbsp almond milk
1 tsp vanilla essence
juice of ½ lemon

LEMON LAYER
1½ cups soaked cashews
¾ cup coconut cream
3 Tbsp maple syrup
1 Tbsp coconut oil
juice of 2 lemons
1 tsp turmeric
 (for yellow colour)
handful of freeze-dried
 raspberries (optional)

OPTIONAL TOPPINGS
chopped pistachios,
 lemon slices, freeze-dried
 raspberries

1. Line a tart tin with baking paper.
2. Combine all the base ingredients in a bowl and pat into the bottom of prepared tin.
3. Blend all the lemon layer ingredients until smooth. Pour on top of the base and set in the freezer for 1–2 hours.
4. Remove from the fridge, add topping of your choice if desired, slice with a warm knife and EAT!

Makes/serves: 12 slices | Prep time: 20 minutes | Set time: 1–2 hours
Nutritional information: DF, RSF, V, GF

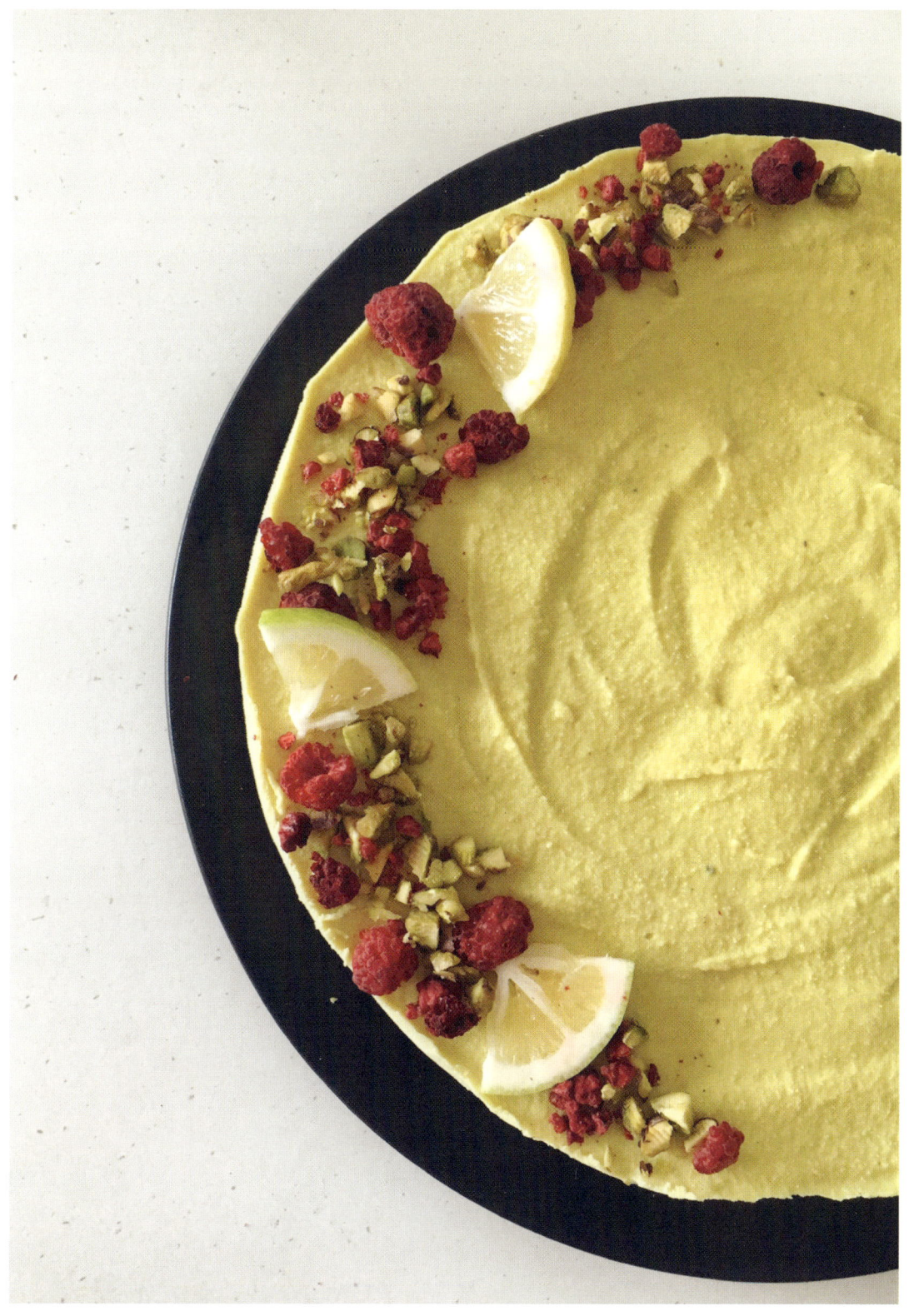

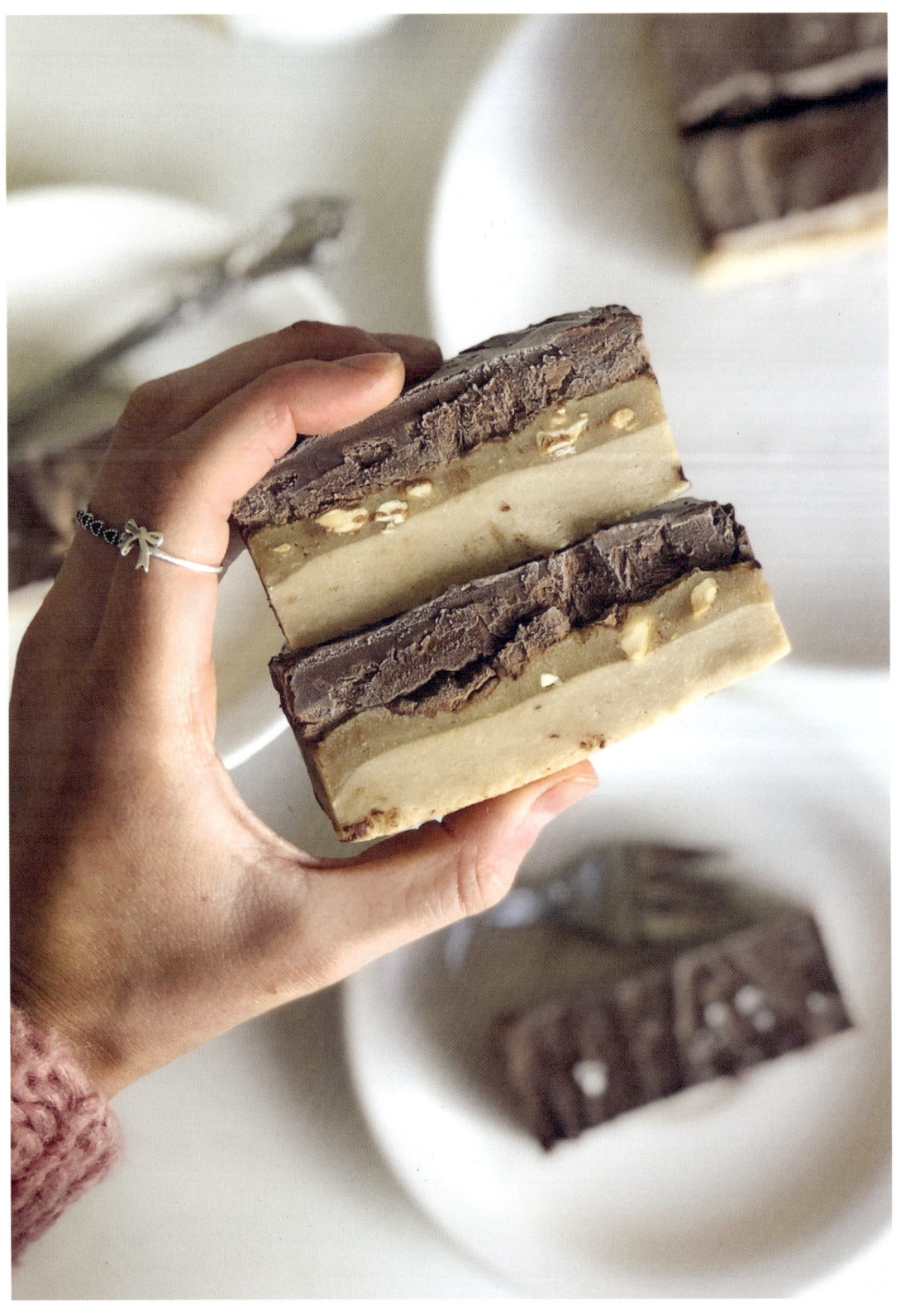

Salted Caramel Slice

BASE
2 cups ground almonds or rolled oats
3 Tbsp maple syrup
3 Tbsp coconut oil, melted
1 tsp vanilla essence
½ tsp salt

CARAMEL
½ cup tahini
½ cup peanut butter
½ cup coconut cream
1 Tbsp coconut oil, melted
2 Tbsp maple syrup
1 tsp vanilla essence
½ tsp salt

CHOC TOP
100g dark chocolate, melted
¾ cup coconut cream

1. In a bowl combine all the base ingredients. Pat into the bottom of a lined loaf tin and place in the freezer while you make the caramel.
2. Combine all the caramel ingredients in a bowl and pour on top of the base. Set in the freezer for 2–3 hours.
3. Remove from the freezer and combine the choc top ingredients in a bowl. Pour on top of the caramel and set in the freezer for 2 hours.
4. Remove from the freezer and let it defrost for 5–10 mins, slice with a warm knife and EAT!

Makes/serves: 12 large slices | Prep time: 20 minutes | Set time: 1–2 hours
Nutritional information: DF, GF, V, RSF

Cacao Peanut Butter Raspberry Brownie

3 eggs (or, for vegan option: 3 Tbsp chia seeds and 1 heaped tsp baking powder)
150g dark chocolate
100g coconut oil
200g coconut sugar
200g ground almonds
125g raspberries (frozen or fresh)
½ cup cacao nibs
2 Tbsp peanut butter

1. Preheat oven to 180°C, and line a square tin with baking paper.
2. For a vegan version, soak chia seeds in half a cup of water until they form a paste.
3. Melt 100g of the dark chocolate in a saucepan with coconut oil.
4. When these have melted, take the pot off the stove and stir in sugar, beaten eggs/chia seeds, ground almonds (and baking powder if making the vegan option).
5. Roughly chop the remaining chocolate, then add this, along with half the raspberries and all of the cacao nibs, to the mixture.
6. Pour the brownie mix into the tin and drizzle the peanut butter over top.
7. Place in the oven for 25–30 minutes.
8. Once the brownie is cooked (we like it crisp on top but gooey in the centre), take it out and leave it to cool before sprinkling with the remaining raspberries.
9. Dig in!

Makes/serves: 16 slices | Prep time: 20 minutes | Cook time: 25–30 minutes
Nutritional information: DF, GF, RSF

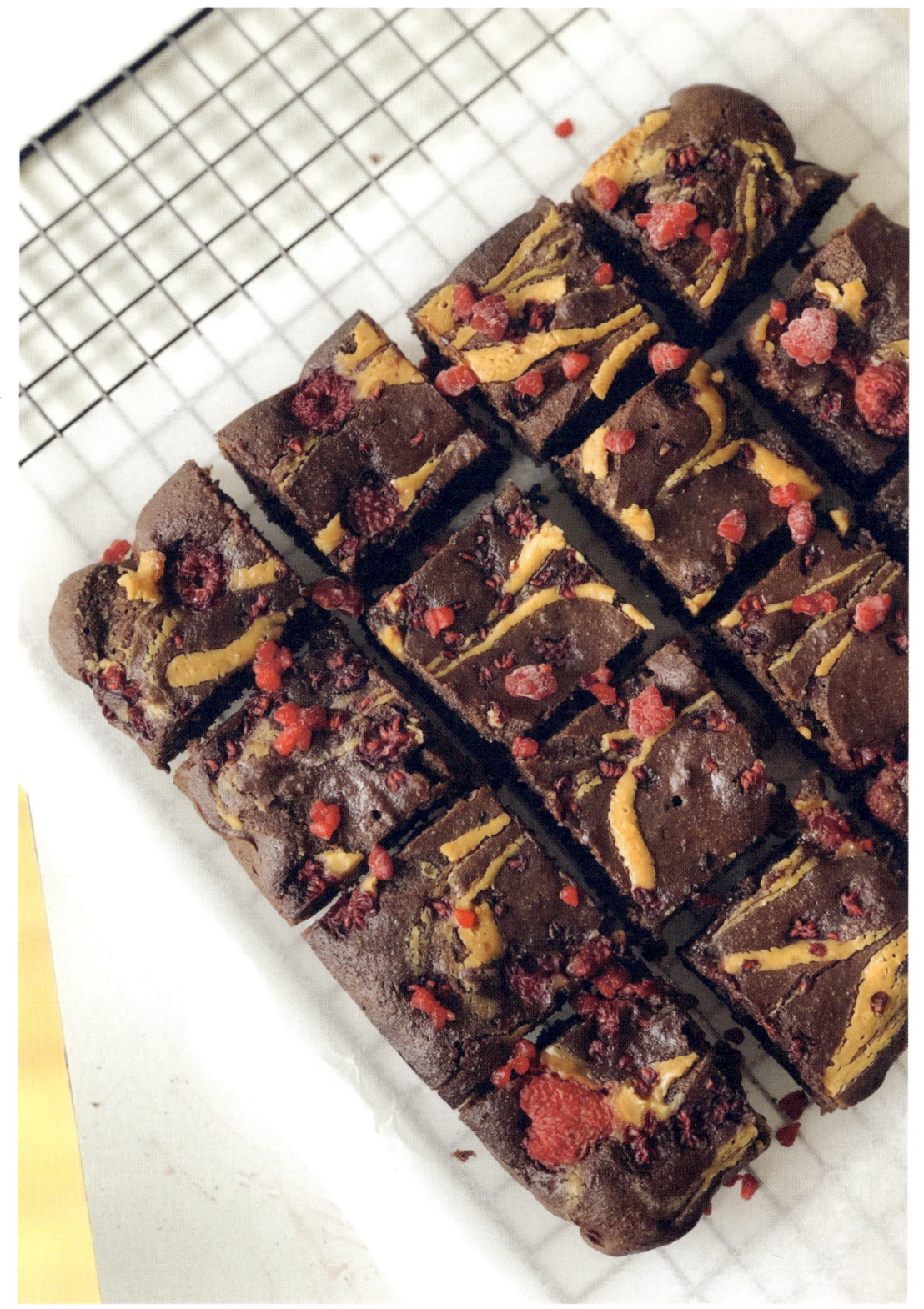

Absolute Bliss

Who doesn't need a good snack supply when they're studying? Whether it's pre-lecture inspo, a post-gym energy buzz or just a midday pick-me-up, the Tasty Twins have got you covered! Bliss balls are pretty much a vital part of our daily routine, and we've put together some of our faves just for you. These recipes are super easy, packed full of nutritious ingredients and totally delish! We have heaps of variations on our fave snack, featuring some iconic flavour combos for you to choose from.

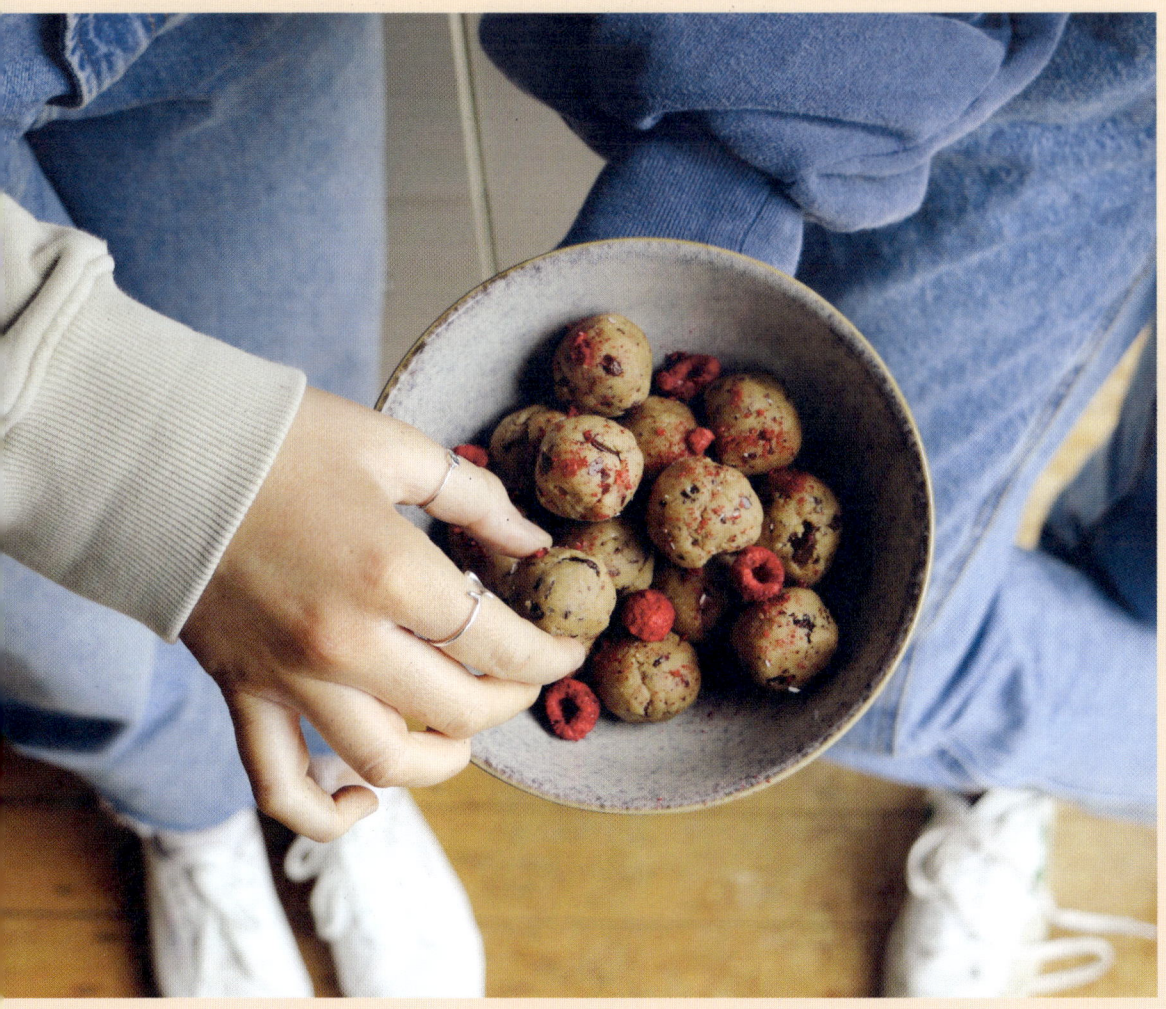

Cookie Dough Bliss Balls

1 cup ground almonds/ oat flour
4 Tbsp maple syrup
½ cup peanut butter
¼ cup chopped dark chocolate
1–2 Tbsp almond milk (if too dry)
1 scoop protein powder

1. Combine all ingredients and roll into small balls.
2. Set in the fridge for 1 hour.

Makes/serves: 10–12 balls | Prep time: 5 minutes | Set time: 1 hour
Nutritional information: DF, RSF, V, GF

Caramel Bliss Balls

1 cup ground almonds/ rolled oats
½ cup dates, soaked in hot water for ½ hour
1 Tbsp peanut butter
120g dark chocolate, melted

1. In a blender combine all ingredients (apart from the chocolate) until smooth.
2. Roll into balls and set in the freezer for 1–2 hours.
3. Remove from the freezer for 10 minutes and then coat each ball in dark chocolate. Place back in the fridge to set.

Makes/serves: 14 balls | Prep time: 5 minutes | Set time: 1–2 hours
Nutritional information: DF, RSF, V, GF

Coffee and Cacao Bliss Balls

1 cup ground almonds/ oat flour
½ cup peanut butter
4 Tbsp honey
2–3 Tbsp ground coffee
¼ cup cacao nibs
1 Tbsp cacao powder
1–2 Tbsp water (if too dry)
100g dark chocolate, melted (optional)

1. In a bowl combine all ingredients (except the melted chocolate), roll into balls and place on a plate to set in the fridge. Just before removing from fridge, melt chocolate (if desired).
2. Remove balls from the fridge and dip in the melted chocolate (if using). Place back on the plate and back into the fridge to set.

Makes/serves: 10–12 balls | Prep time: 5 minutes | Set time: 1 hour
Nutritional information: DF, RSF, V, GF

Peanut Butter Cacao Protein Balls

1 cup rolled oats
½ cup peanut butter
8 dates
1 Tbsp cacao powder
1 cup mixed nuts
¼ cup shredded coconut
2 Tbsp water
1 Tbsp coconut oil, melted
1 tbsp protein powder

1. Finely grind the oats in a blender.
2. Add remaining ingredients and blend until smooth. If it seems a little dry, keep adding water until the mixture is moist and well-combined.
3. Roll the mixture into balls.
4. Leave balls to set in the fridge for around two hours.
5. Snack away!

Makes/serves: 12 bliss balls | Prep time: 10 minutes | Setting time: 2 hours
Nutritional information: DF, RSF, V

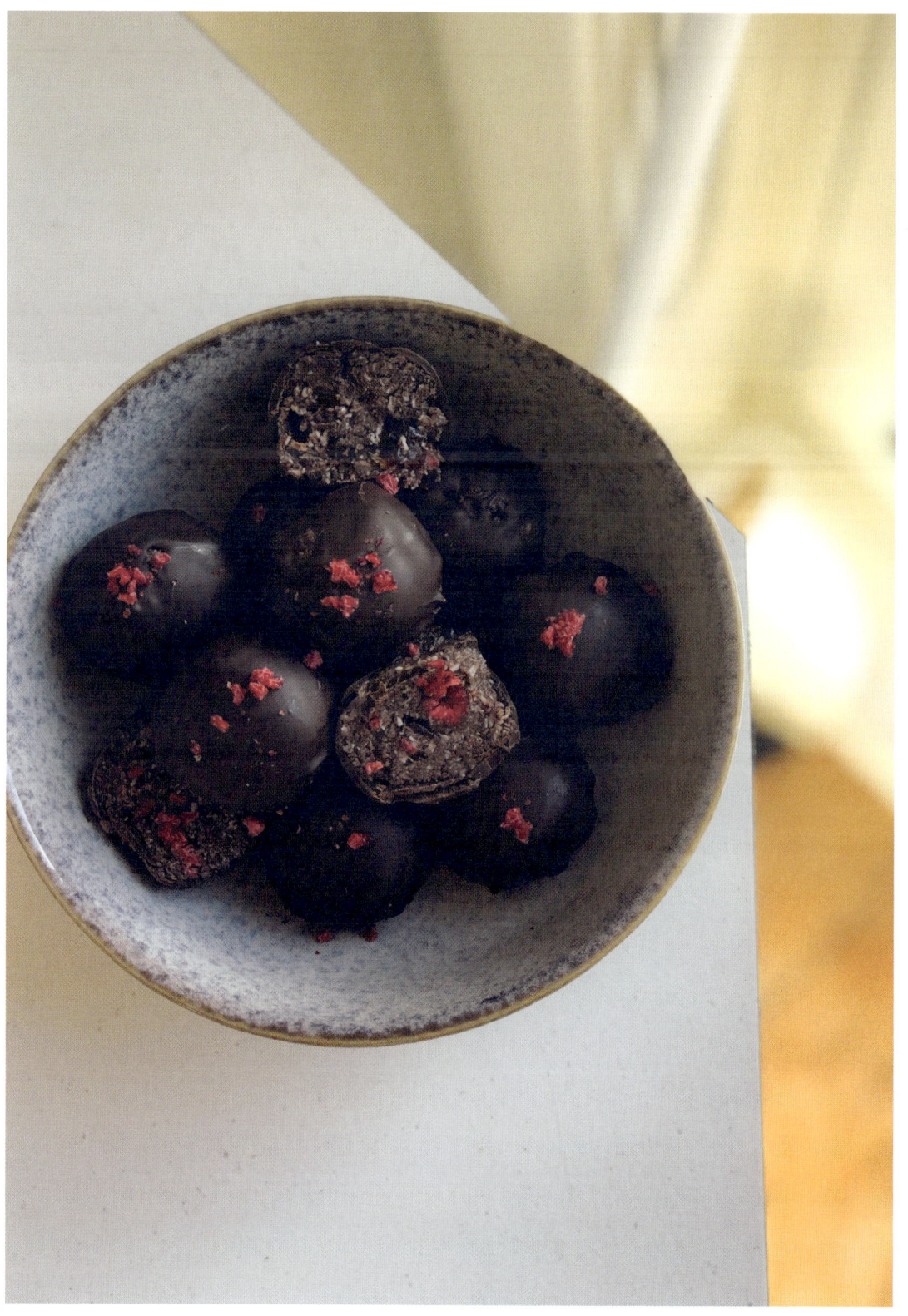

Black Forest Bliss Balls

1½ cups ground almonds or rolled oats
½ cup desiccated coconut
½ cup dried cranberries or freeze-dried raspberries
½ cup chopped dark chocolate
3 Tbsp maple syrup/honey
2 Tbsp almond milk/coconut cream/water
1 Tbsp melted coconut oil
100g dark chocolate, melted

1. Combine and mix all ingredients in a bowl (except the melted dark chocolate).
2. Roll into balls, place on a plate and set in the freezer for 1–2 hours. Just before removing from the fridge, melt the chocolate.
3. Remove from the fridge and coat each ball in the melted dark chocolate.
4. Place back on a plate and set in the freezer for 5–10 minutes.
5. EAT!

Makes/serves: 10–12 bliss balls | Prep time: 5 minutes | Set time: 1.5 hours
Nutritional information: DF, RSF, V, GF

Peanut Butter-filled Bliss Balls

1½ cups ground almonds/oat flour
¼ cup chocolate protein powder
2 Tbsp maple syrup
2 Tbsp peanut butter
120g dark chocolate, melted (optional)
coconut flakes to garnish

1. Combine ground almonds, protein powder and maple syrup in a bowl and roll into ping-pong-sized balls.
2. Make an indentation in the middle of each one with your thumb. Add a small teaspoon of peanut butter to the thumbprint and shape back into balls around the peanut butter. Refrigerate for 1 hour.
3. Remove from the fridge and dip in the dark chocolate, if using. Return to the fridge to set.
4. Sprinkle with coconut flakes and serve.

Makes/serves: 10–12 balls | Prep time: 5 minutes | Set time: 1 hour
Nutritional information: DF, RSF, V, GF

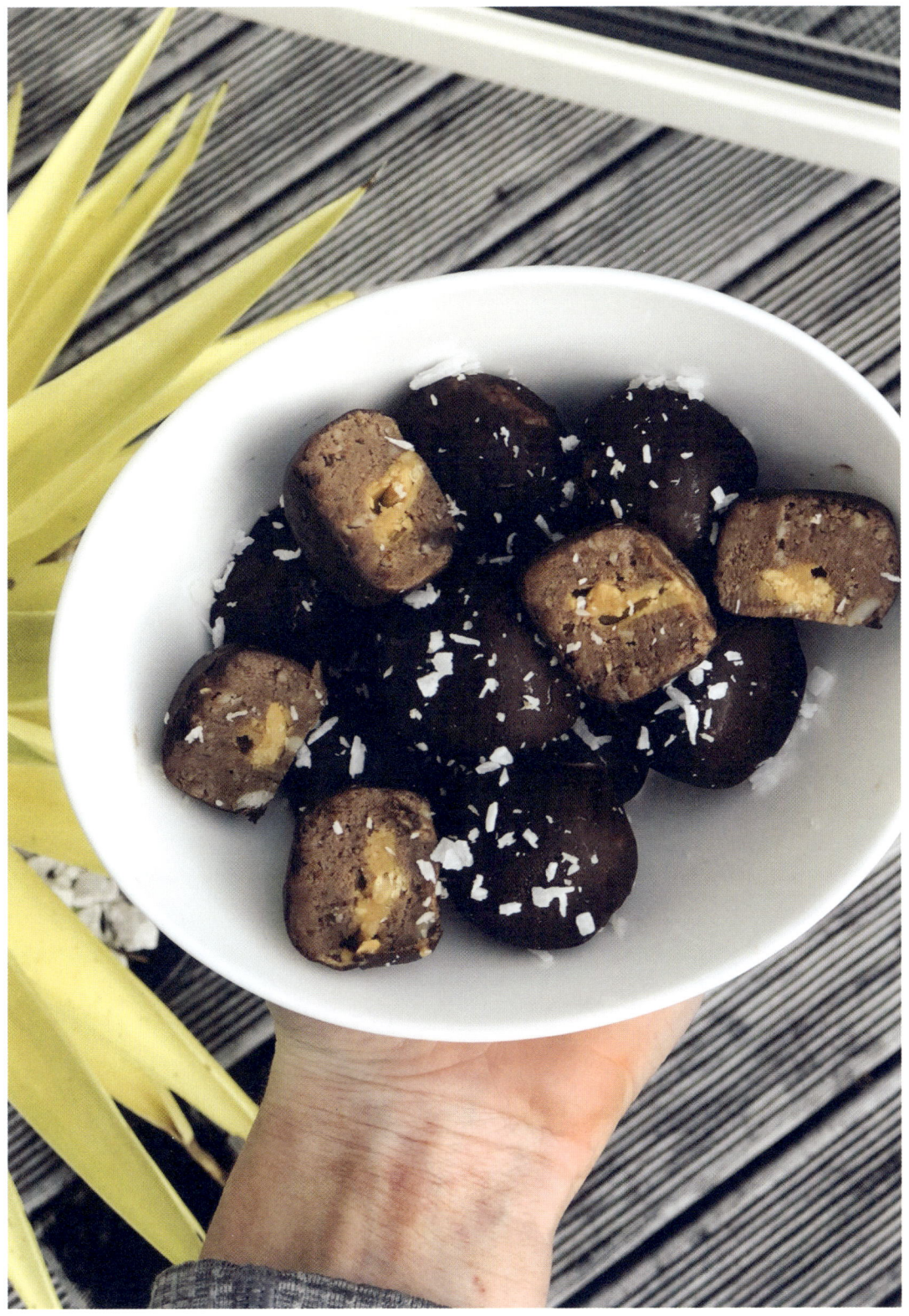

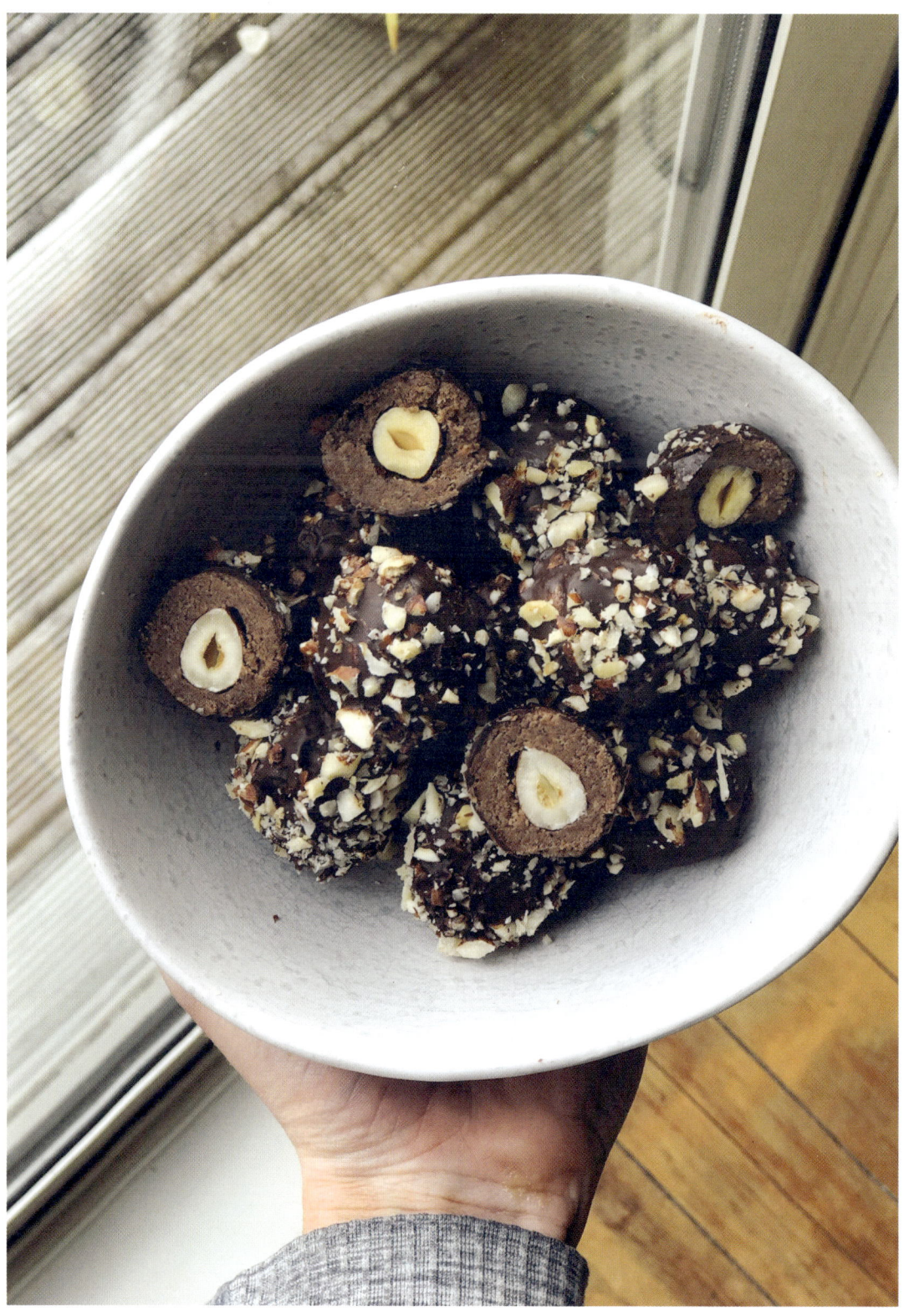

Hazelnut Truffle Bliss Balls

1 cup ground almonds/ oat flour
3 Tbsp peanut butter
3 Tbsp maple syrup/honey
1 tbsp chocolate protein powder
1 Tbsp cacao powder
20 hazelnuts
120g dark chocolate

1. In a bowl combine all ingredients (except hazelnuts and dark chocolate).
2. Take 1 hazelnut and form a ball of mixture around it. Repeat until the rest of the mixture is used up. Set in the fridge for 1 hour.
3. Melt the chocolate and chop the remaining hazelnuts up into fine pieces.
4. Dip each ball into the chocolate and roll in the chopped hazelnuts. Place back on the plate and set in the fridge for 30–60 minutes.

Makes/serves: 10–12 balls | Prep time: 5 minutes | Set time: 1 hour
Nutritional information: DF, RSF, V, GF

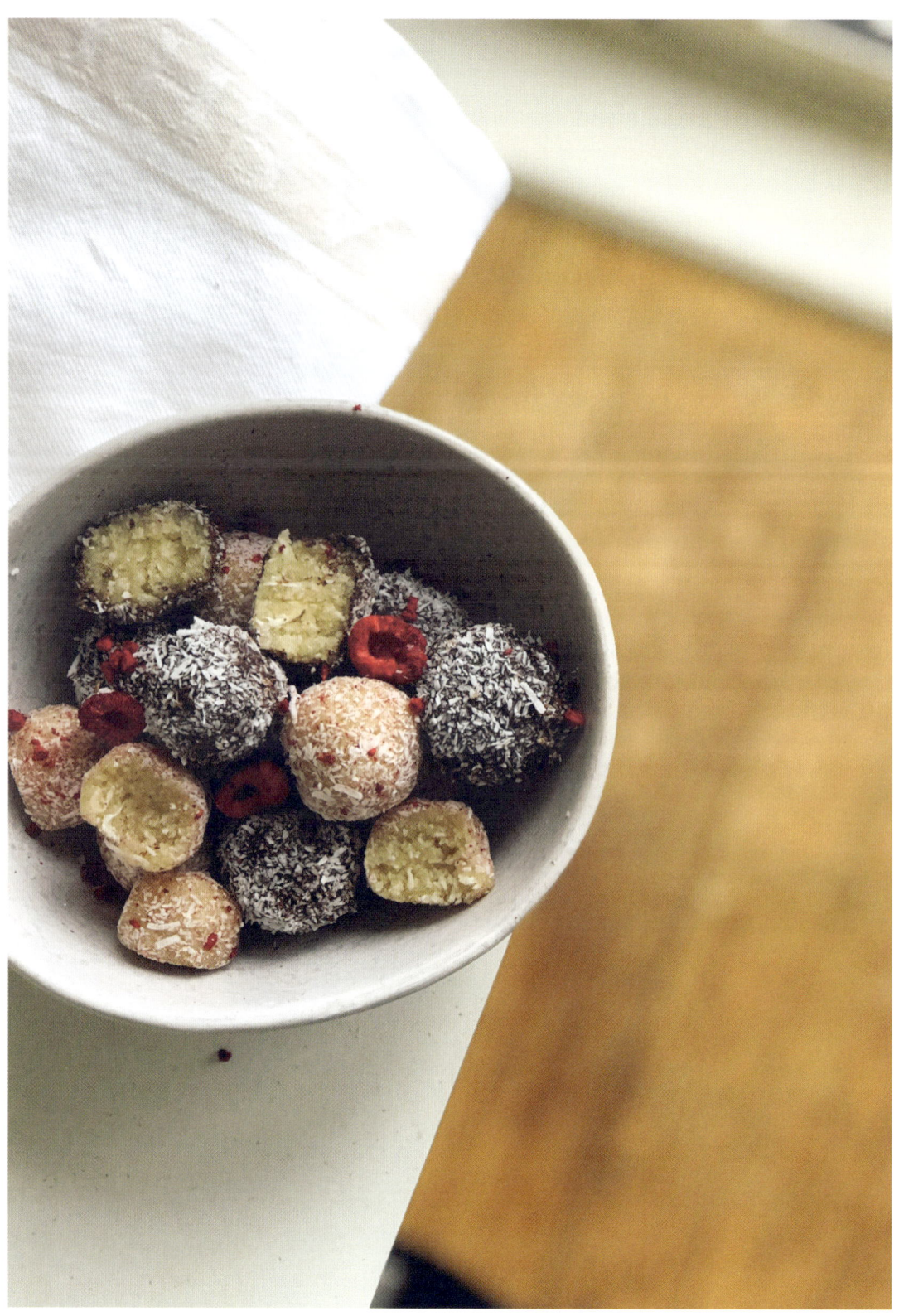

Lamington Bliss Balls

BALLS
1½ cups ground almonds
3 Tbsp maple syrup
3 Tbsp coconut oil, melted
¼ cup coconut thread
1 tsp vanilla essence

CHOCOLATE COATING
100g dark chocolate, melted
½ cup desiccated coconut

RASPBERRY COATING
½ cup desiccated coconut
½ cup freeze-dried raspberries

1. In a bowl combine all the ingredients for the balls (if too dry add water, and if too wet add more ground almonds). Roll into balls and place on a plate in the fridge to set for 30–60 minutes.
2. For the chocolate coating, dip each ball in the chocolate and then roll in the coconut. Place back on a plate and set in the fridge for 30 minutes.
3. For the raspberry coating, blend the coconut and freeze-dried raspberries until fine. Roll each ball in this mixture, place on a plate and set in the fridge for 30 minutes. If the coating doesn't stick, then use a bit of water to help it stick to the balls.

Makes/serves: 14 balls | Prep time: 5 minutes | Set time: 1 hour
Nutritional information: DF, RSF, V, G

Coconut Ice Bliss Balls

JELLY
1 cup ground almonds/
    rolled oats
½ cup desiccated coconut
2 Tbsp mashed berries
    (we used raspberries)
2 Tbsp maple syrup/honey
1 Tbsp coconut oil, melted
1 Tbsp coconut cream/milk/
    water

VANILLA
1 cup ground almonds/
    rolled oats
½ cup desiccated coconut
3 Tbsp maple syrup/honey
1 Tbsp melted coconut oil
1–2 Tbsp coconut cream/
    milk/water

CHOCOLATE COATING
100g dark chocolate, melted

1. In a bowl combine all the jelly ingredients.
2. In another bowl combine all the vanilla ingredients.
3. Roll a small ball of each flavour and then press and roll them together to make 1 large ball. Repeat with the remaining mixtures, place on a plate and set in the freezer for 30–60 minutes.
4. Remove from the fridge and dip each ball into the choc coating. Set in the fridge for a further 15–30 minutes.
5. EAT!!

Makes/serves: 14 balls | Prep time: 5 minutes | Set time: 1–2 hours
Nutritional information: DF, RSF, V, GF

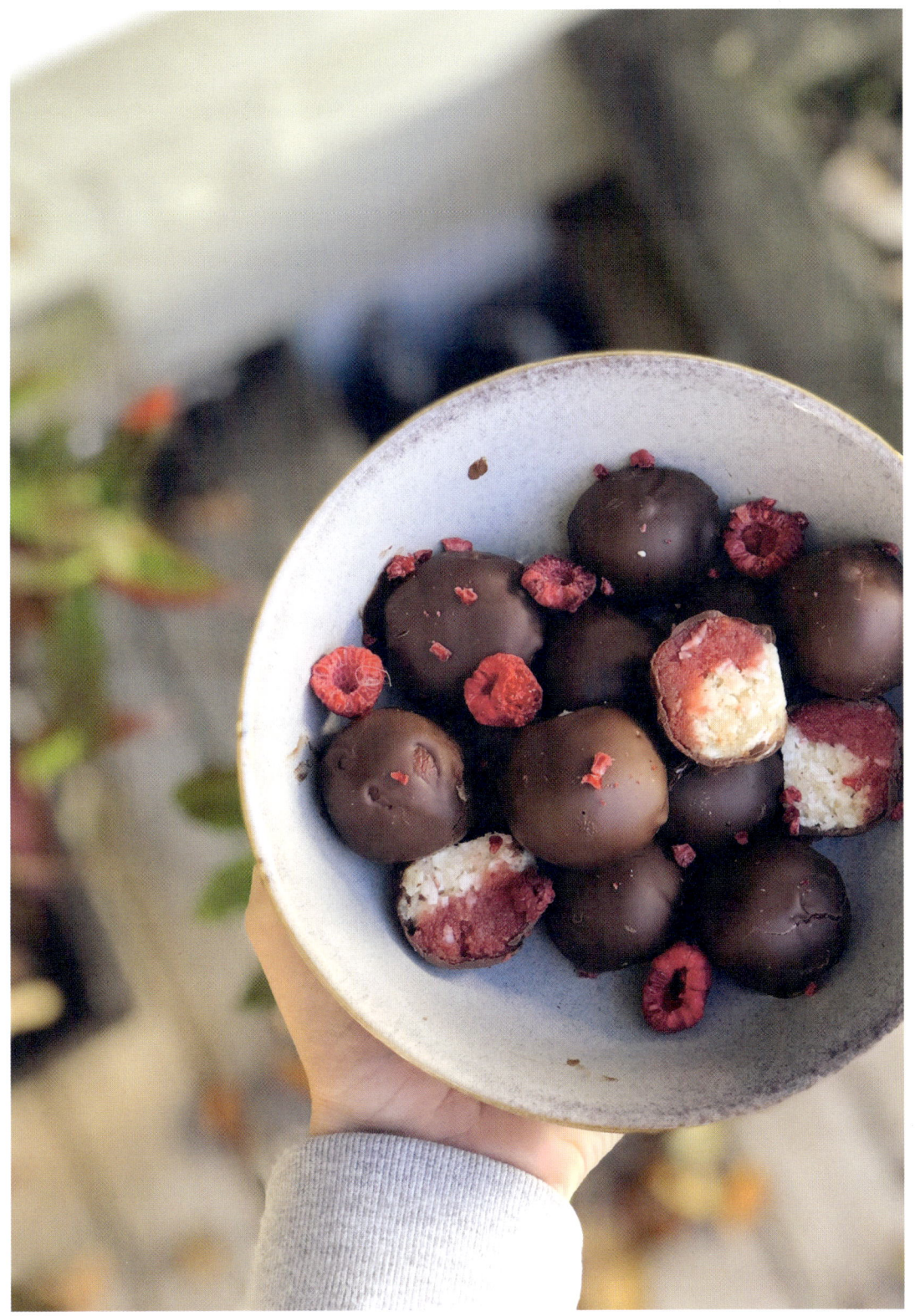

Fitness

When you get to uni or tech, life becomes very busy. What with all the lectures, labs, tutorials, assignments, exams . . . it can sometimes seem impossible to find the time to fit in anything else! But honestly, exercise is something you should always prioritise, if you can. Moving your body can take you into a new environment, a new focus and help you get some perspective.

    Working out looks different for everyone. Some people love getting sweaty with HIIT, some like to lift big, while some like stretching it out, and others can run or walk for miles. There are SO many ways that you can get moving: outside, inside, using equipment, with bodyweight, solo, with friends . . . there's definitely something that will work for you — you just have to find it. We recommend trying out a few different forms of exercise until you find your thing. Maybe go along to a gym class, test out a YouTube workout or go to the gym with a friend to put some different activities to the test. Eventually, you'll find something that you love.

    Finding your fave way of moving your body is the best way to ensure you stick with exercise. We absolutely love group fitness — going to classes is probably the highlight of our day. Working out with friends to some bangers — you can't beat it! Most gyms tend to do free trials, so you can go along and give them a go and see how you feel about it. If you're like us, you won't look back. Group fitness offers so much more than simply exercise. It's super social — you can bring a friend, or even make friends in your class. We met some of our closest friends through the gym. It also holds you accountable. If you're someone who struggles with motivation, group fitness instructors can motivate you to push through, and keep going even when you think you've hit your limit. And group fitness is just fun!

    Exercise has been a lifesaver for us throughout uni. It's a space away from hall drama and study pressure, where you can just focus completely on yourself. It lets you clear your mind, relieves stress and gets those endorphins pumping. The psychological aspect is critical for us. That feeling of leaving the gym, dripping sweat with tomato-red faces, but knowing you just smashed a workout, is pretty tough to beat. Exercise can become your happy place, if you find what works for you.

    We have started this section with a description of all the exercises and equipment we recommend that are ideal for doing at home (or at the park — wherever you like really). We follow this up with some of our fave workouts which incorporate different variations of these exercises. We've included photos with the workouts too, to help you master the right positions! These workouts are perfect for those days when you just can't make it to the gym, or if you're just starting out with fitness and need some workouts to try. These workouts are all approved by the incredible Kris Madsen, Group Fitness Manager, Group Fitness Instructor and Personal Trainer at Les Mills Hutt City. We hope that you enjoy them, and get a bit of a sweat on too.

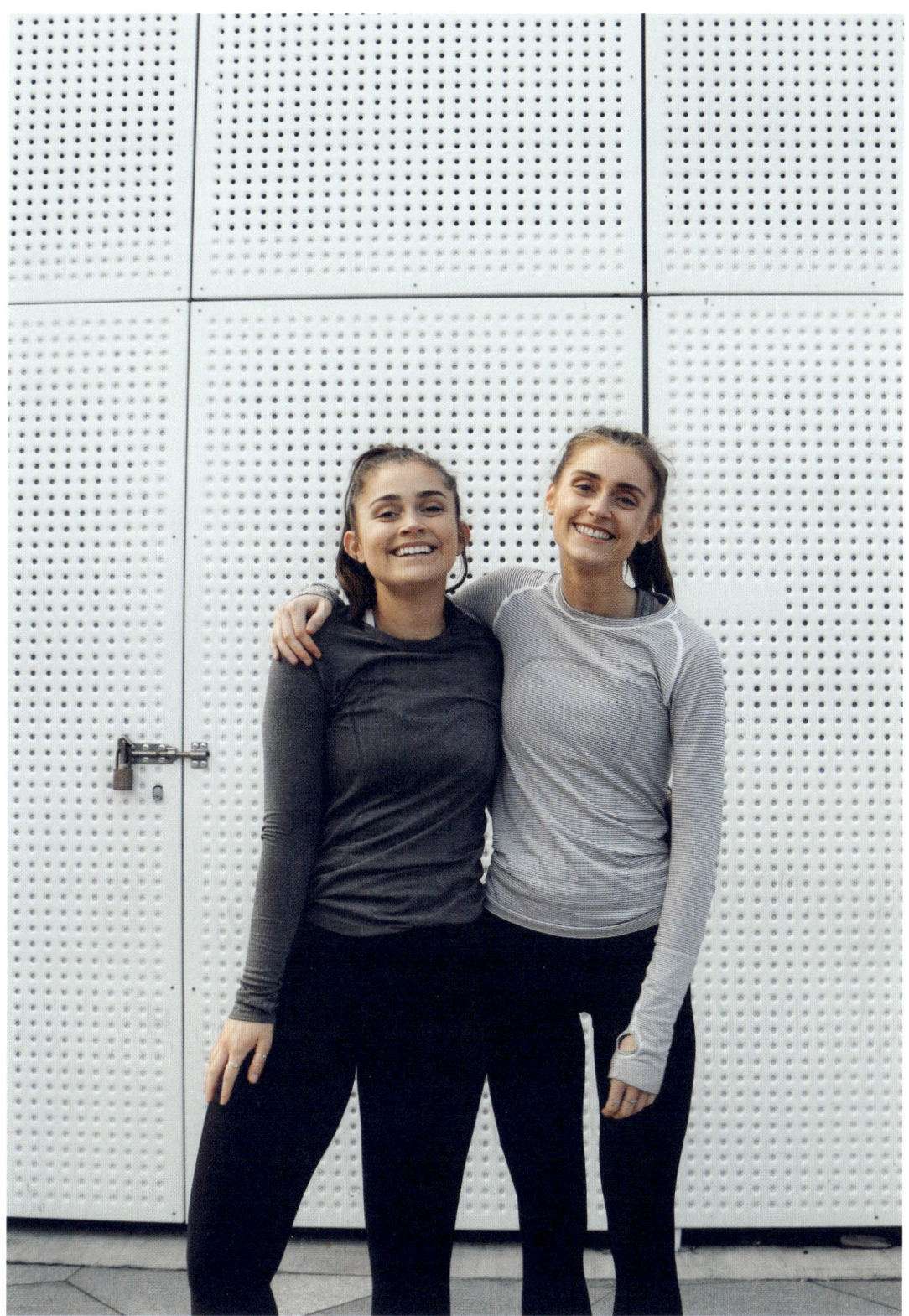

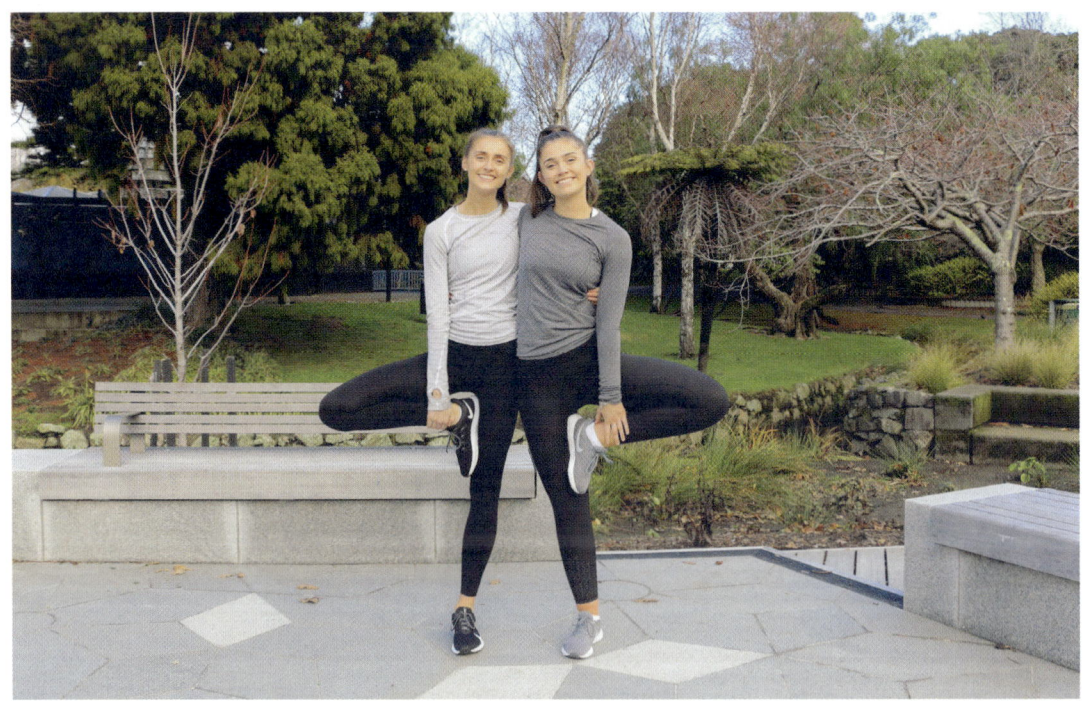

Tasty Twins' Exercise Tips & Tricks

Terms

EMOM, tabata, HIIT . . . if you're new to the exercise world, terms like these may as well be a different language. Well, we're here to help. In this section you'll find the A–Zs of fitness terminology, from your AMRAPs to your Zumba. We'll walk you through every single move that feature in our workouts, with photos to demonstrate, and describe all the equipment you need to smash out a good old sweat sesh!

AMRAP: Stands for 'as many reps as possible'; meaning that within a particular time limit, you are required to perform as many 'reps' of a given move as you can.

Circuit: A style of training whereby you perform a series of exercises, with rest between each exercise.

EMOM: Stands for 'every minute on the minute'; meaning that within a particular time limit (often 1 minute), you must perform a certain number of reps. If you complete those reps within the timeframe with time to spare, you can rest until the end of that specified period.

HIIT: Stands for 'high intensity interval training'; a type of interval training whereby you perform short, high-intensity blocks of work between short recovery periods.

Rep: The number of times that you perform one particular exercise.

Set: A number of reps performed multiple times in a row.

Tabata: A type of interval training in which you perform one exercise for 20 seconds, rest for 10 seconds and repeat 8 times.

Exercises

Alternating jumping lunges: Take one leg back, keeping your back knee and shin parallel to the floor and your front knee and shin straight and directly over your toes — try to aim for 90-degree angles. Jump and switch legs while in the air so that the opposite leg is back. Keep your chest up and use your arms to get a higher jump.

Alternating lunges: Stand upright with feet shoulder-width apart, holding your plate at your collarbone. Take one leg back, keeping your back knee and shin parallel with the floor and your front knee bent over your toes. Aim for 90-degree angles. Switch legs by standing up and taking the other leg back.

Back step lunges: Lift the barbell over your head and, still holding each end, rest it on the meaty part of your upper back, keeping your shoulders back and down and core tight. Step one leg back and lower hips until both knees are bent at a 90-degree angle. Keep your front knee over your big toe and back knee and shin parallel with the floor. Stand up and switch legs so that the opposite leg goes back into the lunge position.

Back squats: Stand with the barbell on the meaty part of your upper back, position your feet shoulder-width apart. Bend your knees and sink your hips back to knee level into a squat position. Squeeze your glutes, keep your knees bent and chest up and return back to a standing position.

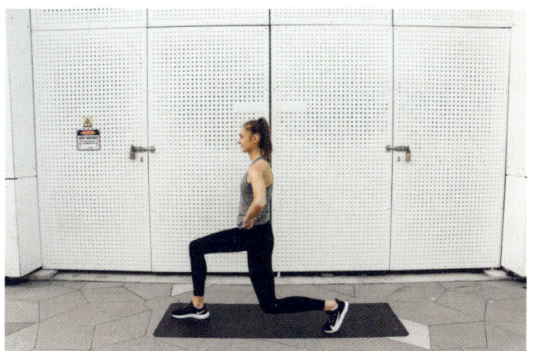
Alternating jumping lunges (1)

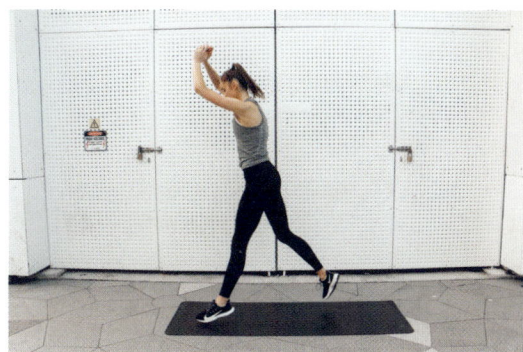
Alternating jumping lunges (2)

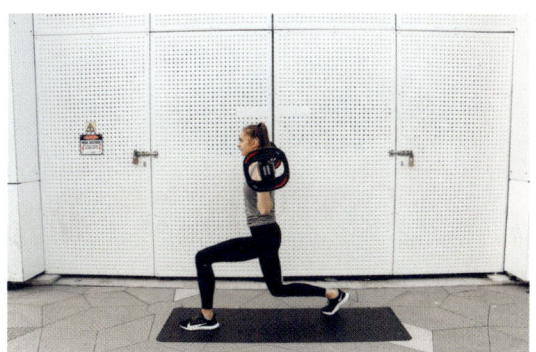
Back step lunges (1)

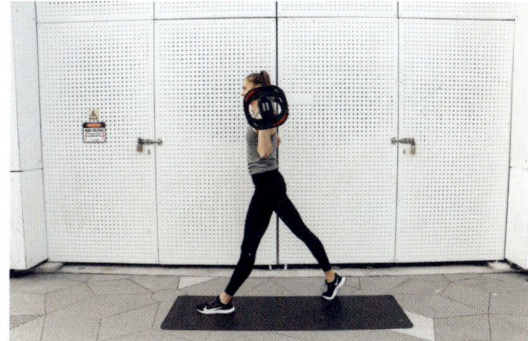
Back step lunges (2)

Bicep curl to shoulder press: Stand upright and hold dumbbells or plates down at arm's length. Curl the dumbbells up to your shoulders, rotating your palms outwards so that they are facing forward. Press the dumbbells overhead until your arms are straight. Reverse the movement back to the starting position.

Bicycle crunches: Lie on the floor with your lower back pressed into the floor and your knees bent. Put your fingertips to your temples and your knees at a 90-degree angle, lifting your feet off the floor. Go through a bicycle motion by bringing one knee to your armpit while straightening the other leg. Rotate your torso so that the opposite knee touches the opposite elbow. Twist to alternate so that the other knee comes forward.

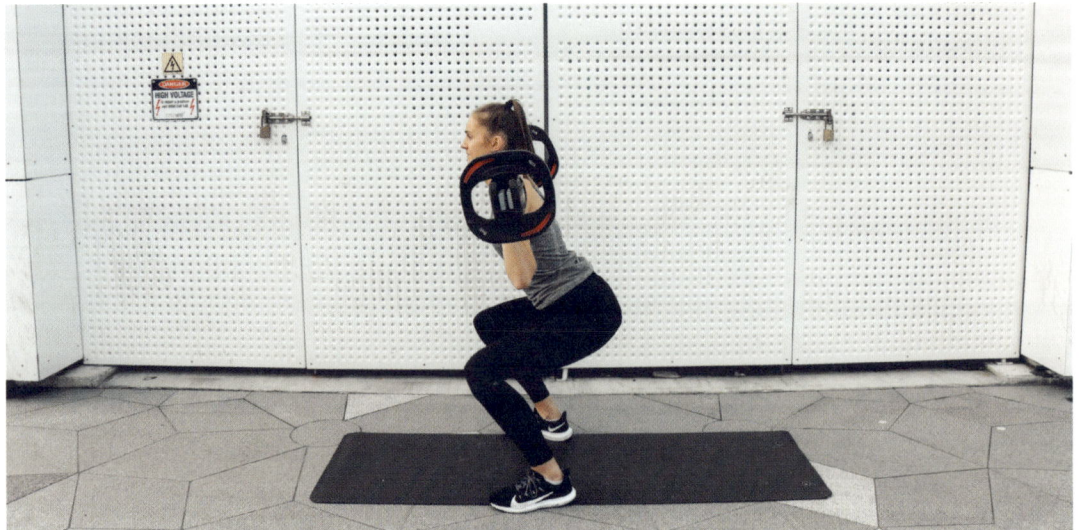

Back squats

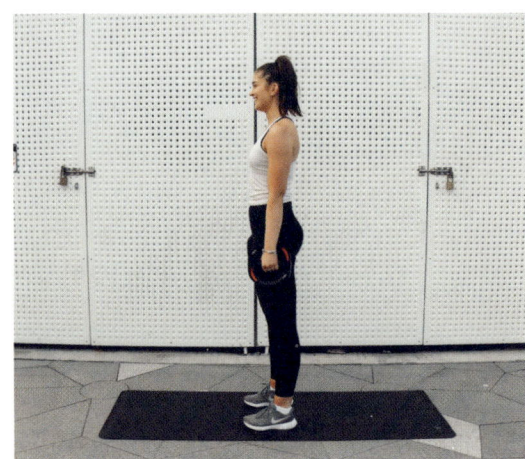

Bicep curls (1)

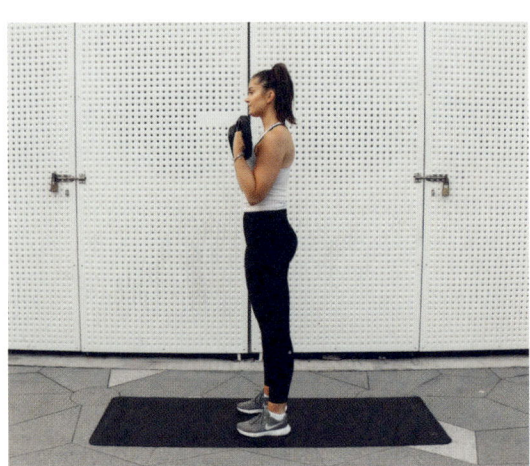

Bicep curls (2)

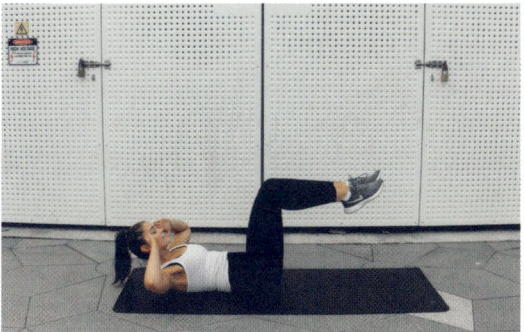
Bicycle crunches (1)

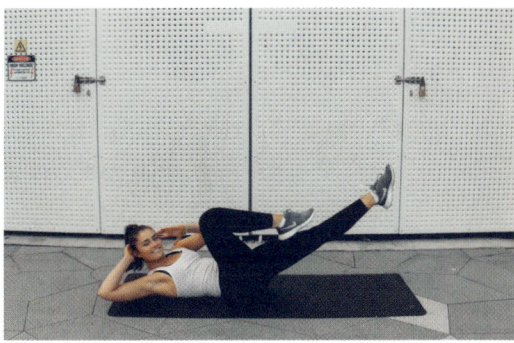
Bicycle crunches (2)

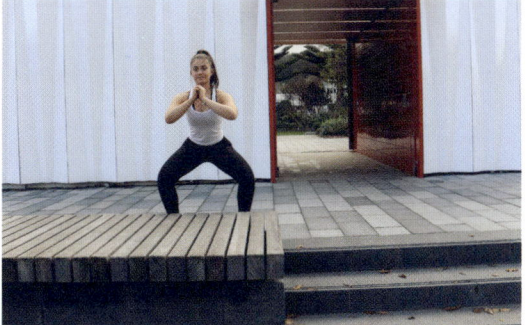
Box jumps (1)

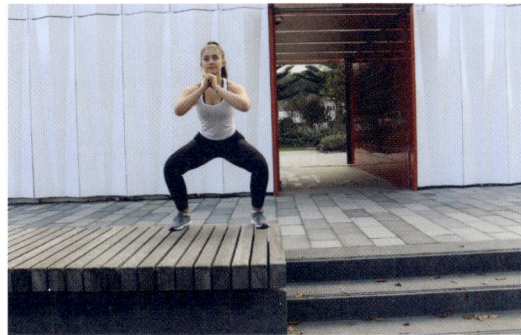
Box jumps (2)

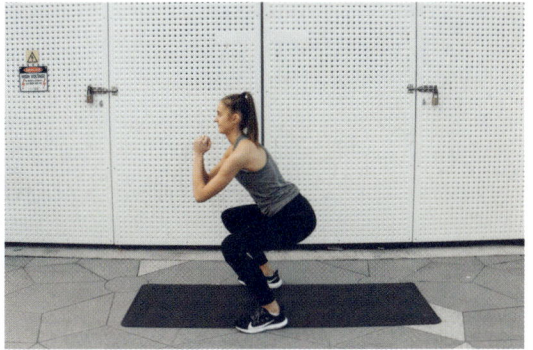
Burpees (1)

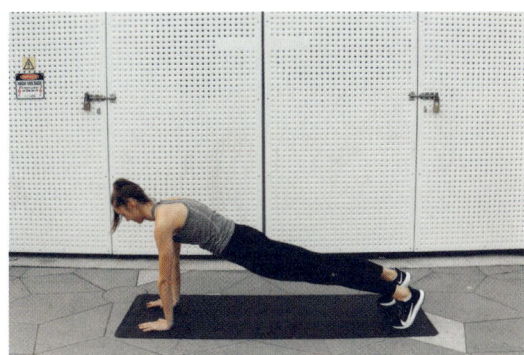
Burpees (2)

Box jumps: Brace your core, bend your knees and drive your hips and feet up onto the box. When you jump off the box, bend your knees as you land to absorb the landing.

Burpees: Position your legs shoulder-width apart and sink your hips back into a squat position, keeping your knees over your toes. Put your hands on the ground, brace your core and jump your legs back to plank position. Jump your feet back to squat position and stand.
OPTION: Step back to squat instead of jumping.

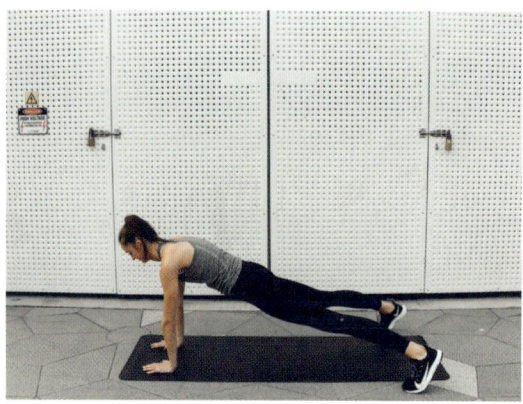
Chest push-ups (1)

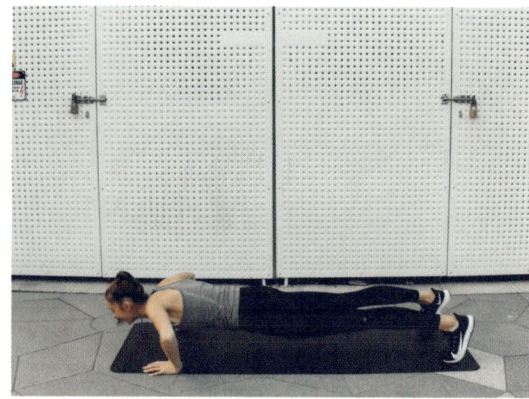
Chest push-ups (2)

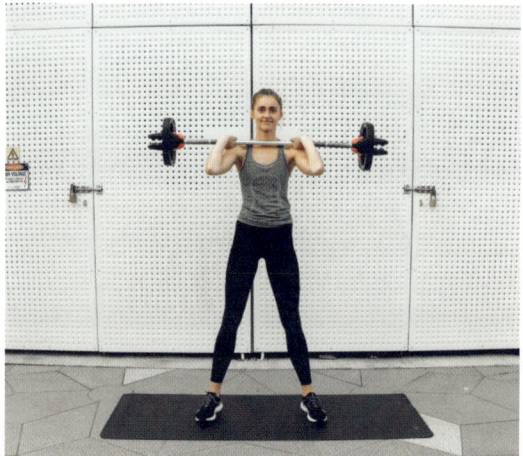
Clean and press (1)

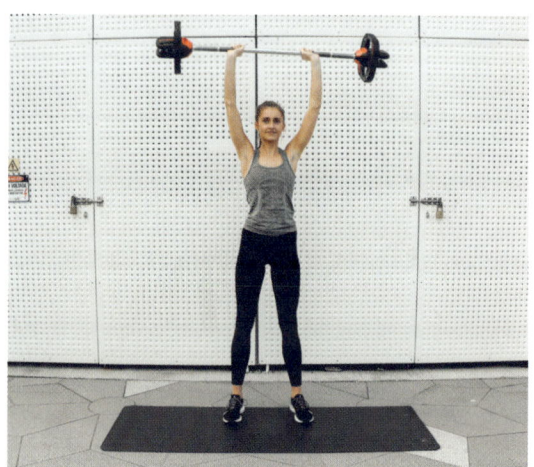
Clean and press (2)

Chest push-ups: Set yourself up in a plank position on your knees or toes. Position your hands outside of shoulder-width, brace your core and lower your chest to elbow height. Brace your core and reset back to a plank position. Squeeze your glutes tight.

Clean and press: Begin holding the bar with an overhand grip, resting it against your thighs. Keeping the bar close to your body, flick the bar up to your collarbone, so that your elbows are underneath. Lift the bar overhead so that your arms are straight, and the bar is above your head. Bring the bar back down to your collarbone, then back to the start position. Make sure you brace your core throughout this entire movement.

Deadlifts: Hold a barbell down at arm's length. Position your feet just outside shoulder-width, push your hips back, keep your chest up and your core tight. Bend at a 45-degree angle, taking the bar down to your knees. Stand upright and bring the bar back to your thighs. Keep the bar close to your body the entire time.

Front squats: Hold the dumbbells/plates at collarbone height. Position your feet slightly wider than shoulder-width apart. Brace your core tight and squat down by taking your hips back to knee level and pushing your knees out over your toes. Squeeze your glutes and return back to the starting position.

High-knee run: On the spot run, with your knees aiming for hip height and keeping your chest up.

High pulls: Stand with your feet shoulder-width apart, holding the barbell in front of your shins. Position your hands on the bar so they are just outside of each leg. Engage your glutes and brace your core tight, then pull the bar up in one movement, keeping it close to your body. As the bar is lifted, shrug your shoulders to pull the bar up to collarbone height. Lower the bar back to start position.

Jumping lunges: Perform alternating lunges without a plate or press and, instead of stepping to switch legs, jump!

Jumping squats: Position your feet shoulder-width apart and do a normal squat. Brace your core and jump up. When you land, lower your body back into a squat.

Lunge press: Place the bar or plate at your collarbone and take one leg back into a lunge. Keep your back knee to the floor, your chest up and try to aim for 90-degree angles. When you step to switch legs, press the plate overhead so that your arms are straight. As you switch legs, return the plate to your collarbone.

Mountain climbers: Set yourself up in a plank position, bracing your core, weight forward over your hands that are directly placed under your shoulders. Keep your

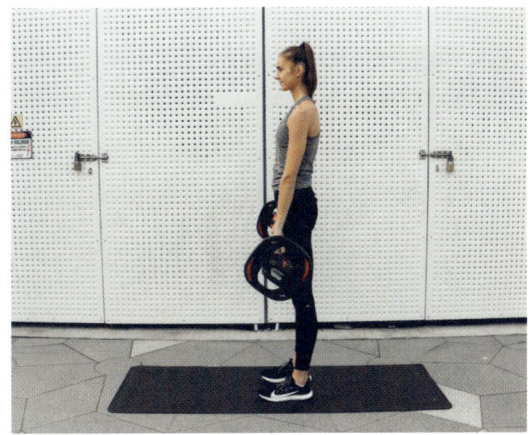

Deadlifts (1)

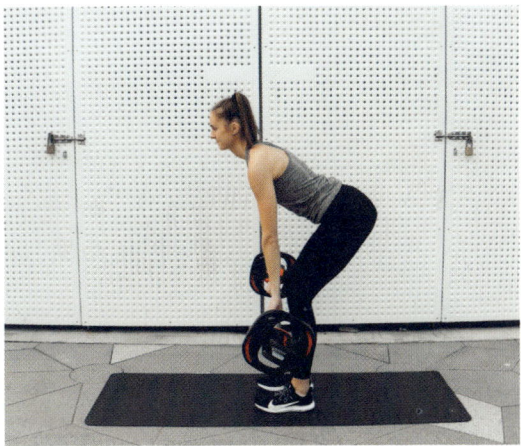

Deadlifts (2)

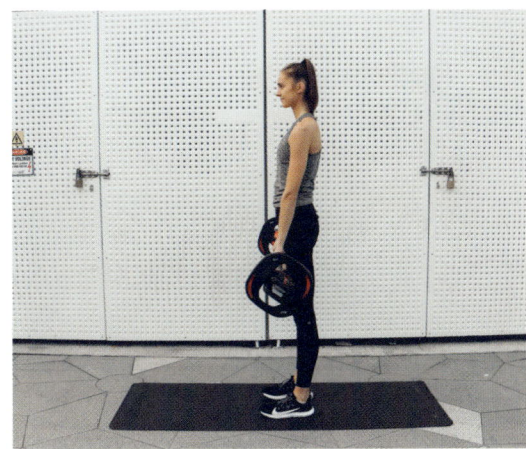

Deadlifts (3)

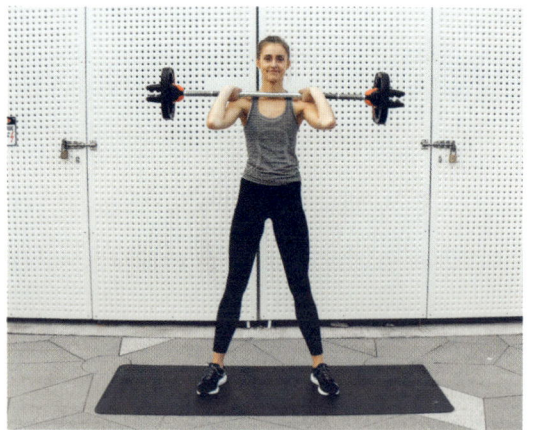
Front squats (1)

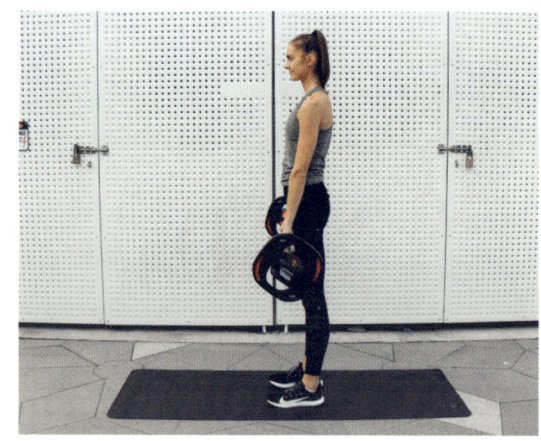
High pulls (1)

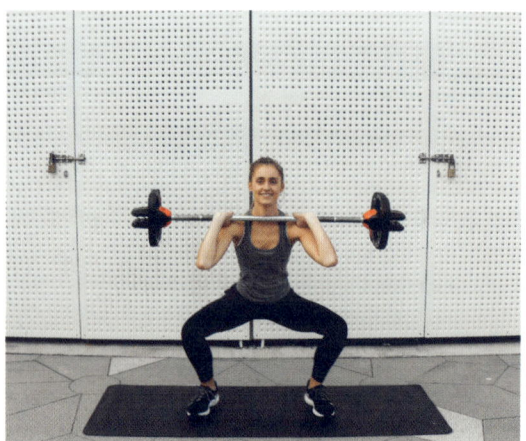
Front squats (2)

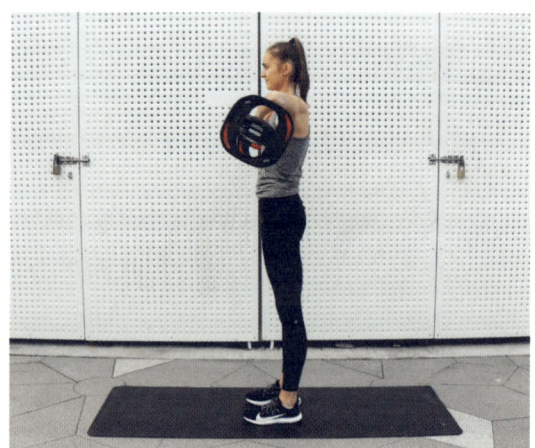
High pulls (2)

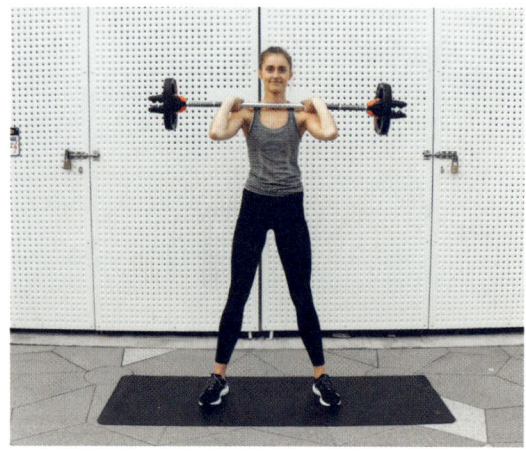
Front squats (3)

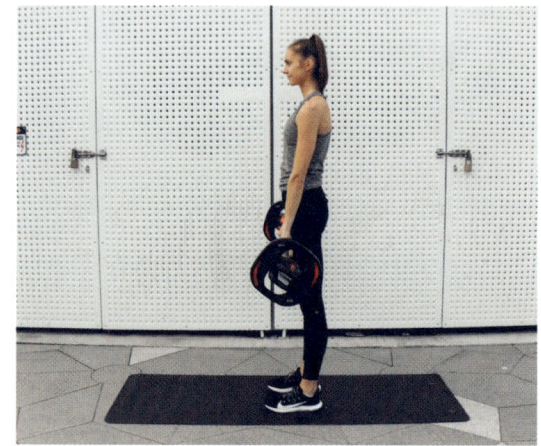
High pulls (3)

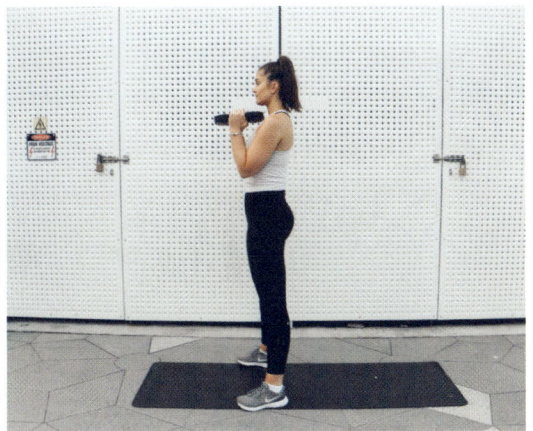
Lunge press (1)

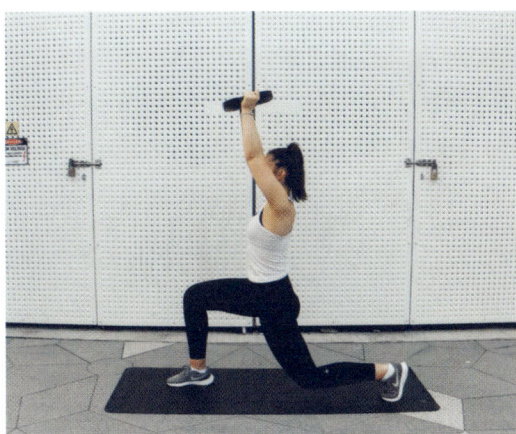
Lunge press (2)

back flat and body square to the floor. Pull one knee into your chest, and then switch so that the other knee is up to your chest. Go as fast as you can!

Plank: Brace your core and keep your back straight. Squeeze your glutes tight and make sure your hips are square to the floor.

Plank jacks: Starting in the plank position, keep your hands under your shoulders and weight over your hands. Brace your core tight and don't let your hips sag. Jump your feet out (to shoulder width) and then back in (so your ankle bones touch).

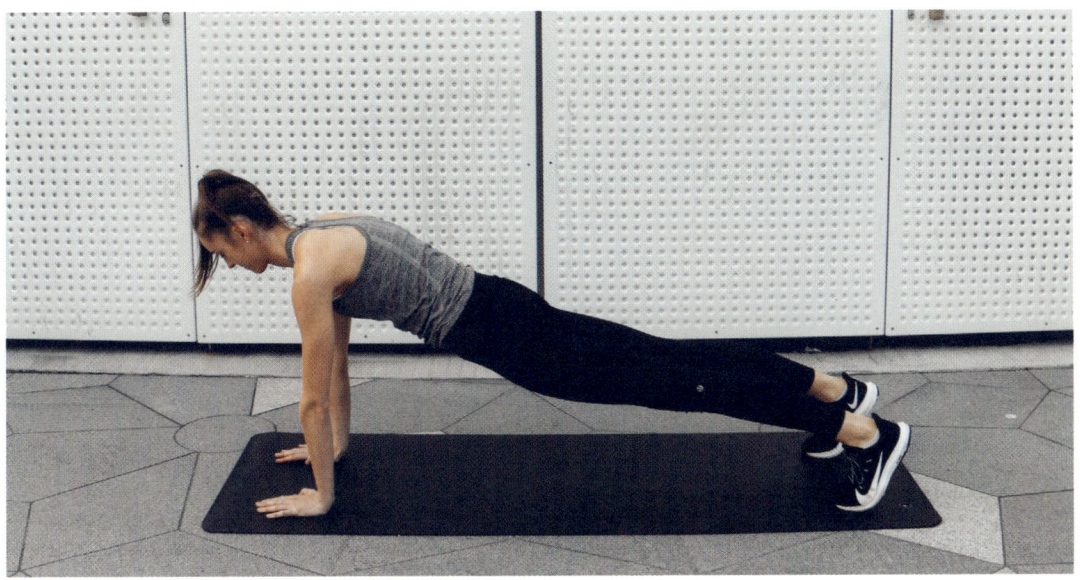
Plank

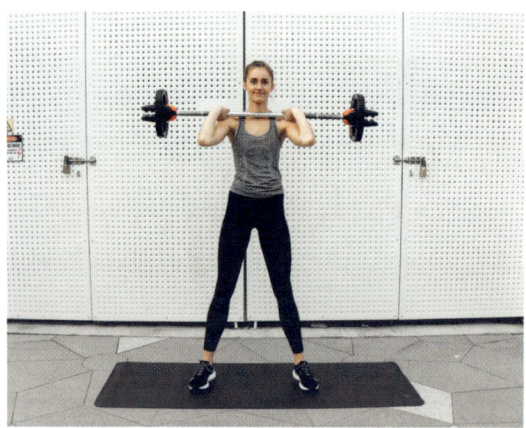
Push press (1)

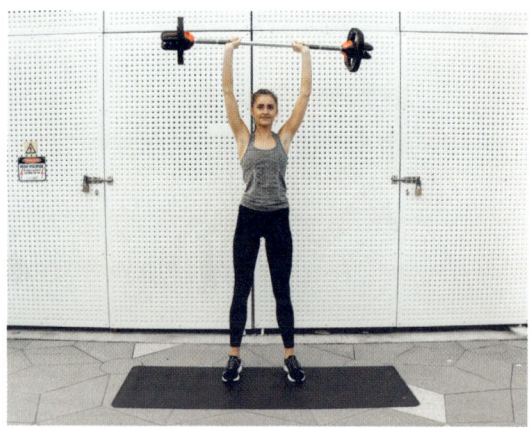
Push press (2)

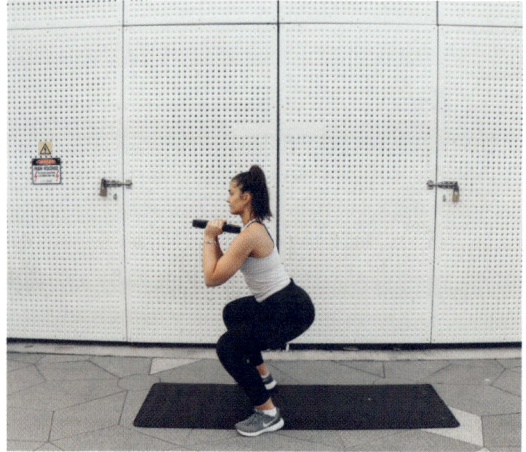
Squat heel raises with press (1)

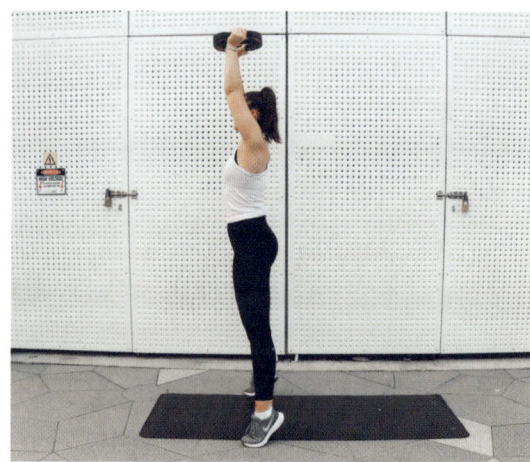
Squat heel raises with press (2)

Plank walk-out and jump: Start standing, squat and put your hands on the ground in front of you. Walk your hands forward until your body is at full length, straight in a plank position. Brace your core in the plank and don't let your hips sag. Walk your hands back to your feet, stand up and jump.

Push press: Stand with your feet shoulder-width apart and bring the barbell from the floor up to your collarbone and drop down into a deep squat. Keep your chest up, knees over toes in the squat and hips back to knee level. Centre your weight under the barbell, press through your heels and drive the bar directly above your head until your arms are straight. Lower the bar down to your chest and return to a squat.

Shoulder taps: In the plank position, place your feet hip-width apart. Keep your body straight and your core braced super tight. Lift one palm to the top of your opposite arm, reset back to plank and repeat on the other side.

Sit-ups: Lie on your back and bend your knees so that your toes lightly touch the floor. Put your hands at your temples and bend your hips and waist to raise your body off the ground. Lower your body back to the ground.

Skipping: Hold onto the handles, flip the rope over your head and jump as it approaches your feet. Keep your knees soft.

Squat heel raises with press: Grab a plate. Standing upright, position your feet shoulder-width apart and hold the plate at your collarbone. Bracing your core tight, squat down by taking your hips back to knee level and pushing your knees out over your toes. Squeeze your glutes and return back to the starting position, this time extending the plate above your head so that your arms are straight. At the same time, squeeze your glutes and raise your heels off the floor. Pull your arms back down to your collarbone and reset to the squat position.

Squat thrusts: Stand with your feet shoulder-width apart. Lower into a squat position, sticking your backside out as if sitting, hips back and knees to 90 degrees. Place your hands on the floor and jump your legs back to plank position. Brace your core tight and jump or step your legs back to a squat position.

Tuck jumps: Standing upright, position your feet just outside your hips and perform a normal squat jump. As you jump, lift your knees to chest height by bracing your core tight and using your arms. As you land, make sure to bend your knees.

Upright row: Position your feet about shoulder-width apart, holding the barbell against your thighs with an overhand grip. Brace your core and pull the bar up to

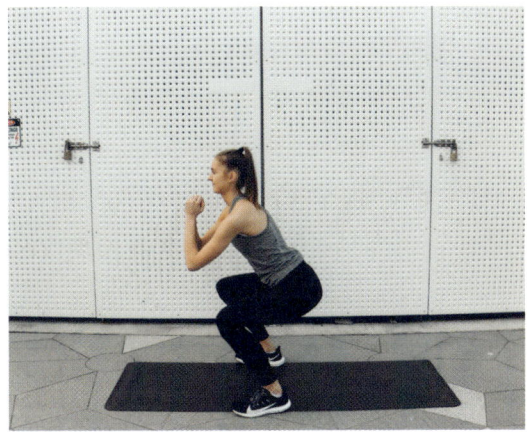

Squat thrusts (1)

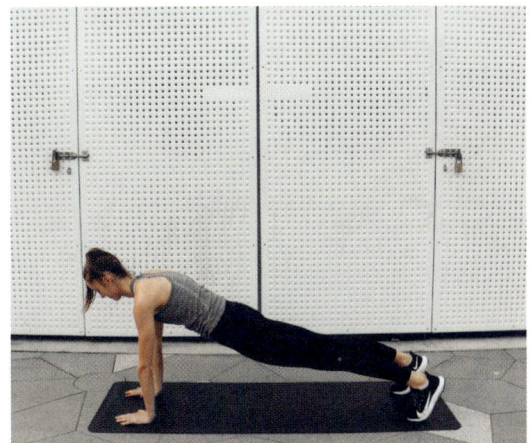

Squat thrusts (2)

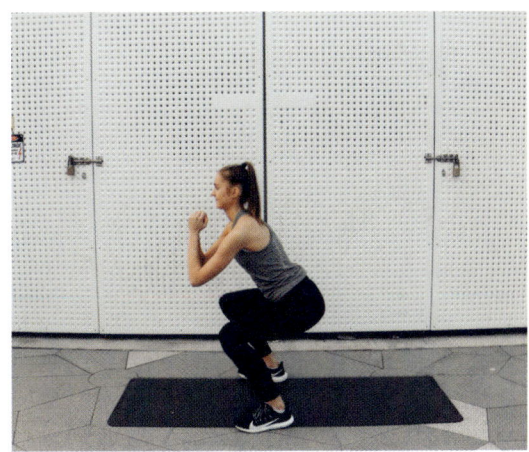

Squat thrusts (3)

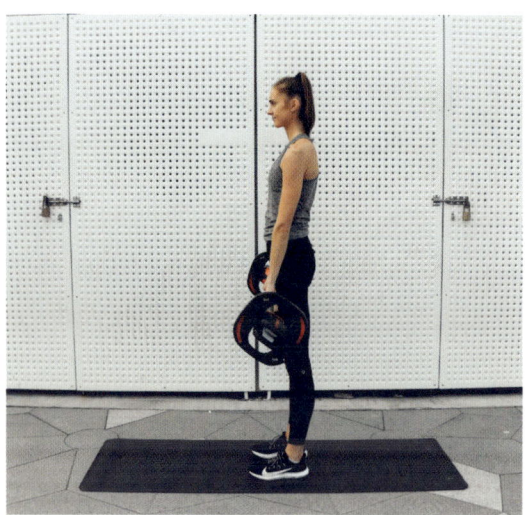
Upright row (1)

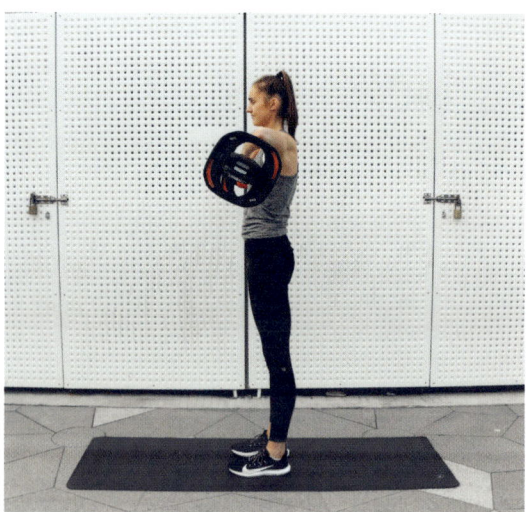
Upright row (2)

chest height, close to your body. Pause at the top and return the barbell back to a starting position.

Weighted squats: Grab a plate. Standing upright, position your feet shoulder-width apart and hold the plate at your collarbone. Bracing your core tight, squat down by taking your hips back to knee level and pushing your knees out over your toes. Squeeze your glutes and return back to the starting position.

Equipment

Equipment is by no means essential to getting a good workout — bodyweight exercises can still be super challenging! However, we love adding in some weights to our workouts for building strength, and taking some of our fave moves to the next level. Below we've listed all the equipment that you might like to include in your exercise regime:
- Dumbbells
- Weight plates
- Barbell
- Kettlebell
- Skipping rope

However, you don't need fancy equipment or a decked-out gym to get a sweat on! Feel free to make the most of anything you have at home. Cans of food, wine bottles, backpacks . . . anything can be a weight if you think about it!

Recovery

While a challenging workout is a great way to push yourself, and leaves you feeling super satisfied afterwards, it's important that you don't push yourself too far. You don't need to work out at 100% effort 7 days a week, 365 days a year. High-intensity exercises like these are best in moderation, perhaps 2–4 times a week, depending on what feels right for you. And, of course, don't forget to stretch afterwards.

You can mix up your types of physical activity, of course — maybe add in a social sport, or try a lower-intensity

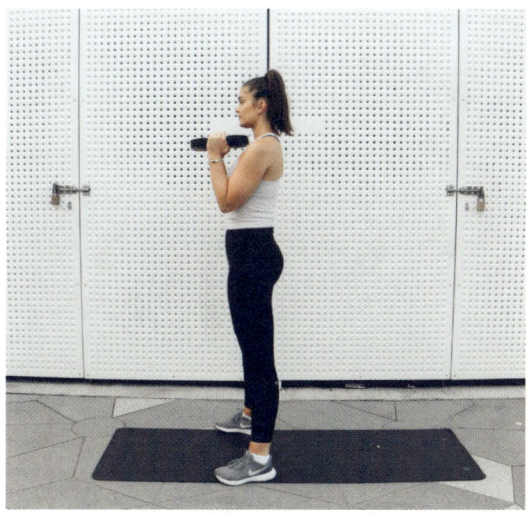

Weighted squat (1)

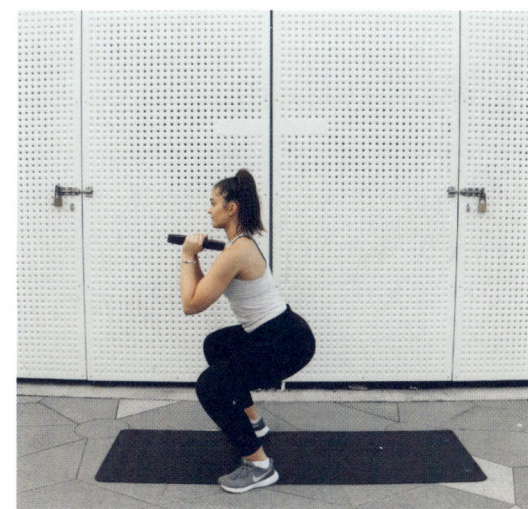

Weighted squat (2)

session, like walking or yoga. Whatever form of exercise you choose, make sure you are taking at least 1–2 rest days a week. Having these days off allows your muscles to recover, and can help protect you from injury.

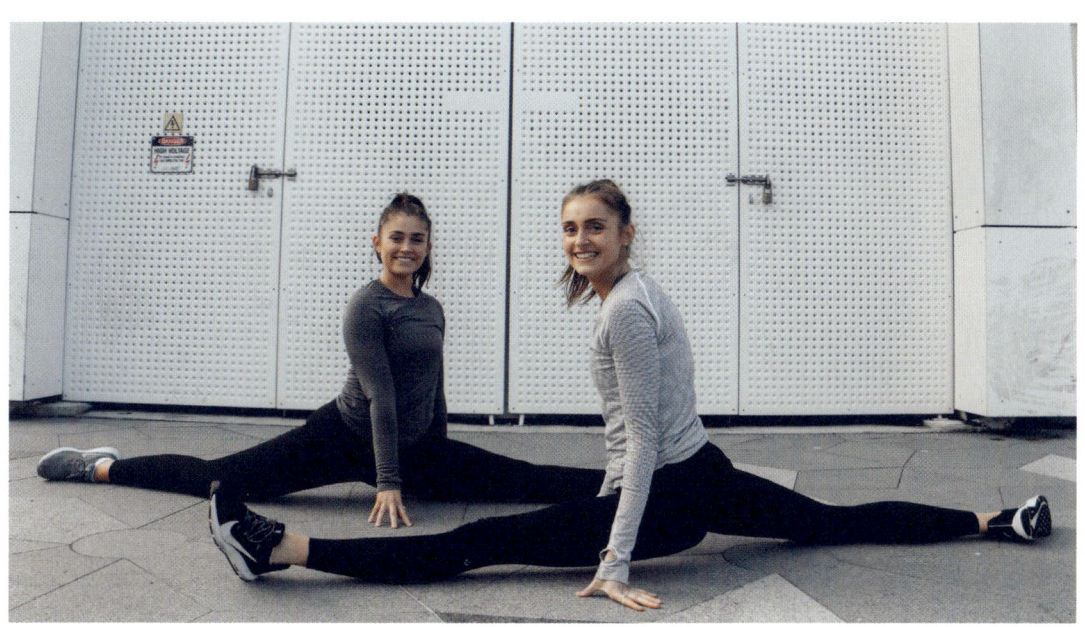

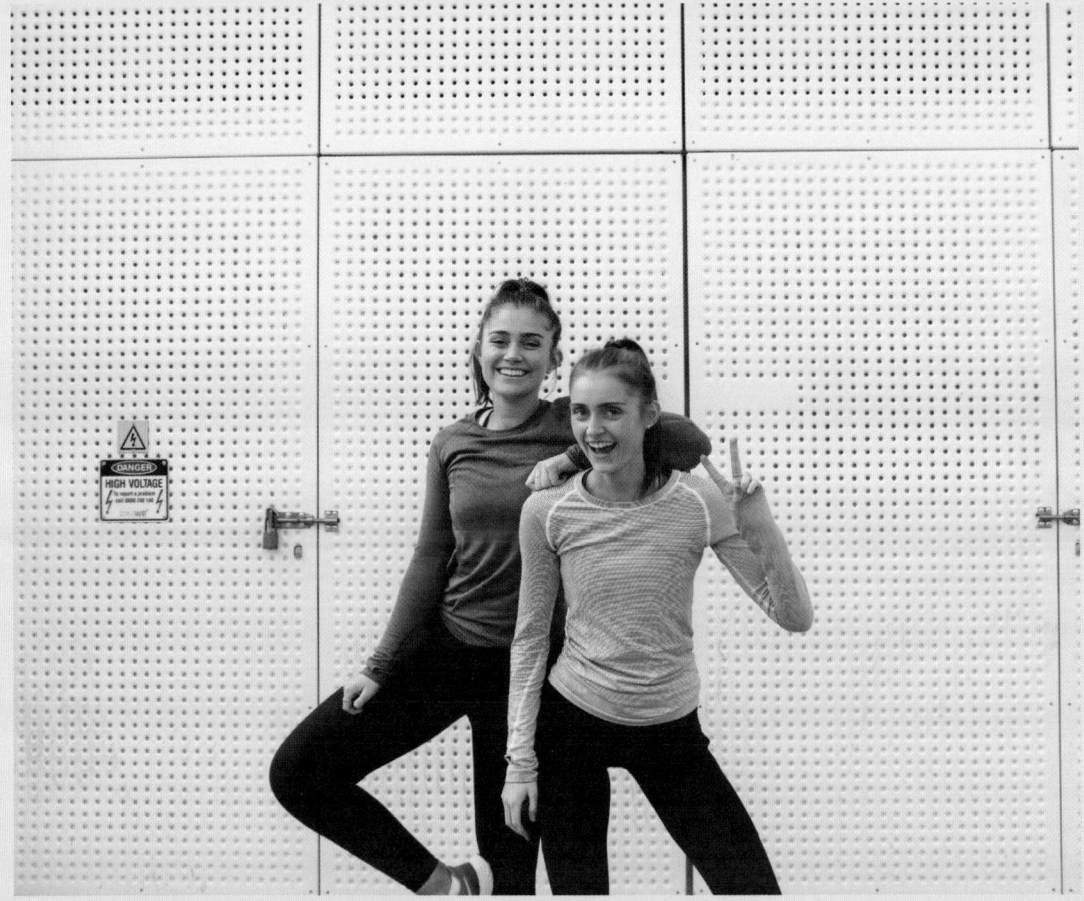

Workouts

Exercise should be a celebration of moving your body, not a punishment. So, we have a whole range of super-fun workouts for you to choose from that target all the muscle groups. These will lift your heart rate, get your endorphins going and leave you feeling accomplished afterwards. You'll find some dynamic bodyweight exercises, where you don't need anything but a bit of space to get a great sweat on, and some challenging equipment-based workouts too. So, whether you're at home or hitting the gym, you'll be able to smash out one of these in no time!

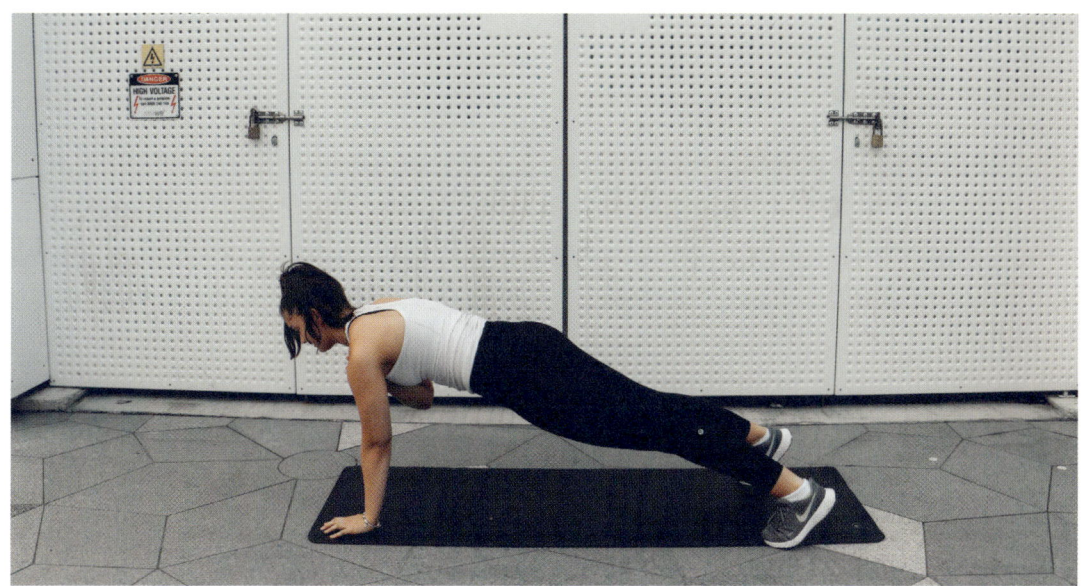

Shoulder taps

Workout 1: Full Body
40 seconds on each move, 20-second recovery, repeat three times:
- Plank walk out and jump (p. 118)
- Plank jacks (p. 117)
- Squat thrusts (p. 119)
- Alternating jumping lunges (p. 111)
- Burpees (p. 113)

Workout 2: AMRAP
4 blocks of work, 7 minutes of work for each block, 2 minutes rest between each:
Equipment: 1 x weighted barbell, 2 x weighted plates or dumbbells

Block 1: Using a weighted barbell
- 7 x push press (p. 118)
- 14 x alternating lunges (7 each leg) (p. 111)
- 21 x squat thrusts (p. 119)

Block 2: Using 2 x weighted plates or dumbbells
- 7 x bicep curl to shoulder press (p. 112)
- 14 x alternating lunges (p. 111)
- 21 x front squats (p. 115)

Block 3: Using weighted barbell
- 7 x high pulls (p. 115)
- 14 x deadlifts (p. 114)
- 21 x squat thrusts (p. 119)

Block 4: Bodyweight
- 7 x chest push-ups (p. 114)
- 14 x shoulder taps (p. 118)
- 21 x plank jacks (p. 117)

Workout 3: Upper Body
4 x moves, repeat 3 times, 2 minutes rest between each set:
Equipment: 1 barbell

Exercise	Reps	Sets
Deadlifts (p. 114)	12	3
Upright row (p. 119)	10	3
Clean and press (p. 114)	15	3
Chest push-ups (p. 114)	12	3

Workout 4: AMRAP
Set a timer for 30 minutes and repeat as many rounds as you can:
Equipment: Bodyweight
- 25 squat thrusts (p. 119)
- 20 alternating lunges (p. 111)
- 5 chest push-ups (p. 114)
- 24 bicycle crunches (p. 112)
- 24 mountain climbers (p. 115)

Workout 5: AMRAP
4 blocks of work, 7 minutes of work for each block, 2 minutes rest between each:
Equipment: 1 x large plate, 1 x medium plate, 1 x heavy bar

Round 1
- 7 x weighted squats (large plate) (p. 120)
- 14 x squat heel raises with press (large plate) (p. 119)
- 21 x jumping squats (p. 115)

Round 2
- 7 x lunge press (each leg) (p. 115)
- 14 x alternating lunges (p. 111)
- 21 x alternating jumping lunges (p. 111)

Round 3
- 7 x chest push-ups (p. 114)
- 14 x plank jacks (p. 117)
- 21 x bicycle crunches (p. 112)

Round 4
- 7 x tuck jumps (p. 119)
- 14 x mountain climbers (p. 115)
- 21 x burpees (p. 113)

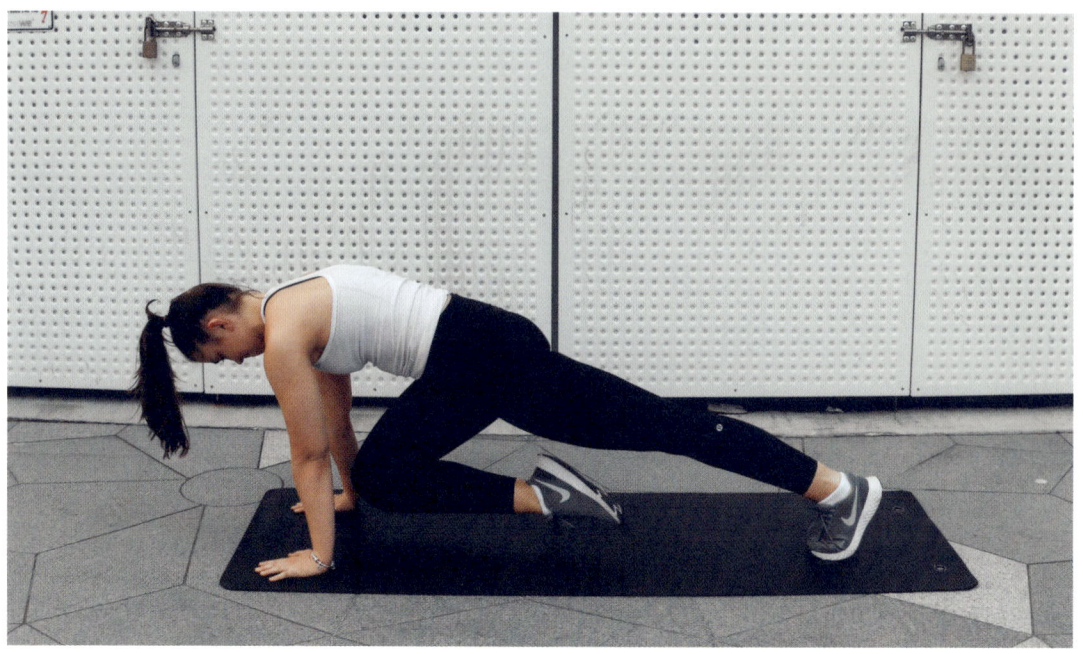

Mountain climbers

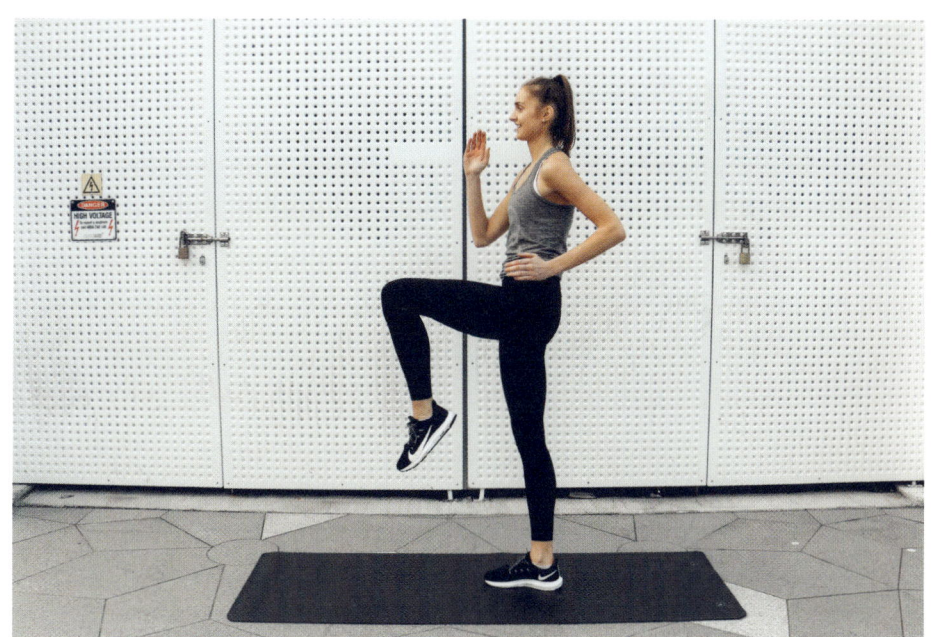
High-knee run

Workout 6: Lower Body Workout
4 moves, 4 rounds, 30 seconds recovery:
Equipment: 1 x large plate/kettlebell,
    1 x medium plate

Move 1: 10 x lunge press (each leg) (p. 115)
Move 2: 10 x weighted squats (p. 120)
Move 3: 10 x squat heel raises with press
    (p. 119)
Move 4: 30 x burpees (p. 113)

Exercise	Reps	Sets
Lunge press (p. 115)	10 each leg	4
Weighted squat (p. 120)	10	4
Deadlifts (p. 114)	10	4
Squat heel raises with press (p. 119)	10	4
Burpees (p. 113)	30	4

Workout 7: Partner Circuit Workout
3 minutes per station, 30 second rest.
Repeat the whole workout 3 times:
Equipment: 1 x medium-heavy plate
Grab a friend and try this partner workout! One person is on the move with a set number of reps to complete, while the other continues with the alternate move until their partner has completed their reps. Then switch. Keep going until the time is up.

Circuit 1:
Partner 1: 12 x lunge press (bar or plate)
    (p. 115)
Partner 2: Continuous burpees (p. 113)

Circuit 2:
Partner 1: 15 x squat heel raises with press
    (plate) (p. 119)
Partner 2: Continuous high-knee run (p. 115)

Circuit 3:
Partner 1: 20 x plank jacks (p. 117)
Partner 2: Continuous tuck jumps (p. 119)

Workout 8: Ladder Workout
Equipment: Rowing machine, medium plate/kettlebell

Warm up: 1km treadmill run

Round 1:
- 500m rowing machine
- 10 squat heel raises with press (p. 119)
- 10 burpees (p. 113)
- 10 chest push-ups (p. 114)
- 10 sit-ups (p. 119)

Round 2:
- 400m rowing machine
- 10 squat heel raises with press (p. 119)
- 10 burpees (p. 113)
- 10 chest push-ups (p. 114)
- 10 sit-ups (p. 119)

Round 3:
- 300m rowing machine
- 10 squat heel raises with press (p. 119)
- 10 burpees (p. 113)
- 10 chest push-ups (p. 114)
- 10 sit-ups (p. 119)

Round 4
- 200m rowing machine
- 10 squat heel raises with press (p. 119)
- 10 burpees (p. 113)
- 10 chest push-ups (p. 114)
- 10 sit-ups (p. 119)

Round 5
- 100m rowing machine
- 10 squat heel raises with press (p. 119)
- 10 burpees (p. 113)
- 10 chest push-ups (p. 114)
- 10 sit-ups (p. 119)

Warm down: 1km treadmill run

Workout 9: 500 Rep Challenge
Repeat these 5 sets 5 times, to complete 500 reps:
Equipment: Medium plate/kettlebell
- 20 x squat heel raises with press (p. 119)
- 20 x lunge press (each leg) (p. 114)
- 20 x deadlifts (p. 114)
- 20 x burpees (p. 113)
- 20 x shoulder taps (p. 118)

Workout 10: Tabata Workout
20 seconds on the move, 10 seconds recovery — repeat 3 times for an awesome sweaty session!
Equipment: Bodyweight
- Burpees (p. 113)
- Sit-ups (p. 119)
- Tuck jumps (p. 119)
- Plank jacks (p. 117)
- Burpees (p. 113)
- Sit-ups (p. 119)
- Tuck jumps (p. 119)
- Plank jacks (p. 117)

Workout 11: Sweat it Up
10 moves, 1 minute each, repeat 3 times:
Equipment: Skipping rope, medium plate/kettlebell, wooden box/knee-height surface to jump on to
- Burpees (p. 113)
- Plank jacks (p. 117)
- Box jumps (p. 113)
- High-knee run (p. 115)
- Skipping (p. 119)
- Mountain climbers (p. 115)
- Chest push-ups (p. 114)
- Lunge press (p. 115)
- Plank (p. 117)
- Tuck jumps (p. 119)

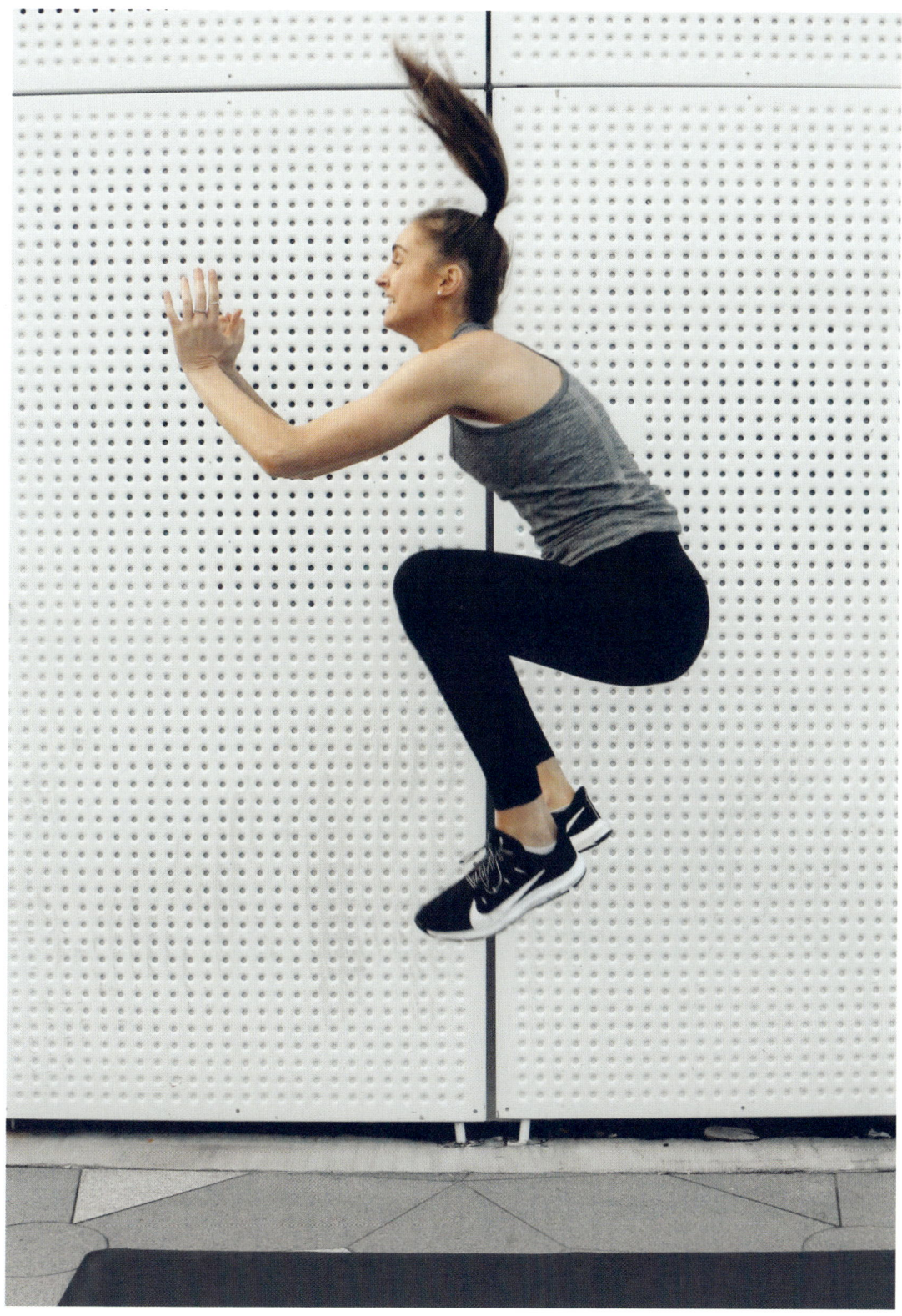

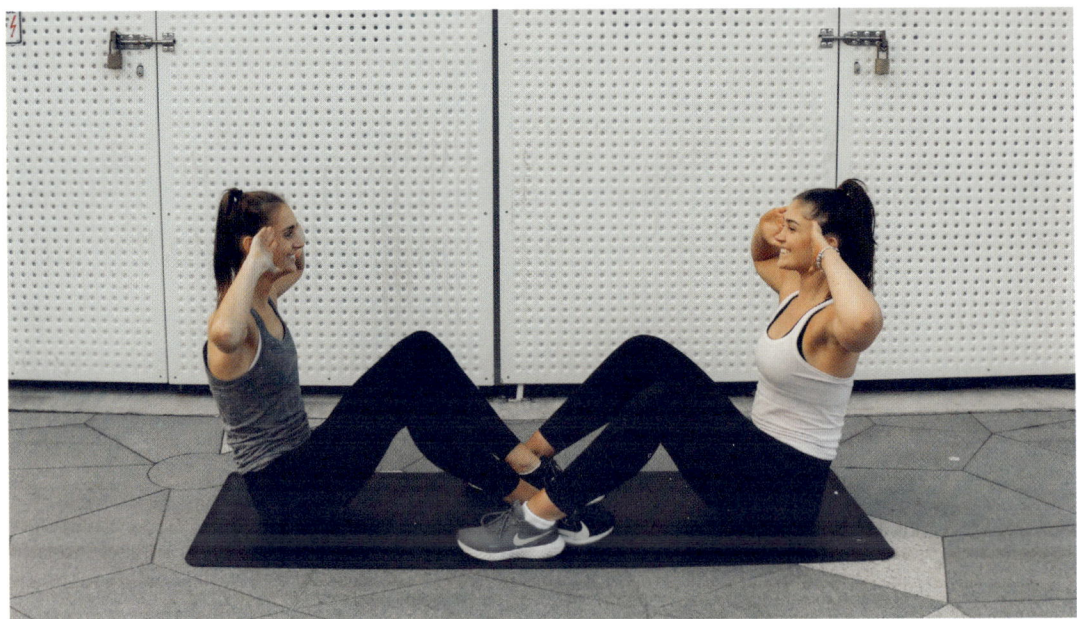
Sit-ups

Workout 12: Full Body Blast
Work your way down the pyramid — 30 reps of each, then 20 reps of each, then 10 reps of each!
Equipment: Bodyweight
- Burpees (p. 113)
- Squat thrusts (p. 119)
- Chest push-ups (p. 114)
- Sit-ups (p. 119)
- Alternating jumping lunges (p. 111)
- Mountain climbers (p. 115)

Workout 13: 2 x AMRAP ROUNDS
Complete as many rounds of each move within the time limit for Round 1, then rest for 1 minute and move onto Round 2. Repeat again for an extra challenge!
Equipment: 1 medium plate

Round 1: 8-minute AMRAP
- 21 x jumping squats (p. 115)
- 15 x chest push-ups (p. 114)
- 9 x burpees (p. 113)

Round 2: 6-minute AMRAP
- 15 x squat heel raises with press (p. 119)
- 12 x chest push-ups (p. 114)
- 9 x burpees (p. 113)

Workout 14: Tabata Core Workout
40 seconds on, 20 seconds recovery. Repeat 3–4 times for a core burner!
Equipment: Bodyweight
- Sit-ups (p. 119)
- Plank jacks (p. 117)
- Mountain climbers (p. 115)

Workout 15: Quick 'n Easy
Set a timer for 1 minute and perform each move for 1 minute. Repeat 4 times:
Equipment: Knee-height surface to jump on to
- Burpees (p. 113)
- Box jumps (p. 113)
- Chest push-ups (p. 114)
- Alternating jumping lunges (p. 111)
- Sit-ups (p. 119)

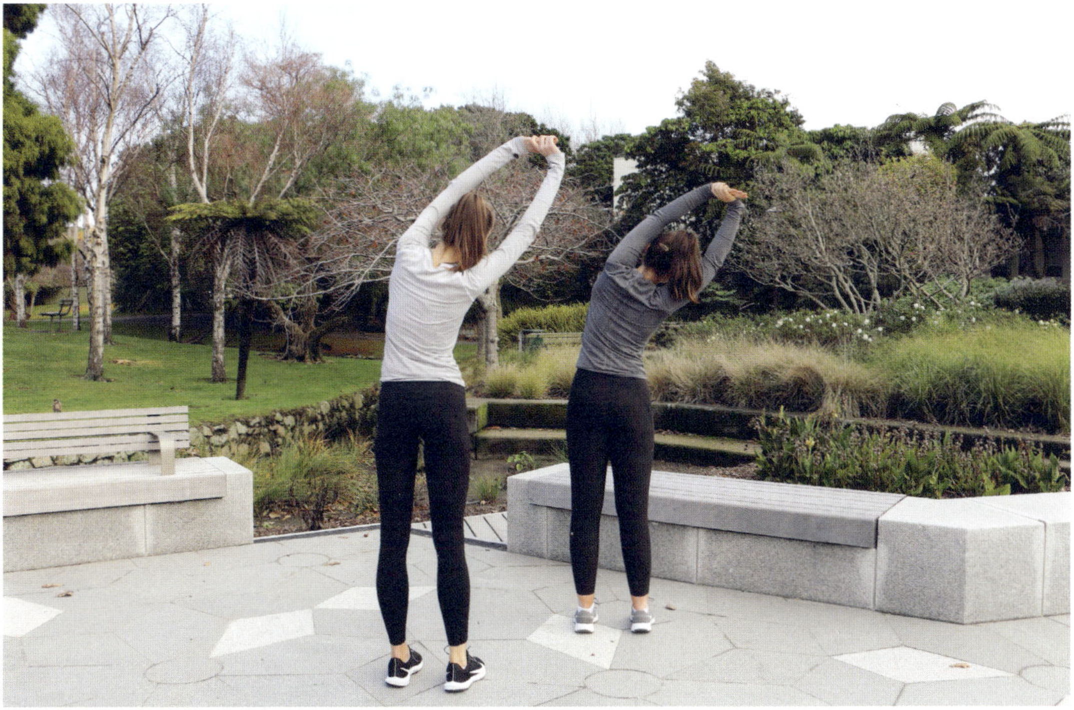

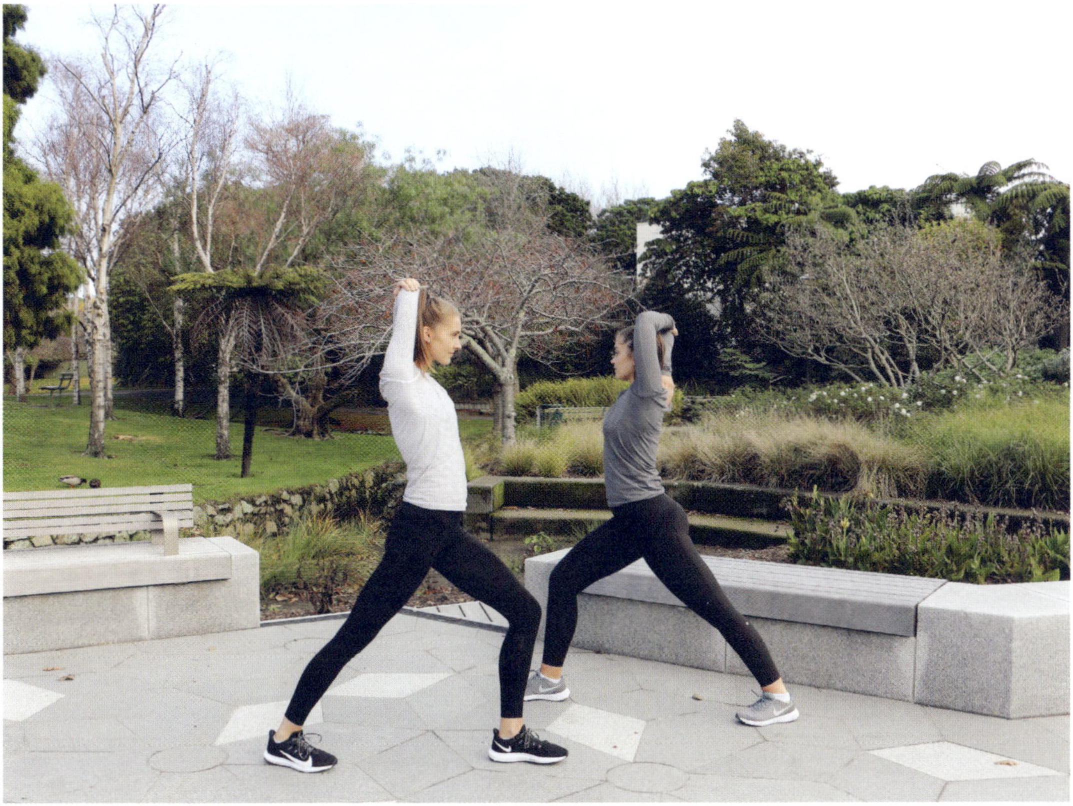

Don't forget to stretch!

Mental Health

We've all had down days, anxious moments or stressful semesters. Sometimes these feelings last a few days, sometimes much longer. We know from experience what it's like to struggle with mental health — but trust us when we say you WILL get through the rough patches.

In this section we describe our own personal mental health journeys, as well as what we perceive to be common emotional upheavals, and little tips on how you can take care of your mind so you are better equipped to ride out the tough times and come out the other side stronger and more focused.

If you're struggling, please believe us when we say that you are not alone — there will always be people you can talk to and steps you can take towards feeling happy again.

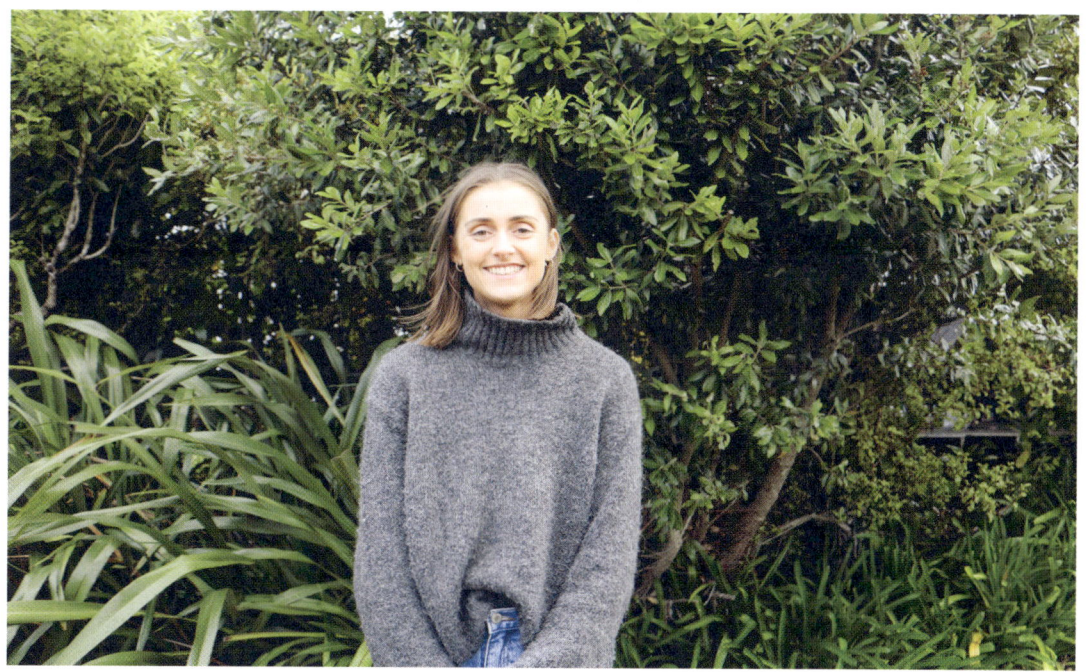

Soph's Story

My experience with anxiety began early in life, in primary school. At the end of Year 6, I experienced stress for the first time. I was worried about starting a new school, afraid of leaving all my friends behind, and stressed about the prospect of new routines. All these things combined began to make me super anxious.

This stress, and my reaction to it, caused pains in my stomach. I started to feel convinced that there was something physically wrong with me. I began to live in fear of getting sick or injured, or of any health-related issues, which caused me to feel constantly on edge. Around once a week, these anxious thoughts would accumulate and become overwhelming. I started to have panic attacks, sometimes so bad that I would have to go to the after-hours medical centre. Initially I didn't even know what a panic attack was, and I worried that there was something seriously wrong with me.

Thankfully, my parents intervened. They recognised I needed some extra help to get on top of my worries and anxieties. They booked me in to see a psychologist in Wellington, where I continued to go once every two weeks. Here, I learnt skills to cope with my anxious thoughts and feelings, and was able to create a whole new mindset.

After about a year, I was able to get on top of my anxiety. I learnt how to recognise my worries for what they were — just thoughts, with no ability to truly hurt me. However, it wasn't always smooth sailing. My anxiety definitely came and went, and sometimes it was worse than others. During my final year at high school, similar thoughts and worries reappeared and I went back to a different psychologist to get on top of it all. But these days, I'm thriving! I've been able to implement the skills I've learnt. I accept that anxious thoughts will always come and go for me, yet now I have the strength and strategies to let them pass me by.

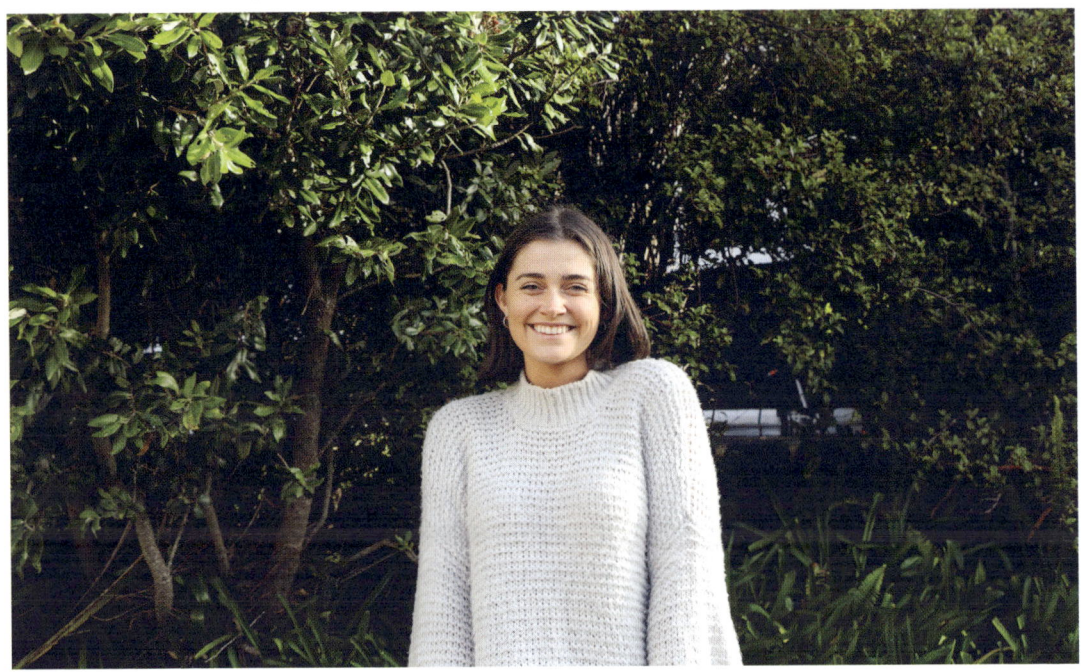

Em's Story

My experience with anxiety started during my second year of university. My first semester started off well, but slowly, things started going downhill. I had never suffered serious anxiety before, though I had always been a worrier, and a pretty stressed-out kid. But then, all of a sudden, everything just all piled up on me. I was worried about not getting the grades to get into the course I wanted to study, and about constantly feeling watched and judged, as well as having gut issues that made me incredibly anxious about the state of my health.

All of this took its toll, and eventually I started having panic attacks at the thought of going into public places. Going to lectures became a massive effort, and going to communal mealtimes at my hall was even harder. I even struggled to go to group fitness classes, something that had previously been my happy place — suddenly it had become a source of fear. It took so much courage on my part, and support and encouragement from my friends and family, to attend any events with lots of people. I felt as though people were constantly talking about me, and every time my stomach played up, I became convinced it was something serious. It seemed to me that as soon as one aspect of my life became a source of stress, everything else started piling up, to the point where I felt buried under an avalanche of worries. I honestly believed I would never be able to see through to the other side.

Somehow, I got through that difficult period. I made it to the other side, burnt out and exhausted, but I made it. And slowly, I started to feel better. Once the external pressures in my life at that time had relented, I was able to focus my energies on my mental health. I went home for the semester break, saw a psychologist and, for once, gave myself a break. It was this shift that helped me to get my mind back on track, and begin my journey back up towards positive health.

It wasn't linear, and it wasn't quick. Sometimes, even now, I still slip back into old unhelpful thinking patterns. But now, I know the signs. I recognise the way my mind operates, the way my body feels, and I can consciously counter the anxiety when it starts creeping back in. While that dark time in my life was unquestionably a struggle, I can now look back and know that it made me stronger. I became closer with friends and family. I learnt skills that I still come back to today, that help to keep my anxiety at bay.

My experiences were in no way as bad as some of the hardships a lot of people go through in life, and they certainly do not compare to more severe mental illnesses. But they helped give me an insight into what anyone suffering may appreciate in their darkest moments. The kind of skills and strategies that may be of some benefit, and the importance of social support in getting better.

Tasty Twins' Mental Health Tips & Tricks

In the following section we would like to offer you some general tips for when you feel as though your mental health is spiralling. We know for a fact that so many of you feel this way. Our hope is that by sharing some of the things we have learnt on our own mental health journeys we'll help some of you get through the tough times. If you're reading this and you identify with any of what we say, don't be afraid to seek out the help you need. Similarly, if you suspect one of your friends might be going through something similar, we encourage you to reach out and try to help them too. Don't overthink it — just do it.

The best advice we can recommend to anyone suffering with depression or anxiety is to talk to someone about how they feel! We know everyone preaches it, but it honestly would have saved us both so much suffering if we had asked for help earlier. It may not feel like it when you're in the dark place, but you can and you will go back to living your 'normal' life again. Remember, too, you can't pour from an empty cup. The only way to care for someone else is to care for yourself first.

Our psychologists were absolutely incredible, and gave us techniques that we still use today if we ever feel anxiety creeping back (which we will describe in the following pages). There is no quick fix to anxiety or depression, but talking to someone is definitely the first step of the journey. This could be anyone you feel comfortable with — a parent or family member, a friend, or a medical professional. There are also some awesome services that you can reach out to if your mental health is dwindling. See p. 135 for the helplines and websites of these various excellent organisations.

Another way you can look after your mental health when you're struggling is to try and take some time out away from the source of some of the stress, if that's possible. If you're living away from home, and it's possible for you, it could be helpful to go home for a weekend. Having someone else look after you for a change or even just having a change of scene can ease your state of mind. Also, it can sometimes help bring mental clarity to the situation when you have that physical and psychological distance from it. If your environment is really getting you down, you may need to look at your options – perhaps physically removing yourself from the situation, whether this means changing flats or courses, may be the best way to go. On the other hand, you may not even have to do anything as drastic as that — sometimes a simple walk in the fresh air, a workout at the gym, or even a ten-minute meditation can reset your mind and give you the space to breathe. Time with friends is also valuable, but so is time to yourself. Balance is key. Putting yourself first doesn't mean you are being selfish. Don't be afraid to take some time out if that is what you are craving.

Remember, though, these are just our experiences. We are sharing them in the hope that they help you — or someone you care about — to feel less alone and happier in yourself.

Whether you recognise your own experience, or that of a friend, in our stories; or whether you simply need a reminder to check in with yourself from time to time, it's so important for all of us to look after ourselves, not just physically but mentally too. Our lives are so busy and it can be very easy to get run down or emotionally depleted.

We all get caught up in our day-to-day to-do lists, our never-ending stream of entertainment through our phones, the overwhelming demands of life in the 21st century. It is so easy to throw yourself into study, into work, into fitness, into socialising . . . into anything that distracts you from your own mind. So how about you try slowing down? Put down your phone now and then, place your work aside, even right now — just put this book aside for a minute and let your thoughts float on by. Distance yourself from those thoughts and let yourself breathe. Give yourself space and time. If you notice feelings arise that you have been trying to push aside, now might be the time to confront them. If they feel too big or too overwhelming to deal with on your own, talk to someone. We promise — even though you may feel certain there is no one to turn to and there is no solution — there is always someone willing to listen and there is always someone who can help.

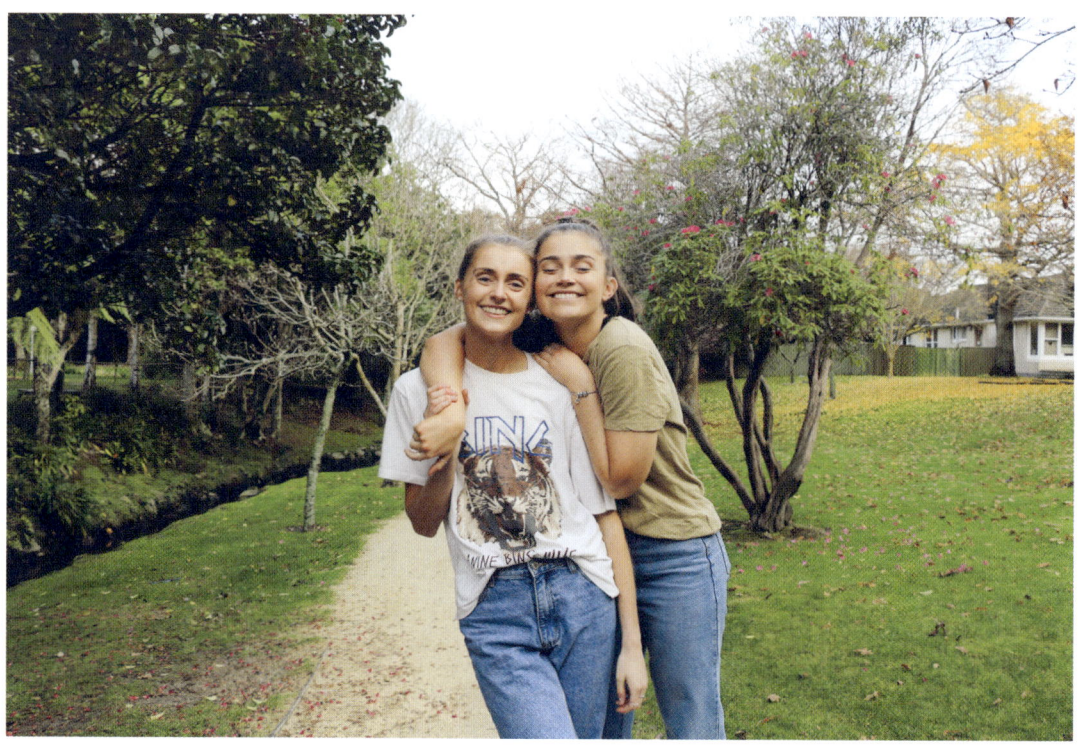

Even if you've never experienced a blip in your mental health yourself, it is likely that you know someone who has. Just getting a little bit of insight into people's personal stories might help you empathise with them, too. Sometimes, if your friends are suffering, it may seem like they're deliberately shutting you out. You might feel hurt, left out or useless. This is often because those suffering can feel like the situation is hopeless and that there is nothing to be gained by opening up. However, please don't stop trying. Your support and friendship is not going unnoticed, and it is not unappreciated. Even silent support and company are invaluable tools to someone going through a rough patch. Your friend who is struggling may not be able to open up or express their gratitude at that moment, but at the very least they will know that you care, which is so important. A phonecall, a 'how are you, really?' text, even a hug, a coffee delivered to them, a card in their letterbox — the smallest actions can have the biggest impacts. Never underestimate your power to help!

Helplines
Youthline: 0800 376 633 or text 234
Suicide Crisis Helpline: 0508 828 865 (0508 TAUTOKO)
Healthline: 0800 611 116
Lifeline: 0800 543 354 (0800 LIFELINE) or free text 4357 (HELP)
Samaritans: 0800 726 666
What's Up: 0800 942 8787 (available Monday-Friday 12PM-11PM, Saturday/Sunday 3PM-11PM)
Depression Helpline: 0800 111 757 or text 4202
Anxiety Helpline: 0800 269 4389 (0800 ANXIETY)
Rape Crisis: 0800 883 300 (support for survivors of sexual assault)
Shine: 0508 744 633 (confidential support for survivors of domestic abuse)
Women's Refuge Crisis Line: 0800 733 843 (0800 REFUGE)
OutLINE: 0800 688 5463 (LGBTQIA+ counsellors available 6-9PM to discuss topics around sexual orientation and gender identity)
EDANZ: 0800 2 EDANZ
Supporting Families in Mental Illness: 0800 732 825

Websites
www.depression.org.nz — information about depression and anxiety.
www.thelowdown.co.nz — support for young people experiencing depression or anxiety.
www.auntydee.co.nz — a free online tool for anyone who needs help working through problems.
www.sparx.org.nz — an online self-help tool that teaches young people the key skills needed to help combat depression and anxiety.
www.ry.org.nz/what-we-do/online-support — online chat support with Rainbow Youth, providing guidance for young people seeking advice surrounding sexuality and gender identity.
www.whatsup.co.nz/ — online chat to discuss problems young people may be going through. Aimed at kids, teens and their families.
www.mentalhealth.org.nz/ — mental health support for young people, or for those looking to support others who are afflicted.
www.mentalhealth.org.nz/home/our-work/category/13/common-ground — helping whānau, parents, family and friends support young people through difficult times.

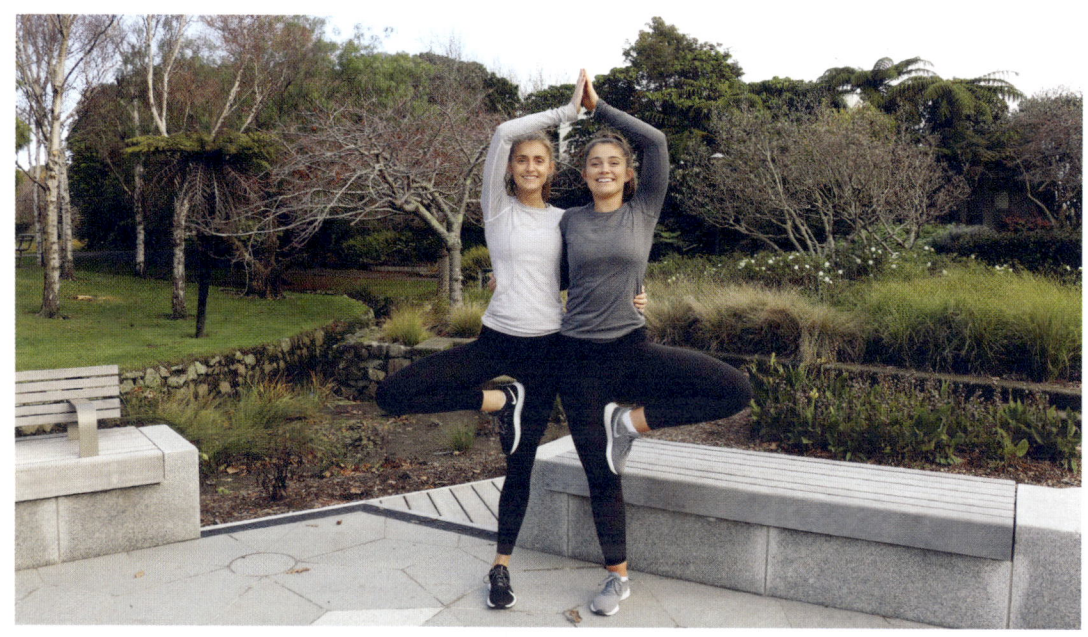

Comparing Ourselves to Others

Maybe you figured it out by now . . . but just in case you haven't . . . we're twins! And we wouldn't have it any other way. Having a sister and a best friend all rolled into one is unbeatable. There's always someone to chat to in awkward social situations, someone's wardrobe to raid when your Saturday night outfit really doesn't look like the model online, and someone to keep you grounded when things get a little rough.

But it's not all twin telepathy and finishing each other's sentences. While we LOVE being twins, the constant comparisons can become exhausting. Labelling comes naturally to most people, so it's not surprising that we were often pitted against each other when we were younger. To everyone else, someone always had to be the sporty/smart/quiet/loud/pretty/ugly/better/worse twin. And honestly, it's something we both still struggle with. External comparison very easily becomes internal — those voices in your head can be very destructive. It can be hard to develop your own identity when you feel pressured to become who everyone expects you to be. While this often felt like a 'just us' problem, we have come to realise just how common this experience is, and not just amongst twins.

We live in an age of comparison. We are constantly compelled to compare ourselves to others. How do our bodies measure up? Our clothes? Our diets? Our exercise regimes? Our incomes? The list goes on! Social media has only increased this pressure. While admittedly social media can sometimes be motivating, encouraging us to work harder to achieve our goals, it can be very easy for this to tip over and become an unhealthy and unrealistic pursuit of perfection. Suddenly, a half-hour run isn't good enough — instead you have to be grinding at the gym for hours on end, lifting massive weights and pulling off some crazy cardio moves. Maybe that way you'll achieve that fitspo Insta-model butt. Oh, you made it to your 9am lecture? Great, but you know what? Someone else got up at 5am and has been studying ever since. This all contributes to sending you a singular message: if you're not working as hard as you possibly can, you're not going to make it.

Maybe you recognise the feeling — sometimes it seems like, no matter how hard you try, you are not good enough. But trust us when we say, YOU ARE ENOUGH. You are comparing your original, evolving, unpredictable, messy, authentic self to a polished image someone chooses to present online. Maybe you feel that you are working your hardest to maintain your grades, but follow someone who seems to be juggling studying, running businesses and partying 'with ease', all the while looking absolutely flawless.

We hear it all the time — Instagram is a highlight reel, and it's true! We are only seeing a fraction of the lives of those people we follow; only those bits deemed interesting enough to make it online. Of course they seem flawless! But that doesn't make our feelings any less valid. They are completely natural and understandable, given the nature of social media today. But it doesn't have to be that way. It is up to us how we let social media influence our lives, whether in healthy or unhealthy ways.

How you can overcome comparisons

1. If someone's online presence is making you feel inferior, UNFOLLOW. The button is there for a reason, so don't be afraid to use it. Your mental health comes first, always.
2. If you find yourself feeling inadequate, it might be time to take a little digital detox. Whether that means trying to cut down your screentime, choosing to start your day with something other than scrolling Instagram, or completely disconnecting for a day — whatever works for you! It's easy for social media to take on a huge significance in our lives, sometimes without us even realising it, but remember: life is so much bigger than a screen. And logging off for a while can help you remember what else is going on in the world that is worthy of your attention.
3. Find a new hobby outside of the Internet. Honestly, a few years ago if someone had asked what we liked doing, it would have been hard to think of something that wasn't Netflix or YouTube. And while there's nothing wrong with a little screentime every now and again, unplugging yourself and re-engaging with the world can help to keep you grounded.
4. Follow your friends and the kind of social media accounts that make you feel better, not worse. There are some amazing people out there, spreading messages of authenticity, positivity and offering advice. People are starting to be a bit more real on social media now, and we are all for that! These people inspire us, but are also relatable.

Honestly, we are both still working on freeing ourselves from the constant need to compare ourselves to others. It's not easy — in fact, it goes against human nature. In many ways it's so much easier to remain within others' expectations of you. But it can be oppressive not to be true to yourself, to try out different ways of being, and to grow and change in the way that feels right for you. You are so much more than people's perceptions of you.

Besides, there are SO many things that are more important than what people think of you, such as what you think of yourself!

Instead of worrying about how people may or may not see you, try investing your energy into building yourself into the kind of person that you want to be, independent of others' opinions. Again, it's not as though you are striving to an end goal of becoming the 'perfect' person — this is impossible, as you will spend your lifetime evolving due to aging, education and life experiences. It is all part of the process of life: adapting, changing and growing.

Reflection
Try shifting your focus. Let's move away from worrying about what everyone else may or may not be thinking, and think about YOU! What can you do well? What motivates you to succeed? What are you most proud of about yourself? Instead of comparing ourselves to some idealistic other, let's celebrate who we are in ourselves right now!

Celebrate you!

I feel inspired by . . .

The thing I am proudest of is . . .

In the last week I achieved . . .

I dream about achieving . . .

I feel happiest doing . . .

I love these things about myself . . .

Failure

At some point in our lives, we are all going to fail at something. Failure is uncomfortable, upsetting, and entirely unavoidable. Remember, by the time you get to uni, you've already survived high school, which — let's face it — is a feat in itself. Getting through years of NCEA exam stress and teenage angst is by no means easy. But you've made it through in one piece, and now you're on to new challenges.

Uni is a whole new world, with hundreds of opportunities at every avenue. But with those opportunities can come setbacks. Maybe you don't get the grade you were aiming for, make it onto your desired sports team, or finish that assignment on time.

No matter the situation, failure isn't a very nice experience. When something like that happens to you, it might feel like the end of the world, like you've screwed up so massively that you'll constantly be living in the shadow of your mistake.

You are allowed to be upset. Your feelings are entirely, completely and utterly valid. There is no rule that says you have to immediately pick yourself back up and move on. Failures allow you to grow and become stronger for it. But first, give yourself time to grieve. Rather than suppressing your feelings, let yourself feel them. Then, once you've expressed your feelings to yourself, try and give yourself some distance. Observe the situation from a different perspective. Once you are able to take a step back, the feeling of failure may start to subside. Try thinking about what you would tell a friend if they were in your situation. Then, take your own advice!

We're going to be those people that tell you 'everything happens for a reason'. Maybe you believe that, maybe you don't. But we can both sincerely say that moments that seemed like our biggest failures have pushed us onwards to work harder, see a little more clearly and reach goals that may have seemed impossible before. From our experience, failing sucks. But it is so important to go through it. If you haven't failed, you're missing out on a fundamental human experience. You will fall down, but you will pick yourself back up again too.

We are so much more than our failures. Even just shifting your appraisal of a particular event or situation can help remind you of that. It's possible if you don't get the grade you wanted on a test, that it will motivate you to be more organised with your studying next time. Or, if you don't get that job you had your heart set on, the fact you updated your CV and went through the interview process may better prepare you for the next job you apply for. There is a silver lining in every cloud — so train your mind to hunt out those silver linings whenever you can, and use the experiences to grow. Every misstep builds resilience, every loss plants the seed of something new. That same strength will allow you to confront the next failure (because, let's face it, no matter how small, chances are you will come across another obstacle on your journey), and to overcome it. You have the tools, so put them to use!

Also, without failure, we might not be able to fully appreciate the successes in our lives. Every small win is a win nevertheless — even showing up to class the day after you received a grade you were disappointed in, or supporting your friends on the sports team you missed out on, there are many ways we can prove to ourselves that we are winners. Remember also, there will be other, bigger successes waiting for you in life. So maybe give yourself some time to recover from a setback, reframe how you're looking at the situation, and find that silver lining to boost you towards your next win!

Best podcast episodes about failing and overcoming failure
'How to Fail'
    Phoebe Waller-Bridge
    Mo Gawdat
    Elizabeth Day

'Deliciously Ella'
    'Turning Adversity into Opportunity'
    'Learning to Fail'
    'Building Resilience'

'Mindset Zone
    'Failure and the Way to Success'
    'Growth Mindset'
    'Getting a "NO" can be your best goal'

'Hurry Slowly'
    'The Greatest Risk is Not Taking One'
    'To Burnout and Back'
    'Transformation is Hard'

Eating

It's so easy to be caught up in what — and what not — to eat. Instagram is chock-full of people claiming intermittent fasting (a.k.a skipping breakfast) changed their life, celery juice is magic or carbs will kill you. Suddenly everyone has a platform to preach what they believe is the perfect picture of health.

These days, there are so many fad diets that we can barely keep up. From paleo, to keto, to food combining . . . the list is endless! A food trend can take hold, consume the Internet for a couple of months, and then disappear, only to be replaced by a new 'life-changing' diet. Often these trends come and go so quickly that the science cannot keep up. Diets explode across Instagram before there is any empirical evidence to support them. And society feeds this never-ending cycle — every trend provides companies with a new money-making opportunity, and a new way to exploit customers with wildly exaggerated claims.

But how are individuals, generally without any qualifications or scientific evidence, to decide what is the absolute best way for everyone to live? While they may know what makes themselves feel healthy, it is unlikely that one lifestyle will suit everyone.

Health doesn't have to look like salads for lunch and dinner, skipping breakfast, or cutting out anything with a hint of sugar. It can be BALANCED! Maybe you have a lettuce wrap for dinner one night, and a burger the next. And you feel perfectly fine with that!

Food does not have any moral value — eating 'healthy' does not make you a better person, any more than eating 'unhealthy' makes you a worse one. If we have this idea of 'clean eating', then what is the alternative? Eating 'dirty'? Suddenly, even a little chocolate chip cookie or packet of chips may create massive feelings of guilt. And what sounds healthier to you — living by incredibly strict food rules that hinder you, or allowing yourself to enjoy the food that you want to eat, and being able to stop when you feel satisfied?

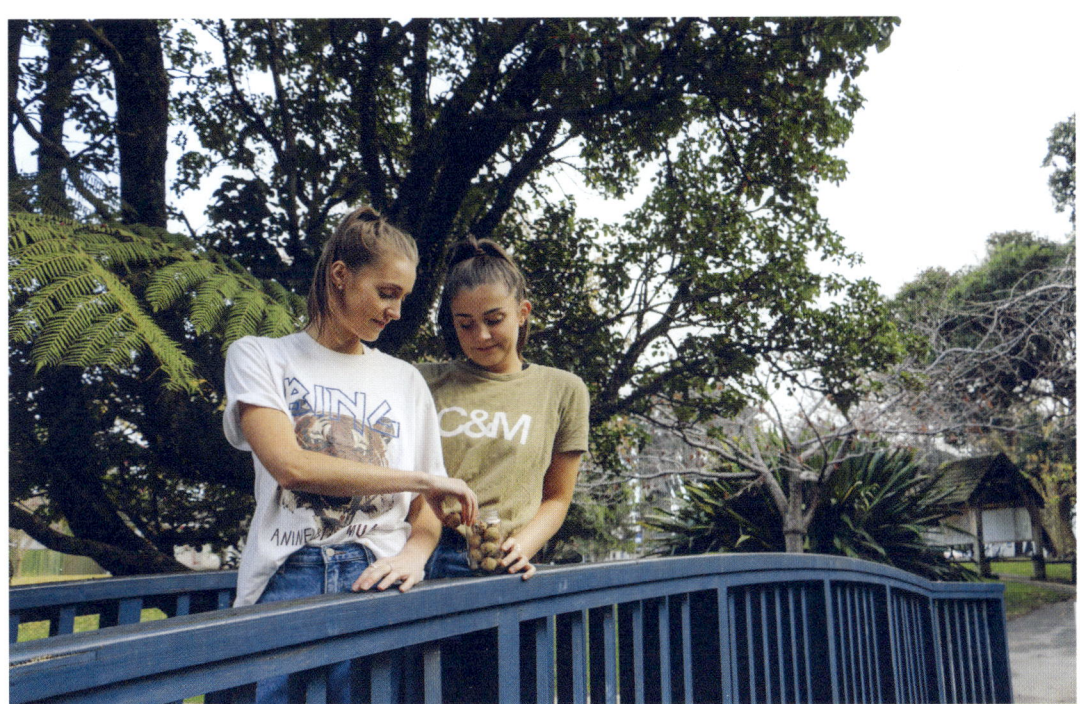

Learning to listen to your body is a skill that develops over time. We are being bombarded by multiple messages from every angle: 'Don't eat carbs after 4pm', 'fruit has too much sugar', 'you need juice cleanses to detox your body', and so on. These messages are everywhere, from our Instagram feeds to the backs of food packaging. So, of course they are hard to overcome! But you know what works for your body, and you know what you feel like eating in that moment. So maybe try tuning in to what your body feels like next time you sit down for a meal. We are by no means dietitians or nutritionists, and we don't want to tell you exactly what and how to live. But we do know what it's like to be made to feel guilty about what you're eating, and how much that sucks. And there are plenty of fully qualified, evidence-based sources of information on the Internet, with all sorts of information that can help you build a healthy relationship with food.

While we can offer advice on what works best for us, we don't assume for a minute that the same diet will necessarily work best for you. You know yourself best. Try compiling a few tips here and there from qualified and evidence-based sources, and find a lifestyle that works for you. If that means eating a few more plant-based meals to reduce your environmental impact, awesome. If that means cutting down on coffee because you've realised it screws up your sleep cycle, go for it. But if it means cutting out carbs and going sugar-free because some dubious Internet forum said it made them miraculously lose weight, think again.

Eating well doesn't need to be expensive or complicated. Instead, food should be enjoyable, simple, affordable and most importantly delicious! Stripping things back to basics and understanding the foundations of a balanced diet will enable you to create tasty, fresh, nourishing meals that will help fuel you to feel your best.

The Inside Scoop: Emma Ternouth

Here's a few handy nutrition tips from our fave nutrition expert, Emma Ternouth. Emma is a dietitian who believes in a holistic no-nonsense approach to food and wellbeing. She is passionate about empowering individuals to feel confident with their nutrition and creating positive relationships with food. You can see more from Emma on Instagram: @nutritionbiteswithemma

What is a balanced diet?
Typically, a balanced diet includes a variety of fruits and vegetables, wholegrains like oats and brown rice, legumes like chickpeas and lentils, lean proteins like eggs, dairy, fish and meat, as well as healthy fats like olive oil and nuts. A balanced diet also leaves room for your favourite soul foods like chocolate, cake or hot chips.

How can you create a balanced meal?
Eating a balanced meal can be the difference between feeling energised and satisfied for hours or tired and ravenous an hour later! The easiest way to create a balanced meal is to include something from each of the four food groups. Use the portion sizes below to help guide you.

Fruit and vegetables: Aim for one piece of fruit or two cupped handfuls of vegetables, about half the size of your plate.
Carbohydrates: Aim for a fist-size portion or a quarter of your plate.
Protein-rich foods: Aim for a palm-sized piece of meat or serving of beans or a quarter of your plate.
Healthy fats: Aim for a few thumb-sized chunks of fat-rich foods.

Remember, everyone is unique. You may need more or less than the next person. Listen to your body and hunger levels.

Top tips for eating well as a student:
- Shop smart: Healthy eating doesn't need to be expensive and can be done on a budget.
  - Allocate a weekly food budget and use this to roughly plan your meals before you shop. This helps prevent overspending and food waste too.
  - Shop seasonally. Fruit and veggies are cheaper and fresher when in season. Look for local fruit and veggie shops close to you as they often have the best deals.
  - Make friends with frozen and canned produce. Frozen produce is just as nutritious as fresh, plus tinned beans and chickpeas make meals go twice as far.
- Don't exclude food groups. Each food group plays an essential role in supporting our health and wellbeing. Intentionally excluding food groups can lead to obsessional and binge-like eating behaviours. Protein-rich foods like eggs, dairy, meat and legumes — which help keep us full — are the building blocks for strong hair, skin and nails. Carbohydrates are our bodies' preferred fuel source, they nourish our gut bacteria and even help to support our mental wellbeing too. Aim to include wholegrains, starchy vegetables and fruit regularly. Healthy fats like olive oil, nuts and omega-3's are essential for happy hormones and brain health. Don't forget about soul foods either — they provide nourishment in a different kind of way, by providing you with joy and treasured memories.

- Cook once, eat twice. Stress less and save time by making the most out of leftovers.
- Ditch the all or nothing approach. Despite what Dr Google says, there's no such thing as a 'perfect' diet. A positive relationship with food is just as important as your vegetable intake. Avoid labelling foods as 'good' or 'bad' and aim for balance, food freedom and enjoyment instead.
- If you're ever unsure, reach out to a qualified professional.

Reflection

Sometimes you may feel like fuelling your body with energy to smash a workout; and other times you may feel like indulging your sweet tooth — both these impulses are absolutely valid. Try filling in our venn diagram below, so the next time you feel like a healthy snack, or a sweet treat, you've got all your choices right there in front of you!

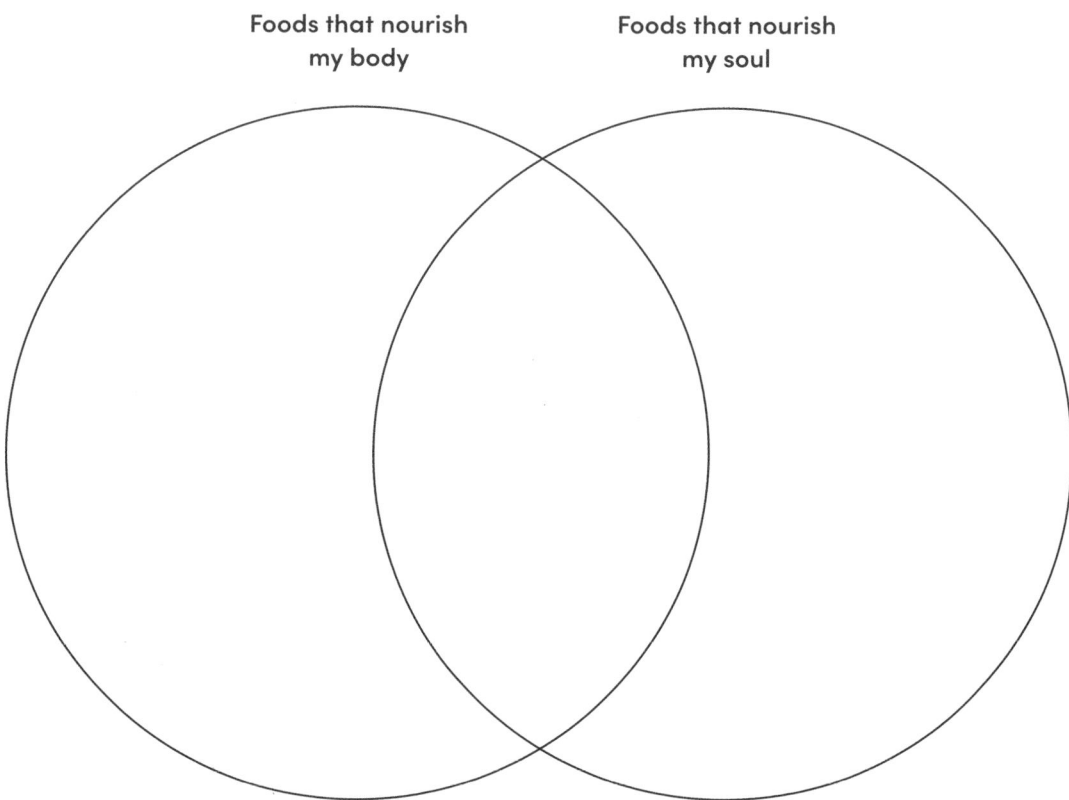

Foods that nourish my body

Foods that nourish my soul

Stress

Uni is A LOT. Anyone who is at or who has been to uni will tell you that. But knowing that uni is going to be stressful may not sufficiently prepare you for the reality. We all implement different strategies for dealing with stress. For some, it's sculling energy drinks, coffee and anything that might help them survive a pre-assignment all-nighter. For others, it's waking up at the crack of dawn and securing a precious seat in the library before the exam hoards stampede in. The stereotype of the stressed-out, sleep-deprived, library-living student is a pretty common one, after all.

We're not going to sugar-coat it and tell you that uni is a piece of cake. But while it is stressful, it comes in waves. Some weeks you'll be able to relax a little, and others you may have to grind a bit harder. And while you're in those peak stressful moments, it can feel pretty overwhelming. Suddenly you might have two assignments and a test coming up, as well as a friend's birthday, a sports training and a shift at work.

It all adds up, and can sometimes feel as though you're facing a mountain that you just will not be able to climb. While other people may seem to stroll up it with ease, you might feel as though the terrain is too arduous. It's easy to become overwhelmed, and when you don't know where to start, it's hard to even make a dent. But while the uni workload can make you stressed, it doesn't have to burn you out. There are ways that you can tackle stress before it even sets in, and make uni that little bit more manageable.

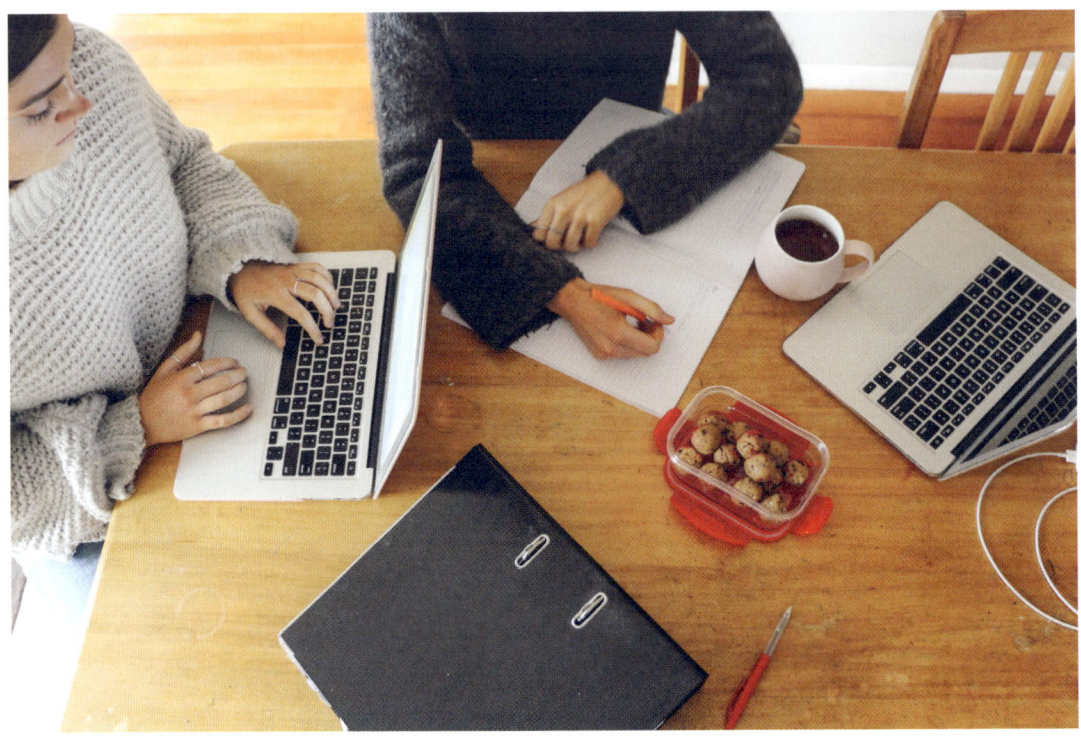

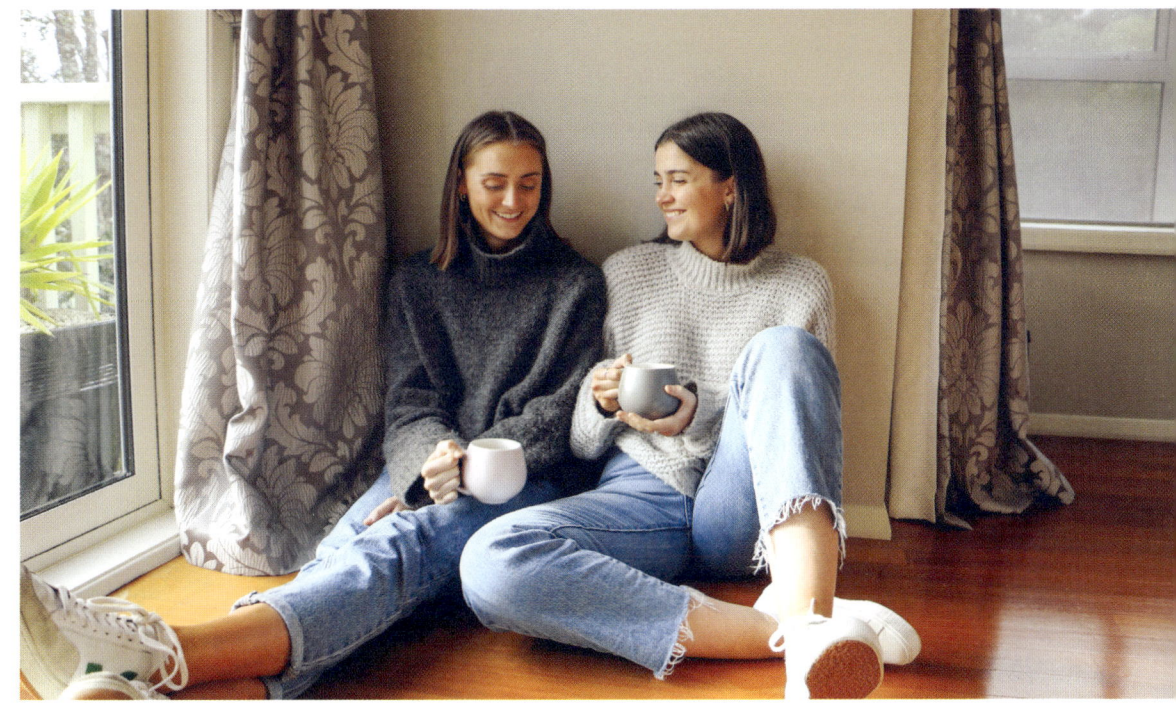

Tips: How we manage stress

1. Know what's coming! For most papers, you will be given assessment dates at the beginning of the semester. So, we suggest finding a yearly calendar and filling in your tests and assignments as soon as you know when they are. That way, you have a bigger-picture idea of what the semester holds, and you can . . .
2. PLAN AHEAD! We cannot stress this enough. If you have some idea of what is heading your way, you can manage your time accordingly. So, you can do this on a semester basis, like planning out which readings/essays/study you will do from week to week, or you can . . .
3. Start using daily to-do lists! Soph especially is a big fan of these. The night before, try writing out everything you have to tackle the next day. Even getting everything out on paper can relieve some of the stress you might be feeling. What's more, it helps you plan your days out. Maybe try numbering the tasks based on their priority, and focus your energy and time on addressing those jobs in order of importance.
4. Find a routine that works for YOU. Some people froth a late-night study grind, and others prefer to get the hard stuff done in the early mornings. Everyone has a different schedule that suits them best, and over your time at uni, you will definitely find your groove! Test out your focus at different times of day to discover when you are most productive, and plan to do your most intense study/work in that time.
5. No matter what routine suits you, make sure you get plenty of sleep! Sleep is honestly the most underrated way to beat fatigue at uni. While we love a good coffee, relying on caffeine to get you through that exam-season lull might affect how you sleep at night, and your performance the following day.

Breathing exercises

Sometimes, things feel overwhelming, unpredictable, and out of your control. But no matter what, there is one thing you can always control — your breath. When you stop and take a moment to focus on your breathing, you will soon realise just how much your breathing can help you through anything.

We've put together a couple of breathing exercises that you can try. We often use them to help us get to sleep at night, but you can use them at any time of the day. If you're ever caught in a situation where you feel fragile, panicky or stressed, you can always come back to these.

If it's possible, find yourself somewhere quiet. If that's too difficult, just take yourself away in your mind's eye, and find your connection to your breath.

1. Breath focus
- Find yourself somewhere where you can be comfortable (in bed, seated, wherever suits you!)
- Close your eyes and tune into your breathing. Bring your awareness to its rise and fall, without trying to change it. Just notice its rhythm.
- If your mind starts to wander to any distractions or thoughts about your day, just allow them to float by. Gently nudge your attention back in the direction of your breath.
- Start to breathe deeper now. Fill your lungs slowly, and empty them just as slowly. Feel the expansion and relaxation in your chest.
- See if you can stay with that slow, deep breath. Give yourself a few minutes to breathe in and out, as deep as you can. Let your eyes close, and let the breath flow.
- When you're ready, bring your attention back into your body. Let your eyes open, and gently start to move around, coming back to the present.

2. Body scan with breath
- For this exercise, find somewhere comfortable to lie down. Close your eyes.
- Bring your attention to your breath. Feel it flow in through your nose, and out through your mouth.
- Imagine your breath, and that sense of relaxation that comes with it, flowing around your body.
- Start with your feet. Let them fall wide, and release all tension.
- Concentrate on your calves, the backs of your knees, your thighs. Imagine them sinking into the floor or bed where you are lying.
- Imagine your breath flowing into your hips. Let them relax.
- Next send your breath back along your spine. From your tailbone, through to your lower back, middle back, upper back . . . and into your shoulders.
- Let your shoulders and neck relax into the floor.
- Allow your breath to flow down through your arms, into your hands, and let them relax.
- Finally, relax your face. As you breathe, let the muscles of your face soften. If you notice any tension, just let it go.
- Close your eyes and stay in this state of relaxation for as long as feels good. Whenever you feel ready, you can reawaken yourself slowly, and bring yourself back into the room.

3. Box breathing
- Wherever you are, take a seat or lie down and find a comfortable position.
- Focus on your breath. Inhale and count slowly to four. Feel the air travelling into your body.

- Once you have reached your count of four, hold your breath for four more counts. Try and keep your body and face relaxed as you count, neither breathing in or breathing out.
- Gently exhale to the count of four.
- Repeat this technique as many times as you need, for as long as you need. Find a rhythm, eyes closed and body relaxed.
- When you feel calmer, gently shift your focus away from your breath and out into your body. Start to move your hands and feet, then open your eyes.

Reflection

One method that you may find helpful for clarity of thought and a calm and happy mind is to start a gratitude journal. No matter what is going on in your life, there is always something to be thankful for. Soph has had her gratitude journal for over two years now, and swears by it as a daily ritual. Such a simple, quick and easy way to get your daily dose of mindfulness.

Take just five minutes each day to think of three things that you're thankful for. One day it might be a gift from a friend, and another day it might simply be that you managed to get out of bed. Nothing is too big or too small to be thankful for. If you feel like extending the ritual, you might choose to list three things that you're looking forward to tomorrow as well.

Use this template for your first week of gratitude, just to get yourself started! And once you're into the swing of it, you can start your own notebook/Word document and make it into a habit.

	Three things I am grateful for today:	Three things I am looking forward to tomorrow:
Monday		
Tuesday		
Wednesday		
Thursday		
Friday		
Saturday		
Sunday		

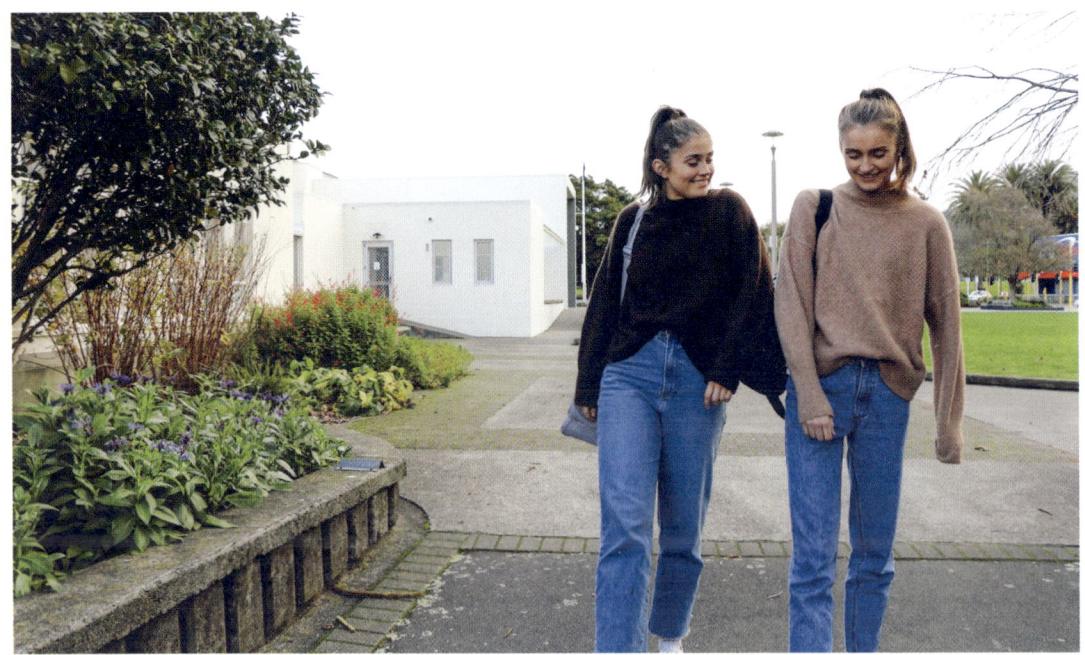

Self-care

It's likely that there will be times in your life when you feel down or depleted but there are things we can do to make ourselves feel better and re-energised. Self-care is perfect for when you're having an off day, and looking for a way to build yourself back up and find happiness again. It doesn't have to cost you money, or even time.

We've compiled a list of our top 10 self-care techniques! Feel free to give these a go next time you're in need of a de-stress or a pick-me-up! Not every method will work for everyone — again, experiment with different things until you find what works for you.

1. Nothing makes us feel more comforted than a hot drink. We love going out to grab a coffee, solo or with a friend. Something about a long black just makes the world brighter. And when we're at home, we love making a cup of tea (or three) and getting super cosy!
2. We love getting out in the fresh air whenever we can. Being outside, especially in nature, can do wonders. Whether we go for a walk or find a spot to sit and just be for a moment, getting outdoors always helps give us some space.
3. Bake something! Being the massive foodies that we are, one surefire moodlifter for us is getting in the kitchen and whipping up a new recipe or an old favourite.
4. Sometimes, we like to find a meditation podcast or YouTube video and give it a go. Being able to switch off from the busyness of day-to-day life and your own thoughts can be a massive relief sometimes.
5. Work up a sweat! Exercise is well-known to be a great release for stress. If you're feeling like challenging yourself, try out some of the workouts in the 'Fitness' section of this book! And if you'd prefer to slow it down, yoga can be a great way to connect your body and breath, no matter your skill level.
6. Reach out to someone you care about! We find that calling a friend and planning

a catch-up can definitely boost our moods.

7. Take a social media break. When we're sad, sometimes scrolling through photo after photo of others having the time of their lives only makes us feel worse. Sometimes we feel the need to switch off and physically put our phones away. Try it for an hour or so and see how you feel.
8. Spring clean! We often find that even doing a five-minute tidy of our bedrooms can make us feel more on top of things. Try going through your closet, or sorting out your pantry. Cleaning can be super therapeutic.
9. Rewatch a beloved movie! This one is a definite fave for us. Whether a cheesy chick flick or one of our throwback favourites, there's nothing like losing yourself in other people's lives for a couple of hours.
10. If we're feeling like we need a bit more self-love than usual, we might have a pamper session. This can be anything — you could paint your nails, apply a face mask, whatever takes your fancy. It doesn't have to be expensive, just something that makes you feel extra special.

Activity

We've told you our favourite ways to take some time out. What are yours? Write them down below and then you'll have a reference guide anytime you need a little bit of self-administered TLC!

1.	
2.	
3.	
4.	
5.	
6.	
7.	
8.	
9.	
10.	

Student Life

There is SO much more to being a student than just getting a degree or diploma. We've put together a few tips and tricks we have learnt throughout our time at uni. From flatting tricks and study tips to how to make the most of your weekly instalment from Studylink, we've got you covered!

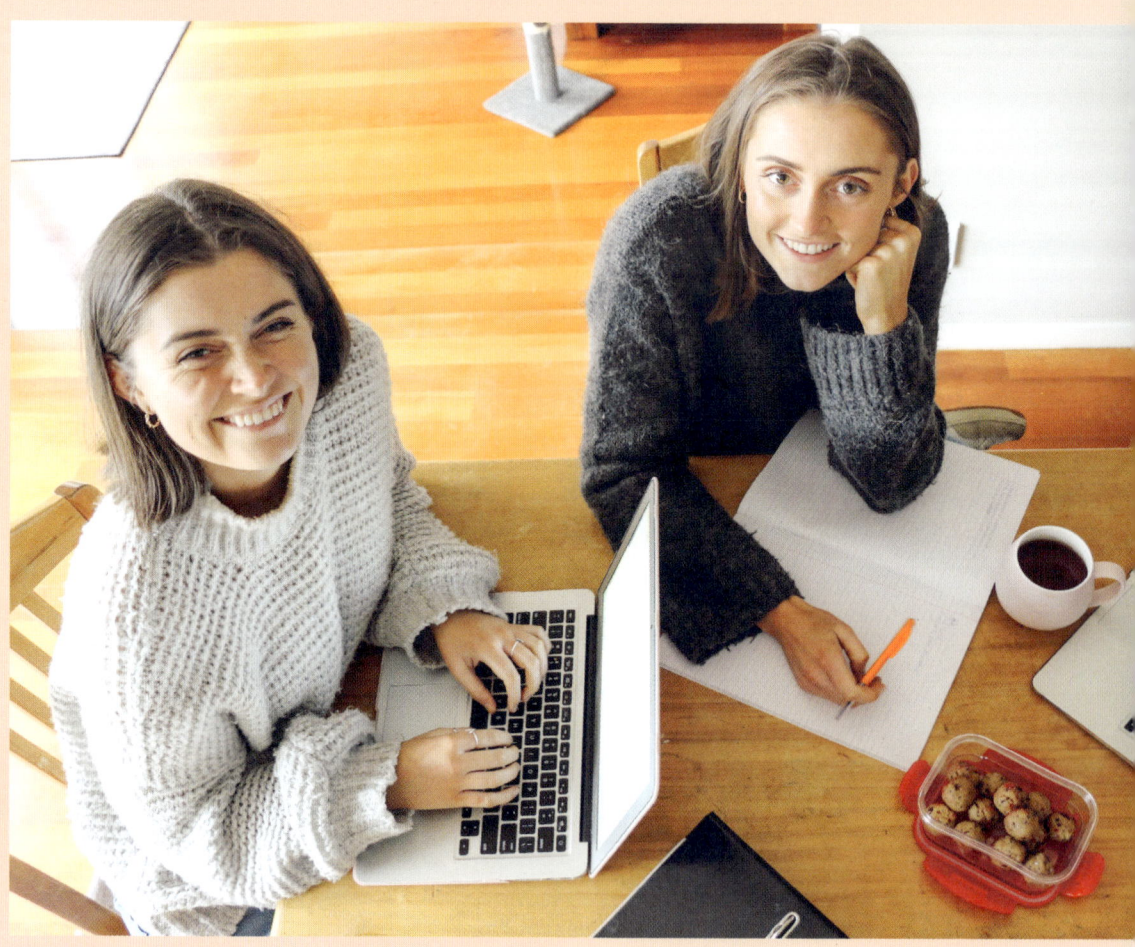

Study Tips

Obviously, the main part of uni is (technically) studying. While uni is a whole lot more than just your course, studying is definitely a key part. If it's your first year of uni, the workload might be a bit of a step up from high school, and it can seem pretty overwhelming at times. But once you find the best way for you to manage, pretty soon you'll be acing those exams. Everyone learns differently, and at their own pace. Just because you're doing something differently from everyone else, doesn't mean it's wrong. Find your way to tackle your course, and stick with it.

We've compiled our top ten favourite study tips. These are only a few ways you can learn, so feel free to do your own research and find what works for you.

1. You can make your life a lot easier early on by writing/typing your notes out after each lecture. Trust me, you'll thank yourself once exam season rolls around. Staying on top of things throughout the semester is one of the best things you can do in order to ensure you are ready for exams. And if you miss a lecture, make sure you rewatch it ASAP, in case the number of lectures you've missed starts to add up.
2. Get your notes sorted. This one is non-negotiable, in our opinion. If your notes are unreadable, spread across notebooks and documents, and completely out of order, it's pretty difficult to learn anything from them. So, try compiling all your notes into one notebook, or one Word document, depending on whether you work best on paper or screen. Make sure they're easy to read and cohesive, and formatted if necessary. This will make studying a whole lot easier.
3. Write it out! This is definitely a method that works for us. Try writing your notes out again and again, each time only writing those things you don't remember or understand, until eventually you have reduced your notes way down. Be warned, this can be a time-consuming way to study, so if this works for you, it's best to start a few weeks before your exam to make sure you have enough time.
4. Quizlet is an absolute life-saver. This app/website lets you make online cue cards, which you can learn through all sorts of methods. You can also print them out, if working on paper is easier for you. You can even find other people's sets who took your paper previously, and use them to help you. Quizlet is super handy if you want to do some 'light' study, and take a break from intense writing/practice tests/etc. You can take it with you on your phone to the gym, and go through your sets while on the treadmill/powermill/bike.
5. Mind maps can also be really helpful as well, especially if you're a visual learner. For each topic, create a one-page summary of all the information you need to know. Go crazy with colours here too, if that helps you learn or makes studying more fun.
6. Talk about it! Going over your notes out loud can help crystallise the information in your brain, especially if you're over writing things out. If you have friends/flatmates in the same paper, discussing it together is super handy too. You can help each other with things the other one finds hard, and find out new info you might not have learnt otherwise.
7. Another awesome app is Flora. This literally got us through the third-year

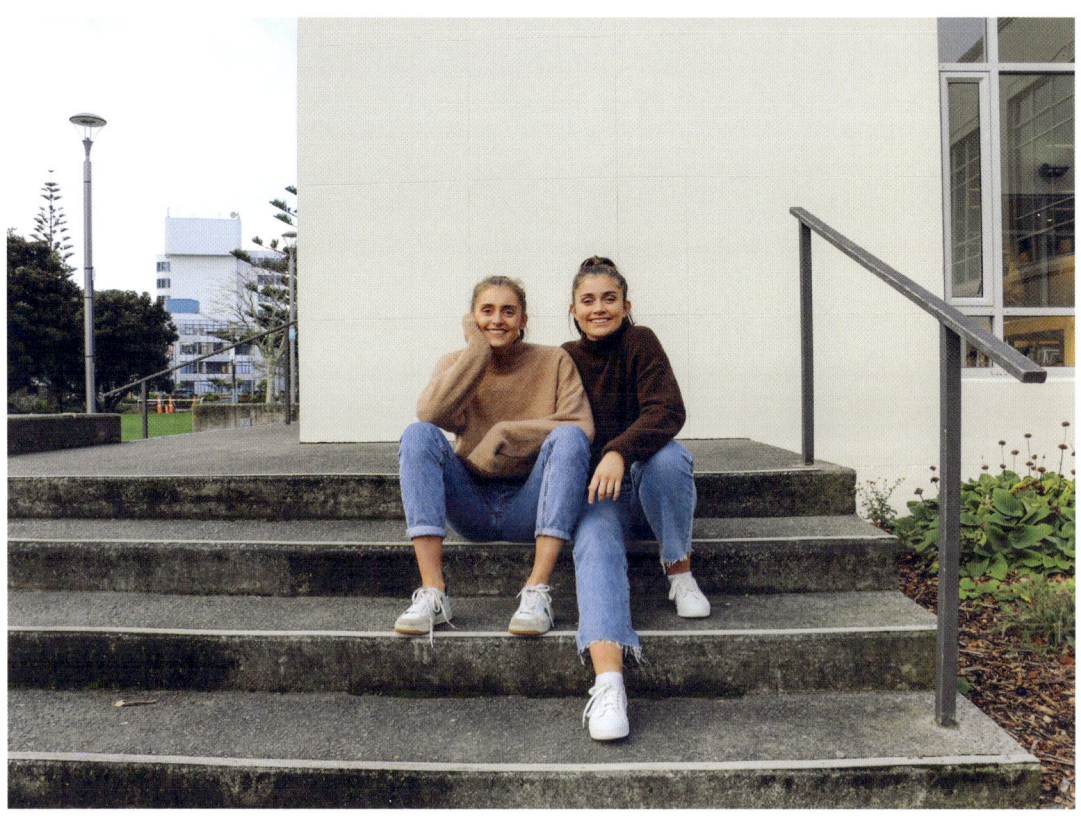

exam season. You download the app onto your phone and 'plant a tree' (a.k.a. set a timer for how long you want to study for). The app stops you from going on your phone until the timer is done, unless you want to kill your tree (which actually feels awful, so it really keeps you motivated). You can grow trees with friends too — and you really don't want to be the one to kill their tree off! Flora is super helpful if you struggle with having distractions during studying. If you can't use your phone, you're basically forced to focus.

8. Ask questions! Lecturers and tutors are there to help you, and (usually) they don't want you to fail. So, go along to office hours and tutorials if you can, and take along any questions you may have, even if you're a little shy about asking them. Chances are half the class is wondering the same thing.

9. Practice, practice, practice. Most papers will have online databases of past exam papers, and these are such beneficial study tools. Once you feel confident about the content, you can sit yourself down, put on a timer, and do practice exams as if they are real.

Reflection

When it feels as if you have so much to do that you can't keep track, sometimes it helps to map it out. We like to do this week by week. The template opposite has been super helpful for us.

Things I can do today:	✓✓✓	Tasks to do this week:
Monday:		Uni:
Tuesday:		
Wednesday;		Life admin:
Thursday:		
Friday:		Other:
Saturday:		
Sunday:		

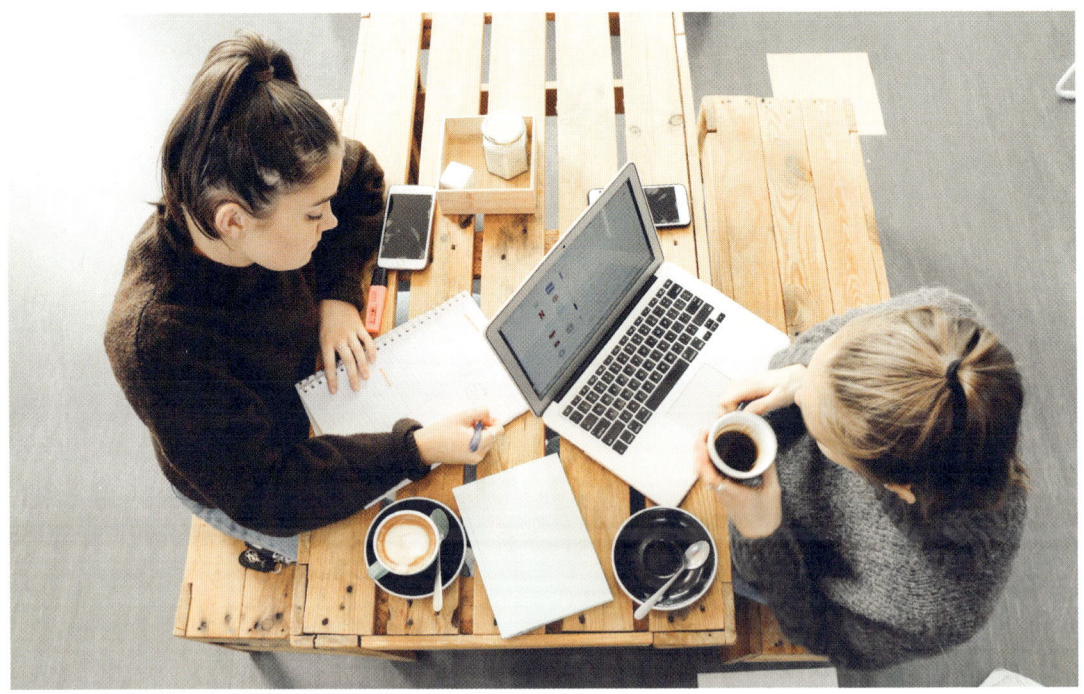

Budgeting

Being a student involves so many costs — from paying rent to grocery shopping and getting a cheeky almond flat white to get you through your studies — it is super important to BUDGET. Here are some tips that helped us make the most of our weekly payment from Studylink:

- Set up automatic payments for rent, power and other bills, and money to your savings. This allows you to get all your essential bills paid, and prevents you from spending money on unnecessary purchases.
- Write a shopping list. Go to the supermarket once a week with this list in hand. This allows you to only purchase what you need (even though that bag of Party Mix or kombucha six-pack might look pretty tempting).
- Shop at bulk food shops, such as the Bin Inn. Take your own reusable containers and jars and fill them up. Not only is this better for the environment, but it is SO much cheaper too ($3.50 to refill a jar of peanut butter — yes please!)
- Start a coffee card for your favourite cafe. Being a student means coffee is ESSENTIAL! This makes the spend on your coffee not quite as hard a hit to your bank account. Limiting your coffee spend in general can be an easy way to save those dollars (and even though instant isn't quite as good, it gets the job done!).
- Get a part-time job. Although not essential, it is always good to have a little bit of extra income on the side to treat yourself to an occasional raw slice or brunch at your favourite cafe.
- Cook as a flat (if schedules and dietary requirements allow). We suggest setting a budget for all flatmates to spend on meals. Not only does this save money, but it allows you to source a variety

of different food and it will also save heaps of time.
- Choose fruit and vegetables that are in season. It is so much cheaper to buy seasonal produce. Check out local fruit and vegetable shops for great deals too.
- Make your own snacks/treats. Not only does it often taste better, but it is so much cheaper. You could always split costs with your flatmates and bake some treats together that you can all enjoy. (Butterscotch pudding was a favourite in our flat!)

Flatting

While you often hear about the horror stories of flatting, the messy roommates and noisy neighbours, living with some of your best friends can actually be a super fun experience. We've both had the best year in our little flat, and thought we'd share a few of the top tips that helped make flatting smooth sailing for us.

1. Spend quality time together. Despite us all knowing each other beforehand, we weren't all super close friends. On our first night in the flat, we all went down the road to a cheap Indian restaurant for a cheeky BYO. This was a fun way to bond a little more, enjoy a glass of wine and eat some yum food. (I mean, how can you turn down a $10 bottle and a chicken tikka masala?)
2. Delegate chores. As a flat we had rosters for all the jobs that needed to be done each week around the flat. As there were six of us, we decided it would be easier to work with partners to get all the jobs done. We had three main jobs that needed to be done each week: kitchen (emptying the rubbish bins when full throughout the week, putting out the bins and cleaning the kitchen on Sunday nights), bathrooms (cleaning the whole bathroom, emptying the bins and mopping the floors) and vacuuming (living room and hallways, and general cleaning of the living room). Each week we would rotate these jobs to ensure our flat was kept in tip-top shape!
3. Cooking collectively. Each night of the week we had a different flat member on cooking duty. We set a budget of $25 for each flat member to spend on dinner items. This allowed us to get a variety of food and meant each member only had to cook once a week. The person who cooked that night got to use the washing machine and dryer on their cooking night and did the washing up that night. This routine worked really well for our flat, and might just suit yours too.
4. Have a flat bank account. Each week we would all transfer money to this account to cover communal items, such as toilet paper, cleaning products, spices and kitchen oils.
5. Communicate. Don't let the little things become big. It's important to remember that everyone is different and has different schedules. So, respect each other, and each other's personal space. But most importantly, have fun! Flatting with a bunch of your pals is such an awesome experience and, who knows, they could become some of your best friends that you'll keep for life.

Activity

Every flat is different, but one thing that is the same for flats everywhere . . . they all need a clean now and again. We found that the best way to keep on top of the cleaning was to draw up a weekly chore chart. You might like to assign one person to each weekly job, or maybe do it in pairs if you have a bigger flat (this method worked really well for us). By sorting out what needs to be done, when, and by who, we were able to keep our flat spick and span (well, mostly). We've given you an idea of some of the jobs we needed to keep track of each week, but feel free to add your own.

Balance

Uni might seem scary, exciting, overwhelming, awesome, hectic — and lots of other things besides — at different stages of the semester, or even all at once! It's a pretty intense journey, but one that you will make it through, we promise. It might feel like you're constantly on the go, always working hard or maybe partying hard. But it's important to make sure you always find your balance.

Balance is the single-most important thing we want you to take away from this book. Whether you're trying to make it through high school, uni, work or just life in general, finding your perfect equilibrium will keep you on track. It's all about trial and error, working out what your body and mind needs, and finding ways to fit them into your lifestyle.

Chore	Whose turn is it?
Putting the rubbish bins out	
Cleaning the kitchen	
Vacuuming the lounge	
Cleaning the bathroom	

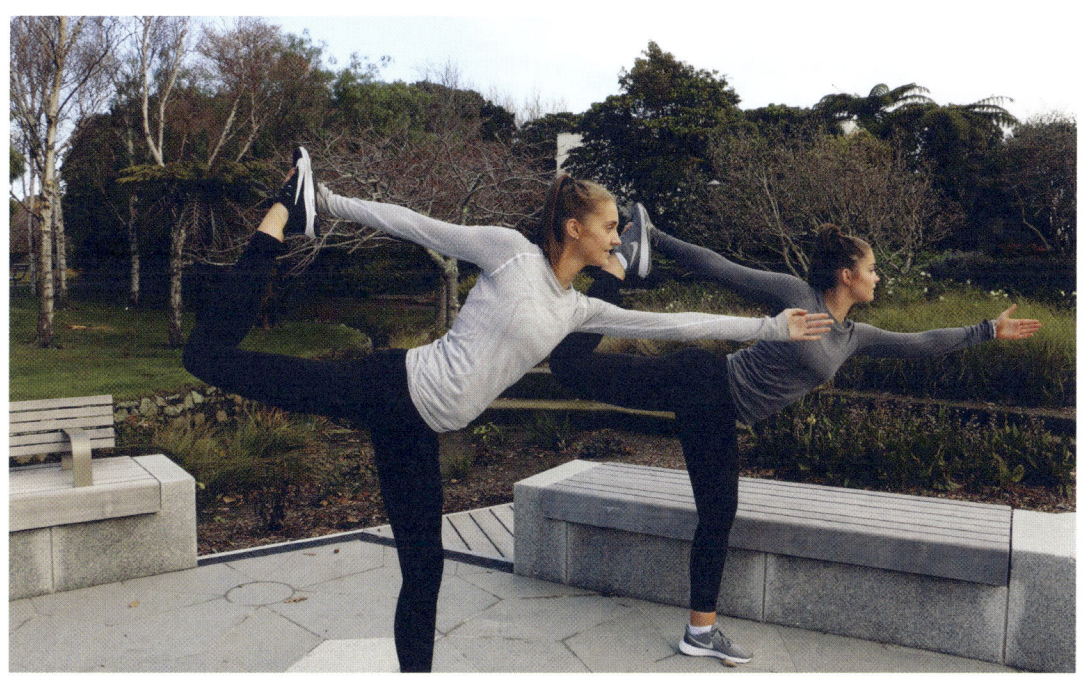

We're all about finding balance in our diet. We both believe that the healthiest diet is one that allows you freedom. By all means, enjoy a salad or a raw slice — we both absolutely love them too! And in the same way, you can enjoy a burger or an ice cream. Our mum is always coming out with iconic sayings, and one of her favourites is 'everything in moderation', which is SO true. A little bit of sugar won't kill you, just like a little bit of kale won't make you perfectly healthy. So, don't be afraid to enjoy yourself every now and again. Food is fuel, but it also brings us together. Whether it's a BYO at your favourite local restaurant, brunch catch-ups or coffee dates, food is a social thing. If you're too preoccupied with avoiding carbs/sugar/'bad' foods, you can become consumed by these thoughts, and distance may develop between you and your friends and family. So why not eat what you enjoy, in moderation, and build yourself a healthy relationship with food in the process?

Exercising is also important to keep in balance. Exercising for the right reasons can help you achieve your performance goals, clear your mind and give you a whole new outlet. And while nothing beats that feeling of reaching a new PB or sweating out your worries, your body won't be able to handle it if you're constantly pushing yourself to its limit. Try swapping out a HIIT session for a yoga flow, or a weights class for a walk. Having at least one rest day a week means you can perform even better when you do push yourself. Listen to your body. If one day, it's asking you to rest, then don't be afraid to take a day off! Finding balance in your exercise routine ensures you're giving your body time to move, and time to recover. Balance can be found in every aspect of your life. At uni, there's a lot to balance. But you will find a way to juggle everything, trust us! Even if it seems a little rocky at first, even if you think you'll never be able to handle it, there is always a way. Hopefully this book has helped you feel ready for the year ahead, armed with all sorts of tools to face university, and helps you to create your own balance in all aspects of life.

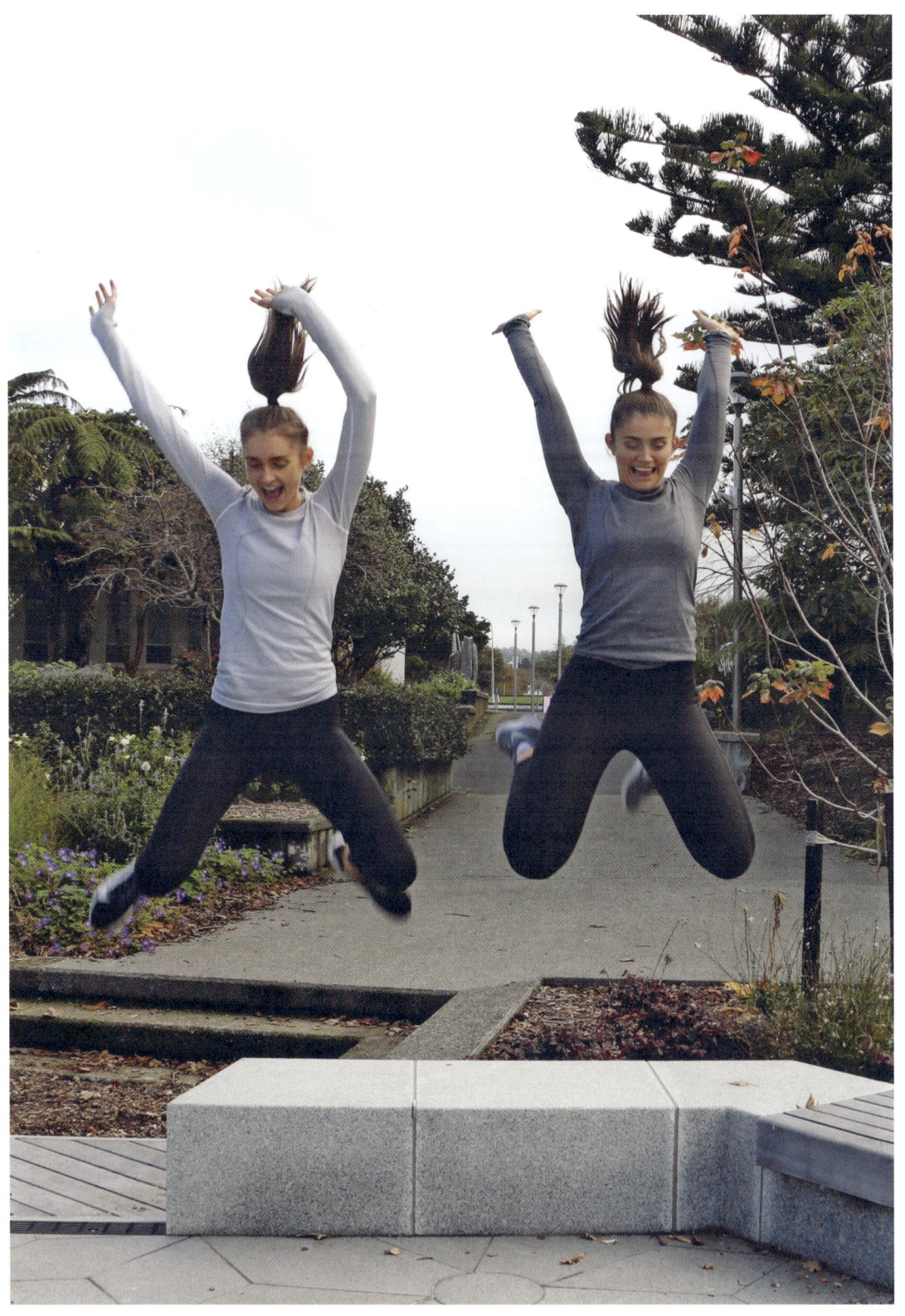

Acknowledgements

This book was a labour of love for us, and couldn't have ever made it to the shelves without the support of an amazing crew behind us!

We'd love to thank Emma Ternouth, for all your nutrition expertise and excellent guidance in the food department. To Louise Russell for all your incredible advice and patience, and the entire team at Bateman Books. Thank you to Kris Madsen — you are the kindest, wisest, most loving person we know. And to our incredible photographer and friend for life, Lauren Reid; we are forever grateful for your talent, advice and unconditional support.

We really couldn't have put this book together without the support of our friends and family. Thank you to our flatmates, for putting up with our recipe testing and giving us brutally honest feedback when they didn't go so well. We are so grateful to all our foodie and not-so foodie friends, for their love and support. To our amazing parents, thanks very much for letting us raid the pantry every summer, passing on your love of food, and for raising us to be the people we are today. And we're especially thankful for each other. Without one another, we would never have made it this far!

And finally, THANK YOU! Whether you've been following us since the beginning, or just picked up the book and decided to give it a go, you can't imagine how grateful we are for your support. So much love from us to you!

Text and photography © Emily and Sophie Martin, 2020
Typographical design © David Bateman Ltd, 2020
The moral rights of the authors have been asserted.

The recipes in this book have been carefully tested by the authors. The publishers and the authors have made every effort to ensure that the recipes and instructions pertaining to them are accurate and safe but cannot accept liability for any resulting injury, illness or loss or damage to property whether direct or consequential.

Published in 2020 by David Bateman Ltd,
Unit 2/5 Workspace Drive, Hobsonville,
Auckland 0618, New Zealand
www.batemanbooks.co.nz
ISBN: 978-1-98-853859-4

This book is copyright. Except for the purposes of fair review, no part may be stored or transmitted in any form or by any means, electronic or mechanical, including recording or storage in any information retrieval systems, without permission in writing from the publisher. No reproduction may be made, whether by photocopying or any other means, unless a licence has been obtained from the publisher or its agent.

A catalogue record for this book is available from the National Library of New Zealand.

Book design: Carolyn Lewis
Printed in China by Asia Pacific Offset Ltd